I0835939

THE PARABLE CONFERENCE

Pablo Helguera

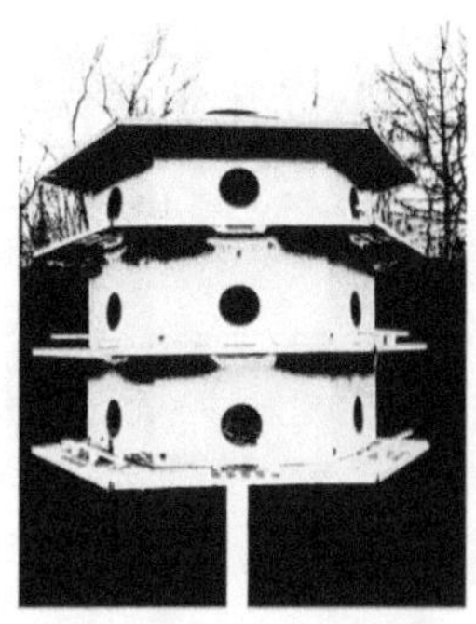

THE PARABLE CONFERENCE

Jorge Pinto Books
New York

The Parable Conference

All images courtesy of the artist.

Cover image PH

Book typesetting: Charles King: www.ckmm.com

ISBN: 978-1-934978-82-5

Someone who supposes that philosophy has never in the world been so near to solving its problems (to explaining all secrets) as now, may well feel it odd, affected, even offensive that I choose the narrative form and do not, in my humble way, lend a hand with putting the coping stone on the System. On the other hand, someone who has convinced himself that philosophy has never been so eccentric as now, so confused, in spite of all its definitions, so very like the weather last winter when all at the same time we heard what had never before been heard, shouts of mussels and prawns and watercress in such a way that someone who attended to a particular shout might at one time think it was winter, at another time spring, at another time midsummer, while someone who paid attention to all these shouts at once might think that nature had become confused and the world could not last till Easter—they will certainly think it right that I should also, by means of the form, try to counteract the detestable falsity which is the mark of modern philosophy; a philosophy which is distinguished from older philosophy by its discovery of the ridiculousness of doing what one said one did or had done—they will find it appropriate and will only be sorry, as I am, that the person who begins this task has not greater authority than I have.

—Søren Kierkegaard,
Johannes Climacus or De Omnibus Dubitanbum

All these things Jesus said to the crowds in parables; indeed, he said nothing to them without a parable.

—Matthew 13:34

Contents

P.S.

In January of 2014, around one hundred and fifty individuals received a letter inviting them to an event that would take place in the fall at an undisclosed location in New York City. Those who accepted the mysterious invitation started receiving individual letters roughly once a month. They were invited to invite in turn other possible interlocutors. Over the months, several other participants joined the project, in the end totaling nearly 400. When the group was finally gathered at the place of the appointment, on October 18, 2014, at the Brooklyn Academy of Music, they experienced at an event with some scripted portions that are detailed in the text at the end of this book.

Over the years I have given much thought to how to individualize the experience of an audience member at a large event. I wanted to create an instance where each participant received different kinds of information from me prior to the performance that would somehow influence their way of interpreting it. One of the ways in which this individuation of communication can happen is through initiating it long before the "performance", that is the official event, takes place. As part of the objective of giving greater meaning to this communication, I decided to send physical letters. Receiving handwritten or printed correspondence has become a rarity for most of us; the convenience of quick communication has made that kind of writing almost obsolete today, it being limited to formal deliveries such as wedding invitations and thank you notes, but mainly to bills and junk mail—that is, mail that we don't want to read or receive. Yet precisely because of that reason, receiving a physical letter—something that still to this day is inexpensive and does not involve that much effort—carries perhaps a greater significance than before. I also found that, by following this approach, I was able to discuss topics that typically I would not feel inclined to discuss in an email, by phone, or even in person. While I am not one of those who lament the demise of "the old ways" per se, I am interested in those "old ways" only inasmuch as they offered ways to connect to individuals that have not been satisfactorily replaced by the advent of avenues like social media. I have also acted on the sense that to the extent that I can produce a relevant text, it is always when I have a clear interlocutor in mind, and specially when that interlocutor is someone who I know and have shared discussions with in the past. This is why it was important to initiate the project with a correspondence with several friends and acquaintances.

A selection of the letters is included here. Although they are presented in the chronological way in which they were written and they interconnect thematically, these short texts are not necessarily meant to be read in a sequential manner. Furthermore, because the texts follow some of the formal conventions of letter writing, the reading of these as if the book were a novel may prove somewhat tedious. The reader must keep in mind that these were letters sent to recipients over the space of many months, that no recipient ever received the same letters, and that each letter was meant to exist as an individual reflection. I considered it important to preserve the original structure of each letter to give the most truthful representation of the project.

I am very grateful to Martha Wilson, whose generous invitation to perform at BAM as part of the Next Wave Festival resulted in this work.

In The Parable Conference I tried to address a number of issues around art using a pre-existing compositional structure. My hope is that the use of this structure, along with my faith in direct communication with individuals who I believe cared as much as I did about the subjects I was addressing, can be seen at least as a sincere effort to frame some of the issues that concern us today about art.

Brooklyn, September, 2014

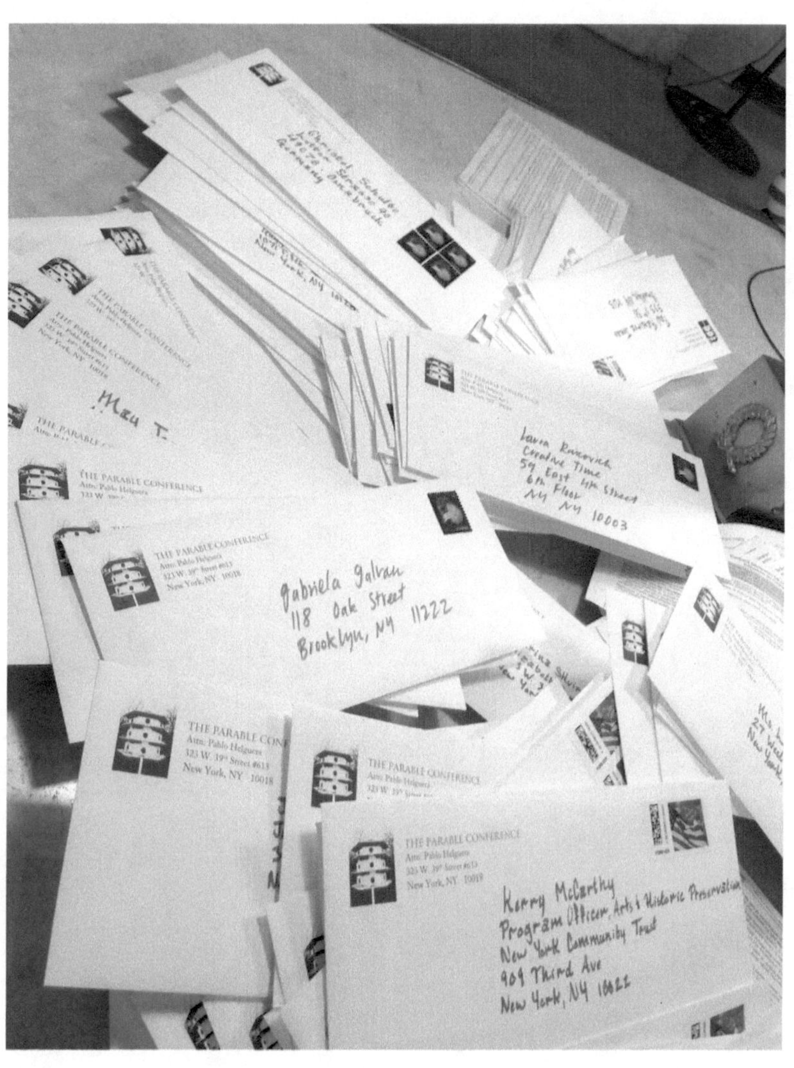
Laura Raicovich
Creative Time
59 East 4th Street
6th Floor
NY NY 10003
THE PARABLE CONFERENCE
Gabriela Galvan
118 Oak Street
Brooklyn, NY 11222
THE PARABLE CONFERENCE
Attn: Pablo Helguera
323 W. 39th Street #613
New York, NY 10018
Kerry McCarthy
Program Officer, Arts & Historic Preservation
New York Community Trust
909 Third Ave
New York, NY 10022

New York City, January 20, 2014

Mr. Tom Finkelpearl

Dear Tom,

I am writing to invite you to be an audience member at an event that will take place on October 18th, 2014 in New York City. This will not be a typical event in the way in which one may generally describe events created by artists. One of the circumstances that makes this event atypical is the fact that prospective audience members are being contacted ten months in advance to confirm their attendance. Secondly, each participating audience member, as soon as he or she confirms their attendance, will be receiving ongoing individual correspondence from me and a few of my collaborators in preparation to the event.

The letters you will receive will be exclusively directed to you and with you exclusively in mind, to help you contextualize what you may experience on October 18th, 2014. In other words, the experience of engaging with this project is not transferrable. You are under no obligation to respond to any piece of mail you may receive up and to the performance. I would only, again, request that you do commit to attending the event as there will be significant effort invested in communicating with you up to an including the event itself.

I fully understand that this invitation may initially appear too vague and perhaps unclear regarding its intentions. You may want to know more about what will happen, or not happen, on October 18th, 2014, before agreeing to attend. This lack of clarity, for better or worse, is an inherent aspect of this project, as I am unable to spell out all that will happen at the event at this time. I can say that I have given a great deal of thought of who to invite. I have selected a group of individuals (of which you are one) that I personally consider in high esteem for their openness to new experiences, their ability to listen and dialogue with others, their understanding and support of the projects that I have undertaken in the past, and the fact that over time I have sustained what I believe has been a meaningful and inspiring dialogue with you. For this reason, and because this event takes place at a very important juncture of my life, I would be very honored by your presence.

I have enclosed a self-addressed RSVP card with prepaid postage for you to reply to this invitation, which is not transferrable. If there were someone else you would like me to invite to partake of this experience, I would love to know about that person. If you can, please enclose this individual's name and address. The event is also open to the general public, and it is expected (and hoped) that as the date gets closer more people will sign up; however this is an event with a somewhat limited capacity. Furthermore, the quality of experience will increase inasmuch I am able to confirm individuals early on.

Please also note that communication for this event will always and exclusively be conducted via regular mail.

I sincerely hope that you may be available and in New York City on October 18th to join me. I anxiously await your response.

Truly yours,

Pablo Helguera Lizalde

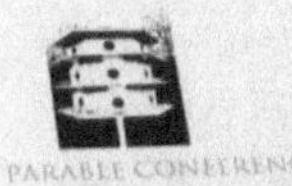

New York City, January 31, 2014

Paco Cao
1075 Grand Concourse Ave. Apt. 5N
Bronx, New York 10452

~~Dear~~ Querido Paco,

I am compelled by many reasons to write you. Mainly, I always wanted to communicate with you in letter format, because I can't seem to find the right time and place where to say what I am about to say. It's also true, and I think I have said this many times, that I am best when I have the calm to write my ideas instead of having to communicate them immediately and in person.

You are a generous individual —someone who has been a critical support to artists—who helps others realize their own vision. I myself have enormously benefited from this natura predisposition of yours to help others. And it is this example that you set, this ability yours to put other's interest in front of yours, that I find most heartening.

the role of generosity in art making. To what extent makers, and to what

1

January 19, 2014

Adeola Enigbokan
Brooklyn, NY

Dear Adeola,

Isn't it significant that we don't write personal letters anymore? It appears that we have relegated their use to official documents, such as applications, recommendations, and other formal occasions. As such, our epistolary voice has all but vanished. Of course, I am sure you will say that email has replaced, and possibly revived the art of writing personal letters. Yet—and I am sure you will recognize once more in me the nostalgic individual who reverts back to the old formats of the past—I can't help but notice that the meaning of receiving an email can't replace the meaning of receiving a letter, in the same way that a face-to-face interaction can't be replaced by any other form of communication. This is why we continue to use letters for truly meaningful moments, often involving critical junctures of marriage, death, and births. But that is not what bothers me about emails. Primarily, they are so ephemeral; all those interactions quickly disappear into the ether. Perhaps it's narcissistic to think that what one writes in private to others has some kind of relevance to posterity. But then again, if we felt that what we do doesn't have any kind of relevance to posterity, is it possible to find meaning to our lives?

This is the question that I wanted to pose in this letter, beyond those cliché debates of the demise of all those things printed on paper. I know you are possibly nostalgic like me, and thus I am even more interested in sharing my thoughts with you.

The question is, what is the relevance of posterity in art for all of us today? Are we fueled by it? To what extent does it determine our decisions and behavior?

Perhaps I first need to clarify what I mean by "posterity." Maybe the easiest way to define it is as the dictionary does it, "for future generations." I would add, "for future generations, after we are dead." Too often I hear artists say they are only interested in the present, but I don't believe them. I have always believed, in fact, that art making is a gesture of existential anxiety, a creative gesture that arises from our very fear of dying, and this very fear triggers a very organic need to create something that is external to us, that in theory can outlive us. This is true, I also believe, of activities that are outside of art, and in fact is connected to our own biology. Why do we choose to reproduce and have children, otherwise?

Let me share a story to illustrate my questions.

There was not to long ago a man that I knew well—let's call him Cristóbal de Sarabia. I met Cristóbal by chance, at a hotel lobby in downtown Mexico City where he was staying at the time. He loved staying at transient places. He immediately said that he knew me and was interested in my work. I was honored, of course, but a bit taken aback, as I am not the kind of artist that one would automatically say that to. I suspected that he was being dishonest. But in reality, now I think that Cristóbal was simply interested in every artist. He was a fast and elegant talker, fueled by his great memory and knowledge. I would say he had a keen curiosity for the world, but perhaps it is more accurate to say that he had an anxiety about not being on top of things. This is a common phenomenon in the art world, where one has to every day check out every single exhibition and event in the world to ensure one is not missing a single artist from view, and that one can be present in a majority of places.

For a while I was part of Cristóbal's circle of professional friendships—it is hard to know in those cases if one is friends, only professional colleague, or both. He was relentlessly self-promotional, but he always did it in such a way that it didn't feel irritating, at least not to me—a very rare occurrence. It was probably because of the excitement and urgency with which he would communicate his achievements, large and small.

Which brings me to his correspondence, which has been on my mind because I am writing so many letters these days. Even though Cristóbal always emailed, he would always write the city, date, and year of the email at the top, as if it was an old fashioned letter. I always thought he did that because of autobiographical vanity, and to show off the city where he was at the time (and he almost always was in a different city). But I loved joining him in that sense that the letter I was receiving perhaps one day would be published and read by historians as valuable material. Mainly, his messages, usually group emails, were long lists of his upcoming social and cultural agenda throughout the world. The excuse for writing them, at times, was to let us know where he would be over the next month or so. It was always something like a week in Helsinki to install a show, a stopover in London to catch the Frieze fair and do a talk, three days in Amsterdam, an opening in Budapest, and then back to a place like Los Angeles and then out to Brazil. He was clearly hyperactive, and seemed to be terrified of being left for one moment without any activity, as if he would suddenly discover his loneliness.

For Cristóbal was, in the end, a very lonely person. There was a vulnerability about him that I always found endearing in a certain way. That was perhaps what made me want to protect him, even though our conversations appeared to be the opposite—he being a curator and me an artist, he always throwing suggestions and ideas of exhibitions he could invite me to do.

He was trying, in fact, to strike a very delicate balance between his immediate impulses and his loftier, and perhaps idealistic, goals. This became clear when he had a brushing with the law, an event that suddenly exposed him in an embarrassing way. After that incident he was never the same. He retreated to a slightly more sedentary life. He became slightly paranoid, and he no longer reached out to others so aggressively. Every now and then he would reply to one of my emails, but he was no longer ubiquitous. He entered into a crisis, perhaps, recognizing that he couldn't live without permanently living his life in public, but also that he couldn't live publicly without suddenly exposing the darker parts of himself.

A few months ago, I received news that Cristóbal had passed away from a complication of a condition that I did not know he had, and that he probably had not communicated to anyone. I suspect he feared it would have made him look weak in the eyes of others. He always wanted to project success and strength, and did all he could to look elegant and camera-ready. I now recognize that he wanted to conquer the present. Further, he thought that to win the battle of the present, would ultimately give him the war of conquering posterity.

I am not sure if he achieved that. It is so hard to look at the balance sheet of someone's life and dare to give a judgment. But, I do think that in his premature departure—while he was caught in a permanent state of anxiety—every moment he lived was only worth as much as the moment he was about to live.

Perhaps the afterlife, if it exists, is also like that: a permanent state of anticipation for something else, which is what keeps you going. And maybe our excitement for what is next is only a coping mechanism to mask the anxiety for what is ultimately inevitable. Maybe Cristóbal was on to something.

All yours,

Pablo

2

January 20, 2014

Caroline Woolard
Brooklyn, NY

Dear Caroline,

I think you know that I like opera. (If you don't know that about me then I would say that you don't know me.) I am by no means a fanatic, but I do like opera for many reasons, mainly because singing is an organic need for me. It is not about the desire to be a famous or professional musician, although I have fantasized with that thought my entire life, and on the day of my death that will probably be my only regret: not having become a professional musician.

I enjoy the unreality of the operatic world. The plots in operas don't make any sense at all; they have contorted logic and follow old-fashioned rationales, they are long, sometimes soporiferous, and sometimes one must wait hours to get to the aria that one really wanted to hear. Talk of the commitment of an audience member. Can you imagine putting yourself through three hours of a terrible video only so that you can see the one minute that you really wanted to see? These days we just fast forward to pleasure.

Why would I suddenly tell you all this? The reason why I bring this up is because I wanted to tell you that I believe that there is something to be learned from strange operatic stories for people like you and me, who are artists and who are forced to continuously reflect on what being an artist in the XXIst century means today.

I believe that you know that over the years I have been interested in individual biographies. I often think I could have been a biographer (but that is definitely not something I will lament not doing on my deathbed; I don't think I could be for three decades writing a book on the life of, say, Lyndon B. Johnson). Mainly, it is what I believe we see reflected of ourselves on those who we know. And I have always been interested in the biographies of artists who have struggled to make the connection between who they are and how the others perceive them. Are we ever able to make the connection? Is it even possible to know?

Let me tell you one of my favorite real-life stories to try to illustrate this question.

Once upon a time there was a woman named Florence Foster Jenkins. She was born in 1868. Her father was a wealthy banker from Wilkes-Barre, Pennsylvania, and wanted his daughter to have a typical Victorian housewife's life. Florence wanted to be an opera singer, but her father forbid it. She at some point eloped with a lover, barely making a living teaching piano. When her father died, turns out he had ultimately forgiven her and left her a huge sum of money. Being now wealthy herself, Florence decided to pursue her singing career in earnest. The thing is—her voice was preposterous. She could almost never sing a single note in tune. And, it appears, she was incapable of noticing it. Thus, she organized huge recitals with elaborate sets and costumes—her favorite was "the angel of inspiration" where she would appear with large silver wings onstage. Audiences were at first small, comprised mainly of wealthy society women like her, without much knowledge of music. She was the butt joke of critics; her inconceivably bad voice, her utter lack of awareness and gall to stage such massive performances was an effrontery to the art and would have probably felt irresponsible if it wasn't because she truly didn't seem to realize her complete lack of talent. But precisely because of that fact, it is believed, something extraordinary started happening. Her concerts became more and more populated, not by people who admired her voice, but simply by audiences who came to laugh at the sheer spectacle of a delusional woman making a fool of herself.

You would imagine that for any regular individual, the embarrassment of such reception would be enough to stop singing altogether. But for Florence it was the opposite: she appeared to relish in the public's attention. It is reported that she never flinched, although when the laughter was just too bad to be ignored she would simply dismiss it as it coming from a small group of "unlettered louts" in her recitals. As they say, only once she appeared to be truly shaken by the criticisms and laughter. On that occasion she said her most immortal phrase: "people may say that I can't sing, but no one can say that I didn't sing."

Florence is one of those individuals that have been in my mind ever since I listened to her recordings as a child. There are many reasons for it, I believe. For one, I think that most of us artists are a bit like Florence: always with a degree with delusion, always with a degree of hopefulness, and always trying to appear invincible—but, in the end containing a delicate fragility that comes with the territory of being an individual with a sensibility toward art.

But what interests me more in the context of this letter is the way in which Florence related to her audience. You know, she was known to sell every ticket to her own recitals *by herself*. She would sit in a hotel or theater lobby or ballroom and people would have to come to her to buy the ticket. She claimed that she wanted to meet every audience member individually. Have you ever heard of an artist who wanted to do that? Isn't there an incredible arrogance by the artist who wants to be appreciated, but could not care less about who appreciates them and who these individuals are?

In the end, I believe, and in a deep sense, those audiences knew how much Florence cared about them. And I also believe that the joke was on them. Florence was a performance artist. And in the end, her audiences were addicted. They thought they were laughing at her—but, at the same time they were completely entranced by her unintentional humoristic delivery.

Her final recital in 1944, at Carnegie Hall, was an unprecedented popular success. The event was sold out months in advance and hundreds of eager ticket buyers were turned away. There were, of course, the laughs, the tears of laughter, but the acclaim was real. Florence, a month before her passing away, received a standing ovation as a tribute of a lifetime of dedication to singing.

In a larger sense, Florence had created a unique experience that went way beyond the status quo performances by able musicians.

Most of those performers of her era are now completely forgotten, yet the name of Florence Foster Jenkins will likely live on forever. I want to think that partially this stems from that organic need to communicate, which is what made it relevant. We say that birds sing; we attribute aesthetic qualities to organic needs. What if we considered the intention behind that organic impulse to make art, as something worth valuing in it of itself, regardless of how it fares in the scope of aesthetic expression?

At the end of every concert, Florence would go to the center of the stage and address the audience, asking them to write to her to give her impressions of the recital and telling her what pieces they had enjoyed the most. "It may not seem important to you—she would say—but it is very important to me."

Over the years, I have also been thinking about what aspects of art making are important to me, and which ones of those that are not important anymore. Sometimes I suspect that if each one of us were to spell them out it would make us feel in the eyes of others, and of ourselves even, as delusional as Florence. And yet, we would probably be so much happier in how we undertake our artistic endeavors. I think you know what I mean.

Yours,

Pablo

3

January 24, 2014

Jane Wesman and Don Savelson
New York, NY

Dear Jane and Don,

First, let me thank you for agreeing to be part of an event of which you still don't know anything about. It shows, besides your openness, generosity and intellectual curiosity, a degree of trust in me and in my work of which I am deeply grateful for. Although the nature of this project will probably reveal itself as we continue, for the time being I can say, as I wrote before, that you are under no obligation to do anything, nor even read this letter, or attend the event on October 18th, although it certainly will make me so glad if you do. I can also promise in a very solemn way that I will not betray the trust that you have placed in wanting to participate in this experience.

Which brings me to the first thing I want to discuss. How many times as participants of art experiences do we want to have it all spelled out? This is a constant reality I have faced over my 25 years as a museum educator (which yes, I believe you know a triple life: artist, museum educator, and father-husband).

It is most common in museums that unseasoned visitors simply want us—the lecturers, tour guides and such—to spell out "what the piece is about." Some groups, who come probably from St. Patrick's Cathedral or Rockefeller Center and have been given a story about the place, expect the same self-contained story about the paintings on view. And as you know, no art work can possibly be described in a self-contained story. In fact, I would argue that the more I can tell you about an art work, the murkier its meaning becomes.

Let me give you an example.

Once upon a time there was a man named Herbert Von Kleipstock. He belonged to a wealthy family, as his grandfather had made a substantial fortune in the steel business. As such, he never had to worry about sustenance, and had privileged access to many artists and intellectuals of his time. He decided to study art, but he also became interested in philosophy and art criticism. This was in the late 1950s, in New York. He was deeply impacted by the Ab Ex artists, by the seriousness of their quest in producing great art. But as the typical youth who seeks to rebel against the previous generation, he was very much against the idea that art had openness of interpretation, as abstract art appeared to suggest. He firmly believed that there was a final translation for each artwork, and that it was possible to spell it out as long as there is enough time and effort invested in it.

His family had a house in Johnson, Vermont that he favored; he was in essence a loner and a lover of nature, and it served him well to spend long periods there, writing about art when he was not in Manhattan or the Hamptons being part of the art scene at the time.

It was through some of the conversations that Kleipstock had with the critics and artists of that milieu that he became increasingly more obsessed with the subject of art interpretation. He favored objective readings of works, and disagreed with the notion that subjectivity determines an interpretation. According to Kleipstock, subjective readings of a work were nothing but the result of the inability of an individual to fully understand the essence of a work itself. He spent a while trying to formulate this idea, and after two or three years of spending time in Johnson, Vermont, he published an essay, which I can't remember how it was titled, but it was somewhere along the lines of "The Problem of Subjectivity."

Kleipstock's book, a self-published limited edition, was courteously received by the local art world, but not enthusiastically embraced. It appears to me, given that his family had a foundation that generously gave to artists and museums, no one had the desire to break his heart and tell him that his theories were the least convincing. But Kleipstock wasn't dumb: he clearly perceived that his conclusions in his book had no effect in the art world at large. He confronted many artists, museum directors, and critics about this; I can only imagine how uncomfortable they must have felt about being pushed to tell him what they really thought. After a few episodes, one individual suggested that perhaps his hypothesis would be better taken if he could provide definitive proof that it was possible, indeed, to arrive to a final reading or interpretation of a single art work.

This idea really resonated in Kleipstock, and became a sort of epiphany for him. He decided to test out this experiment. Kleipstock managed to acquire a painting by Arshile Gorky. It did not really matter whether the art work to examine was a most important one or least important; what mattered is whether what could be said about it could be exhausted.

Kleipstock installed the small painting at an almost empty room in his Upper West Side apartment and started writing about the piece. The work didn't have a title, but it clearly was a preparatory painting for Gorki's famous "Garden in Sochi" from 1943 containing a similar composition, with some of its similar lyrical lines and abstract shapes.

He put an enormous effort to have anyone and everyone he could get into his apartment to spend at least an hour in front of the painting, and describing what they saw. He hired a stenographer by the name of Marcus Rivington to quickly transcribe everything that was said in the session. He sought people ranging from Gorki's widow, Agnes Magruder (who supposedly caused him to commit suicide after she abandoned him), to random individuals such as neighbors and children.

At first the experiment seemed to be going well. Rivington had a great ability to organize information and this helped Kleipstock to come up with a variety of "trends" of data that, he thought, were pointing to what he thought a final reading of the work would be. It was, however, after the first 200 individuals or so that he interviewed where he started having a hard time correlating the data. While there were many instances of similar readings of the works, more and more outliers would emerge. In particular, an Irish policeman, Scott Taylor, had provided such a fanciful interpretation of the painting that it had left Kleipstock dumbfounded. Taylor had had a powerful vision that took him twenty hours to describe, over the course of seven sessions. It was probably one of the most unexpected and intricate interpretations of a painting ever heard. Each session Taylor would keep finding more and more details in the painting, seeing verses from the Bible, images of World War I and of rivers in China where he had once lived. Kleipstock realized that it would take a long time to arrive to a final reading of that painting that would help correlate all other interpretations.

Years went by. Throughout the 1960s it became a ritual in New York inner art circles to meet Kleipstock at exhibition openings and receive later a written invitation by him to join him in making an interpretation of the Gorki painting. Later, Kleipstock decided that the problem was to be limited by audiences in Manhattan, and started traveling with the painting, and with his loyal Rivington, to continue documenting painting responses. It is believed they spent time in Rochester, New York, Schenedtady, Quebec, Santa Monica, Detroit, and Mobile, Alabama, interviewing spectators of the painting. The catalogue of interpretations kept growing over the years, until they had reached around 40,000 readings. In the 1970s Kleipstock hired a team of data analysts from MIT to make sense of the data he had collected. The process of reading the data took them eight years, under a costly process that Kleipstock funded, using much of his fortune to do so. By the time they had concluded analyzing the data, no final conclusion had been reached, and the analysts had had disagreements on how to interpret certain kind of statements from various individuals.

Undaunted, Kleipstock set more than ever to prove that it was possible to create a final reading of that Gorki painting. He grew obsessed with the task and through the 1980s spent the rest of his fortune hiring a wide range of consultants, ranging from an astrophysicist to a specialist in the I Ching to make sense of the growing archive of information. His house in Johnson, Vermont became the place where all the archives were stored; he was forced to build a warehouse on his property to store the more than 100,000 interviews he had collected over the decades.

Von Kleipstock died in 1994, shortly before the internet took off and with it, the digital revolution. He never gave up his life's purpose of offering a final reading of a painting. It so happened, tragically, that after his death, his sister's son Andrew (Kleipstock never married) determined that the material in the warehouse was useless and disposed of it. It took three large trailers to remove all the documents. It is also believed that amidst the confusion, the Gorky painting itself was thrown along with the research materials.

It is rumored (I have no way to confirm this story) that Von Kleipstock never got around to doing his own interpretation of the painting. It seems ironic to think that, consumed as he was by documenting every single reaction, every single idea, thought or feeling that had emerged from looking at that Gorky painting, not even once did he attempt to sit in front of it himself. A local artist from Johnson who knew him toward the end of his life and used to run into him at the local café in Johnson asked him, point blank, what he thought about the painting.

Von Kleipstock looked at the sky in a distracted way.

"I am not there yet."

Truly yours,

Pablo

4

January 26, 2014

Amy Whitaker
New York, NY

Dear Amy,

There are times, like this one, that I am grateful to claim the privilege to be able to write to individuals like you, who I sincerely admire. I hope you won't take this as an empty compliment. The reason I invited you to join this project was somewhat selfish: I was looking for the opportunity to share thoughts in an unhurried way, which the letter helps to provide. I feel handicapped when speaking in person; my mind doesn't move at the pace of a conversation. Too many things distract me during live conversation, including my own thoughts about my own thoughts. For that reason I believe I am more myself when I write. And writing letters is a joy that most of us—I hope you agree—have lost. In letters, we can discuss things that have no connection to any immediate, pressing or current event. As a result, some of the most important things are left unsaid.

Speaking of privileges, I have thought a lot about the topic of the kind of privileges that art bestows to us. By "us" I mean, those of us who have truly dedicated our lives to understanding art to the point that the true pleasure of making and discussing art, of trying to piece apart and put back together the puzzles that it poses to us, is the real thrill. Everything else is secondary: fame, celebrity, money. I don't want, of course, pretend to pose as a purist who doesn't care about the incredible pleasures and conveniences that those things pose, and I am sure that both you and I very much enjoy when some of those supposedly materialistic benefits befall us in one way or another. You may agree that our lack of privilege in some of these areas can help us see more clearly, as long as we are not truly disadvantaged. So where is the line between privilege granting us an advantage, and privilege rendering us blind?

I believe you know that, for whatever circumstances, I have a privileged access to the two defining spheres of the art world: the sphere of the artists, the makers, and the sphere of the museum, the presenters. Many artists work in museums, but quite honestly, I have never met anyone who can call themselves a practicing artist while at simultaneously have the same level of access to conversations and information that I have obtained in my career, even if I am not meant to ever be, or want to be, anything like a museum director. But in any case, this access is the privilege I have to acknowledge I possess. At times it feels more like a burden than an advantage, as when I appear in "the other" side, I have to ensure that a defining aspect of my identity has to disappear, to become invisible. To make it appear at the wrong place makes me feel extremely uncomfortable, and I believe no good is to come of it. At other times, the possibility of not emphasizing an aspect of myself is a relief. In other words, I am equally relieved of not being perceived as an artist in certain situations, as I am of not always having to think of myself as one, although I am one.

Perhaps this whole self-reflection on my condition would have never taken place nor have troubled me so much if I had not met Gaspar de Sandoval.

I met Mr. Sandoval (I am employing a fictional name just to protect this individual's privacy) many years ago when I taught a college art class. He presented himself as any other person, very agreeable and cordial, but I soon sensed something rather unusual in him. He was, let's say, wearing a calculated disguise, similar to the one worn by undercover cops. They wear too stereotypical, too average outfits to the point that it is very easy to spot them. This was the case of Mr. Sandoval, who essentially dressed as someone much younger, and much poorer. He was trying to fit the look of an emerging artist.

I later learned from indirect sources that Mr. Sandoval was fabulously wealthy. He came from a family of privilege for many generations and, needless to say, had never had to worry about any issues connected to work and daily survival, let alone any of the challenges usually encountered by a struggling artist. He was connected to one of the most powerful art foundations in the country; he sat on boards that made decisions with substantial influence on the arts.

None of this would have mattered to me until the day in which, due to pure serendipity, he joined me in the split parallel of realities that I live in. Except that he, of course, entered into these two worlds in a most lopsided way: on the side of the museum, the Olympus. He entered as a bulldozer; I am in that world of no importance compared to him. In contrast, in the netherworld of artists where I pride myself of having paid my dues after so many years of struggle and work, he was absolutely no one.

When I first saw Mr. Sandoval in the Olympus, I was impressed. There he was free to dress and wear his true outfits, which outshone anyone. Being a truly attractive man, his presence had a great deal of impact. Everyone knew who he was, and everyone showed great respect to him. You may have noticed that in the upper tiers of society, there is always a great deal of respect and deference amongst the members of that clan, but there are those who truly wield real power—that is, truly wealthy people—and in that upper tier, absolutely everyone knows the difference and acts accordingly. Mr. Sandoval clearly knew that he owned that place, and completely dominated that world.

We had a good relationship ever since he was my student. I believe that we sincerely liked each other; I certainly did. When he saw me at the Olympus, he embraced me with great affection; pleasantly surprised to see me there, he immediately wanted me to be his confidant. This made me extremely uncomfortable, but I was not in the position to say no. It was an unusual role for me to play, and at times I felt like the main character, "Ol' Sport", of *The Great Gatsby*, reluctantly pulled into the high tiers of privilege by someone, but never overcoming his self-awareness of not truly belonging there. Mr. Sandoval took me to events with extremely wealthy and powerful people like himself, and I would watch in silence as they exchanged their various concerns, most of the time completely oblivious that I was there. Mr. Sandoval could not see the disparity, nor perhaps could have even been able to see it.

What made it most uncomfortable for me, to the point of cringing, was bearing witness of how Mr. Sandoval conflated his role as a museum trustee with his self-imagined role as a major artist. It entered in direct conflict with my innermost core as I have explained. But for Mr. Sandoval that was not even an issue. It is obvious to see why: being the most powerful player in a particular system, one probably doesn't have to concern himself too much with doing anything that may offend anyone, as there are never any negative consequences to what one says or does. One can never get fired, can never be talked down by anyone, and can never be reproached. One can make up the rules if he is the owner of the game.

But none of this would have been an issue if it wasn't for the fact that Mr. Sandoval was a terrible artist. And, as I am sure you would guess, he was completely unaware of that plain fact as well. Like an isolated dictator who surrounds himself with people who only adulate him, no one would even dare say a critical word about Mr. Sandoval's work. Moreover, everyone around him was forced to indulge him, and look at his work for hours, and to discuss each and every random thought he had about what he was doing in the studio. Mr. Sandoval was in reality no different from a freshman art student who sees himself and his concerns as the center of the universe.

The difference, of course, was that Mr. Sandoval had unlimited resources to do whatever he wanted. If one morning he felt like making an installation, he could call Frank Gehry's office and ask them to make it. If he wanted to do a music composition, he could call Philip Glass and ask him to orchestrate it for him. Needless to say, they all would immediately pick up the phone when their benefactor called and would always oblige, charging incalculable sums of money and assigning it to legions of top technical experts. The result was always an odd combination of something with superb production values, but devoid of any point.

It was fascinating for me to witness Mr. Sandoval's degree of delusion. Like many others, I would have kept my opinion to myself about his art, but he provoked me to the point that I could no longer remain neutral.

One day, after seeing an announcement of one of my exhibitions, Mr. Sandoval sent me an email prodding me to be more forthcoming and promotional about my projects amongst my museum colleagues—something that I abhor to do. His tone was, as usual, unintentionally condescending, which quite frankly unnerved me, and to a degree, insulted me coming from someone who I regarded as a ridiculously amateur artist. Then I did something that is very uncharacteristic of me: I replied his email with an objective reading of his personal situation as I saw it. Very delicately, I laid out my own principles regarding keeping one's artistic life private when in interaction at the museum where one works. I went as far to tell him that he, in a position of power, would not be able to determine whether the positive comments about his work by anyone would be sincere, and that abuse of power would ultimately undermine his career.

I immediately regretted sending that email. What was I thinking? He would be deeply offended at my egregious honesty, which he had perhaps never experienced in his life. I had definitely crossed a line. I even had images of getting fired for offending a powerful trustee.

But Mr. Sandoval didn't even flinch. He replied with his exact, calm, confident, unintentionally condescending tone, explaining to me that I was a young artist who still wasn't used to pushing my way through and claiming my rightful place. In a way he was right: I was unable to understand the world of entitlement from which he had come from. I came from a middle class family in Mexico City that used to be upper class. My father had inherited a successful business from my grandfather, but he lost it all before I turned four. I grew up witnessing his humiliation as the rich friends that my family used to have turned their back on him. I came from another world where I had twice the awareness of being a second-class citizen: from belonging to another class and from being an immigrant, seeing my people mistreated. My exchange with Mr. Sandoval only made me even more grateful, in a perverse way, of the fact that my father had lost it all.

But I do often wonder—and this is the thing that really troubles me: am I the one being delusional? And, is that delusion, in a contorted way, another form of privilege?

All yours,

Pablo

5

January 29th, 2014

Douglas Kent Walla
New York, NY

Dear Doug,

I am compelled by many reasons to write you. Mainly, I always wanted to communicate with you in letter format, because I can't seem to find the right time and place where to say what I am about to say. It's also true, and I think I have said this many times, that I am best when I have the calm to write my ideas instead of having to communicate them immediately and in person.

You are a generous individual—someone who has been a critical support to artists—who helps others realize their own vision. I myself have enormously benefited from this natural predisposition of yours to help others. And it is this example that you set, this ability of yours to put other's interest in front of yours, that I find most heartening.

It also makes me think about the role of generosity in art making. To what extent we are seeking to benefit and satisfy our own desires and needs as makers, and to what extent should it be balanced with satisfying the needs and desires of those who we know will experience the work? And, moreover, where is the point where our concessions become such that they are more a direct response to our desire of acceptance by others than a truly integral personal vision?

This is not an easy question. I don't concern myself with those who only want to serve themselves and acknowledge it, thinking that their cynical self-centeredness will make them look truly cutting-edge, while they actually live in a delusional past. In the case of those around us who claim that their work exclusively is made to benefit others, I believe they are fooling themselves, or being hypocritical—perhaps too afraid to acknowledge that they, too, have an ego that needs to be satisfied, even if it is through our collective admiration for their generosity.

But the rest of us usually fall somewhere in between. There is no way that one can become an art professional without a certain high self-opinion, even if we fall within the realm of the eccentric who mainly finds satisfaction in the very making of the work, without much concern on the opinion of others. And in order to be the recipients of positive opinion, we need to care about what we are giving them. The problem is that it is very difficult to know where the balance is.

Let me pose an example.

There is a man amongst us—let's call him Bishop William (I'll use a fictional name to avoid embarrassing him). Bishop William is an art critic, and was well known by every single artist in his country. For many years he has written in some of the most influential art magazines. He wielded enormous power, and even when some people claimed that they didn't read his reviews and commentary they all definitely did, and definitely cared. Bishop William knew this, and overall showed magnanimity in his reviews. He was not shy to be stern when the occasion demanded it, and for that reason he was highly respected. We can also surmise that Bishop William felt fulfilled: his writing showed a dedication and a pleasure in his work that is hard to find these days.

Then the social media revolution happened.

An interesting thing you may have noticed that has taken place in the last few years is that the fact that most of us have created connections amongst each other in social media means that we are capable to debate things large and small and have access to a wide variety of opinions on a given subject, not just the one of the lone art critic whose review would appear in a lone art magazine. I personally will always be much more interested, for example, in knowing what you may think of a given exhibition or book than an "expert" writing a review. This is of course not to completely discard or dismiss expertise; it only means that today we have much wider critical consensus means at our disposal.

The fact of the matter is that Bishop William saw his readership decline, as is the case with all magazines and newspapers. His opinion was no longer the last word on anything, and while he still was very influential, he now had to compete with the commentary of a myriad of bloggers and commenters, both famous and unknown.

At first, Bishop William dismissed the phenomenon, attributing those opinions to people who were just amateurs and didn't have his level of experience and knowledge. However, while there certainly was plenty of irrelevant commentary out there, a lot of that critical commentary was also very informed and objective. I firmly believe that Bishop William, as most people like him, didn't see this coming, regardless of what he may say. I also don't think that he realized that his own writing voice started changing, ostensibly in order to best the competition. Increasingly, Bishop William started being more aggressive in his commentary, exaggerating the positive and negative attributes of a show; he started to wax lyrical in some cases, treating some reviews as prose poetry; he even sounded apocalyptic at times when he attacked institutions. He also started doing a lot of namedropping, as it appears that articles are more likely to be read the more people you mention in them.

But none of this had a significant effect, other than people starting to comment on how Bishop William was starting to lose it.

His behavior in public also changed. He used to come to galleries and museums when no one would recognize him, during the run of the show, trying to be as anonymous as possible. He kept to himself most of the time. But now he started showing up at every opening and gala, participating in every single one of those ghastly art fair panel discussions that are just a pretext to do people watching. He now dressed in a fashionable way, investing a lot in his wardrobe; whenever there was an event photographer in the room, he would immediately push his way to insert himself in the photo op. He would stick around with whoever was the most important person in the room and act as if he was best friends with them. He basically became a socialite.

When none of this worked, he essentially just started writing about himself. Every review started becoming an excuse for him to explore one aspect of his fears, desires and hopes. It is almost as if every artist was now a tool for himself to practice a kind of self-therapy, one that he ensures many people listen. And of course, he now spends all day on Facebook.

I am worried about Bishop William. But perhaps what worries me the most is, in light of the way in which great minds like his are now lost to us, is it going to also happen to you and me? Or has the process already begun?

Yours,

Pablo

6

January 30th, 2014

Claudia Joskowicz
Brooklyn, NY

Dear Claudia,

I have a lot to explain—primarily as to why I have invited you attend an event without any meaningful information about it. In reality, there is no real secret behind this. I am mainly interested in corresponding with people that I care about, people that matter to me. And by doing so, discuss aspects of you that have had a particular impact on me.

I have always admired you because of the sincerity of what you do. Sincerity, in our world, is the kind of attribute that we all praise, and we want to see ourselves as sincere in all we do, but we also know full well that sincerity can also hurt others and us, so we also tend to gravitate to a social milieu where no one really means what they say, and where there are many experts at making that which they say most believable.

A Mexican writer, Julio Torri, once wrote a story about a man who despite acting with utmost sincerity, was always misinterpreted. He is finally told that he is "a poor actor of his emotions." I would like to join this phrase with Marcel Broodthaers' famous comment, expressed when he explained his transition from his failed career as a poet to art: "the idea of doing something insincere crossed my mind, and I immediately put myself to work."

Now, let me suggest, first, that Broodthaers' genius consisted in making people believe that he was being insincere, but his supposedly insincere acts turned out to instead reveal the insincerity of the institutional, formal world around him. And secondly, that most artists, who tend to be poorer actors of their emotions than Broodthaers, end doing the opposite: they present work as sincere when it is not.

And I will submit to you that having real emotions and knowing how to act them are ultimately incompatible things; that we need to choose either to be sincere (which turns us usually into bad artists) or to construct a sincere persona (which usually can only be done by truly exceptional artists).

Perhaps this is why I have been fascinated by the world of politics, and the way in which politicians construct their image. If you really think about it, we all instinctively know that politicians construct somewhat fictional personas, a composite of who they really are in private, and the projections and hopes of who they think their constituents want them to be. We can be disappointed when we suddenly see a glimpse of the "real" individual behind the politician, but it is never that surprising when that wall comes down.

But it all gets more complicated when we think of the persona of the artist or the arts professional, for that matter. We basically have a harder time knowing whether to judge artists in terms of the sincerity of their behavior. This is important because in the end we instinctively search for a kind of authenticity in the individual that is making an art work, and when don't find it we consider that person as betraying us. We hold in higher regard someone who does something that we may disapprove of, but who we know that is doing it because he/she firmly believes in it, than someone who does something out of opportunism. And when it comes to judging the work or actions of others (and let's be honest, we do this every day) we actually obsess about their intentions, and take any indication of those intentions to give our judgment. For example, if it is evident that an artist produced a project about a social issue but in a format that is very gallery-friendly, we may critique it in that the subject matter is subservient to the commercial dimension of the project.

But many times the work is hard to read this way, and thus we need to turn to the individual himself.

I often think of Mr. Loremond S. Finney as the perfect example of what I mean. Mr. Finney (I have changed his name so I can tell you with more liberty) was the director of a major museum. He was a significant public figure, and as such he was often the subject of criticism of people in the media and the art milieu at large, none of which ever seemed to bother him (nothing, in fact, ever appeared to bother him). Whatever one may have thought of him, if one were to meet him in person, he or she would be automatically disarmed. He was an extremely engaging and cordial individual; superbly smart and able to communicate about any subject. Sophisticated and well traveled, Mr. Finney could talk about ski resorts and golf to wealthy donors, but also about foreign and economic policy; he would be equally comfortable at Davos and at the opening of the Venice Biennial; he could engage in contemporary art theory at an impressively high level with curators and academics.

But the key unanswerable question about Mr. Finney was: what did he actually stand for? He appeared to be a Zelig of worldviews, and was able to formulate ideas that appeared to be self-made opinions, but they were invariably references to what others thought and believed. Yet the way he did this was so effective that most of the time one would leave with the sense that he had truly communicated profound beliefs of his own.

The day when I was most impressed by him was on an instance when he was challenged by an artist who is known for being a troublemaker—wanting to claim the mantle of the lead institutional critic of our time. He is an artist who many people admire (including myself), widely known and who has made irreverence and anti-institutionality one of his trademarks. This artist,—let's call him George Cheyne—was invited to an event where Mr. Finney would be present along with a group of museum donors and trustees, thus a delicate environment for Mr. Finney. From the beginning of the event Cheyne started interrupting and challenging Mr. Finney, at every step of the way trying to unveil what he thought was his hypocrisy, tying to show him as an apparatchik of an evil system that only cared about the preservation of power and money. Cheyne took a populist attack approach, trying to make Mr. Finney look like an out of touch elitist.

But Mr. Finney was undaunted. He did not appear to be bothered, or surprised, for a second by Cheyne's assault. Instead, he confronted him in a calm and elegant way, slowly asking Cheyne's questions about himself and about his own ideas about the public. Within minutes Cheyne started falling into contradictions, as if he were an amateur lawyer on his first public trial. On the one hand he was vouching for making museums drastically radical, but he had no way to reconcile how that would connect with the masses of the public that he was also arguing to have access. Every question that Mr. Finney posed to Mr. Cheyne made the latter diminish the audacity in his tone, starting to qualify the things he had originally said. Toward the end Mr. Cheyne had started to support ideas that Mr. Finney had started the conversation with, to the point that it was unclear what he was criticizing in the first place. Mr. Cheyne looked defeated in the end, and somewhat dazzled, not fully understanding what had happened. Perhaps the most elegant touch was when Mr. Finney, before leaving the room, patted Mr. Cheyne telling him: "please continue doing what you do—you are doing very important work."

It was a picture to behold. One of the greatest artists of my generation, who I have always admired for his embrace of radicality, was publicly acknowledging that he wasn't even sure what the radicality he espoused ultimately meant, nor was he able to articulate the soundness of the politics behind it. Meanwhile, Mr. Finney had been able, once again, to turn things around to the point where what he actually thought about any of the subjects discussed remained a mystery. I thought at that point that we will likely never know what Mr. Finney actually thought about any subject. Maybe he didn't, and maybe it was precisely that exasperating neutrality behind every issue that made him invincible, and feelings inexpugnable. We will probably never know.

The incident made me also think of something that was unthinkable in that moment. Looking at that conversation at face value, one would say that Mr. Cheyne had displayed the true character of the bureaucrat of art, and Mr. Finney the true character of the artist. I think you may understand what I mean by that. Certainly Mr. Finney will never be considered an artist in the future in the way we interpret artists to be right now. But maybe that may change? In the future, will we think of art not as the calculated actions of those who presented themselves as artists by acting in the predictable ways, but in the actual effect of those who managed to be the best actors of their emotions, regardless on whether they considered themselves artists or not?

Yours truly,

Pablo

7

February 2, 2014

Andras Szanto and Alanna Stang
Brooklyn, NY

Dear Andras and Alanna,

I am writing you today because I would like to set some things straight in my mind, and I have found that in conversations with you, I can get those "things" best straightened. Too often we find each other in social events initiating discussions about topics that are important to us, but never have the true opportunity to go deeper in them; someone always comes to interrupt, there are always other topics that get in the way, and as a result we don't really get to know what each other is thinking.

I will now tell you something that bothers me constantly, something that is the source of certain disquiet in me. And I hate to have to recur to quote Jacques Derrida to do so, but at this very moment I can't think of any other way to do it.

Derrida once wrote that he desperately was trying to find a way to write outside of philosophy and outside of literature, but without forgetting the memory of either of them. I often feel that we in art are dealing with a similar dilemma, except that the two worlds that we are trying to negotiate are art history and the present world. Are we continuing to be subservient to an art history that only seems to satisfy and reinforce itself and its own narratives? Or by renouncing it do we end up producing art in the void?

Perhaps its best if I provide a practical example about this question in the shape of a story.

There are two artists. Let's name one of them Oxyartes and the other Polygnotus.

Both are professional artists, and both have a robust education and knowledge of their field. The difference is that Oxyartes is just not interested in the artists of the past; art history bores him. He is much more interested in issues about the world and his artwork is a direct, visceral response to that. He could not be less concerned with how what he produces in the forms of art works could be preserved, exhibited to many people, or collected. Polygnotus, in contrast, is obsessed about art history, and knowledgeable. He can accurately recall vast amounts of information about art that happened forty, fifty years ago, and most of his work is a commentary on that art. Polygnotus loves to talk about his art, probably more than making it. It is almost like each work is mainly a prop to illustrate a one-hour lecture on why this particular object is justified. And for the most part he is compelling, if slightly annoying, when he pedantically elaborates each of his points. Oxyartes, on the other hand, doesn't like to elaborate or even talk on top of his work; the work in it of itself generates debate and animated dialogue amongst those who experience it.

The most important museum in these two artists' lives is aware of the work they both produce, and is considering how to support them. But, the museum is dealing with issues of its own. Its collection is essentially of work made forty, fifty years ago, and the question today is on how those works are relevant to our present. More and more this museum seems like a mausoleum of once vibrant ideas.

The curators admire the work of Oxyartes, but it is a work that, because it breaks with almost every convention on how a museum operates or collects, poses formidable challenges for them to present in any way. Oxyartes' work, when discussed or thought about in the context of the collection of this museum, makes the museum's collection look even more old fashioned than it usually looks.

In contrast, Polygnotus' work fits perfectly with those older works. He has spent his entire career studying those pieces and can animatedly exchange academic theories with the museum's curators, who in turn, feel excited to utilize their connoisseurship in those conversations. They can think of many exhibitions they can curate where Polygnotus' works neatly fit in the already existing narrative. And Polygnotus' works can be acquired.

In the end, the museum decides that Polygnotus is the artist they will support for the time being. They purchase his works and give him a major exhibition. Other museums follow suit with his work. Oxyartes continues producing, but at a modest scale since he can't count on the infrastructure of the museum. Many years later, Polygnotus is a rich man, producing works that still dialogue with the works from now seventy years ago. At some point someone asks: who was that artist from Polygnotus' generation that produced un-exhibitable art? Someone answers: "Oh yes, Oxyartes. I believe he abandoned the art world."

Truly yours,

Pablo

8

February 5, 2014

Pablo León de la Barra
New York

Dear Pablo,

There is a story that for some reason I can't stop thinking about; perhaps because it has a particular significance for our time. I mention it to you because you may find certain resonance to our collective concerns.

The story is about a XIXth century French geographer whose name I believe was Maximilien Calmet (although I could be wrong). Dr. Calmet was considered the absolute authority in his field. Growing up, he had become weary of the short-sightedness of people around him. He didn't like the idea that everything would be explained through the eyes and the logic of the place where he grew up. His desire to become a geographer stems precisely from his effort to get away from a mono-centric perception of the world. He soon became a world traveler, going to remote and dangerous places that range from the Arabian desert to the depths of the Amazon; from the Himalayas to Antartica. He became known as an expert in capturing the most minute and defining details of regions and places. He formed many of the most important geographers of subsequent generations.

For many decades he worked on an immense Atlas, his life's work, that was meant to correct once and for all the inaccuracies of previous atlases. Using the most advance measurement techniques, he surveyed every river, every mountain, every small city and town known to exist in the planet. He worked with an army of young geographers. Nothing seemed to escape him. Toward the end of his life, he published the massive compendium, which is comprised of forty huge, heavy volumes. The work was very well received by the specialists and the critics; soon it became the geography textbook for generations.

I think we all, to a degree, at some point in our lives have a fantasy to be the Dr. Maximilien Calmet of our respective professions. Certainly when it comes to art, we usually appear to be in pursuit of the holy grail of definitiveness. Let me explain. We, for instance, try to come up with gestures that represent "the last word" on a particular conversation, something that summarizes everything else behind us. It is the revolutionary and disruptive—yet restorative—spirit that we inherited from modernism. Our challenge is, in a way, to absorb everything that has been done before and then set our best foot forward.

But curators, I believe, are often thrown into (or willingly throw themselves into) an even more narcissistic and fraught game.

Whatever exhibition narrative they produce is expected to carry in itself the most accurate representation of our concerns and knowledge on that subject. It has to be compelling, final, and provide an accurate narration. When I look at those vast collections of works of a large museum, I often think of my beloved Giulio Camillo, the Renaissance creator of the Memory Theater, who imagined a place where all the things of the world could be known and where all the forms of knowledge would meet in a specific *loci*—a system of systems. Needless to say, Camillo's theater was a great failure, starting from his inability to get his theaters construction funded.

The problem with this aspiration to represent totality is that we humans have a great limitation in our ability to absorb vast quantities of information. And perhaps the most difficult aspect of it is not our ability to see what is in front of us, but rather our ability to distinguish what is missing. Think about a museum collection, for instance, and the stories that it purports to tell. Even if the museum would claim to be telling a partial story, there is always the feeling that it is telling a final narrative. And no museum ever tells us the things that are not available to see. Don't you think it would be interesting if every time you walked into a museum you would receive not just a map of what is on view but also a list of all those things that are not on view and will never be?

Which brings me to the end of my story.

Dr. Calmet died many years ago. He was highly revered and continued to be so years later. It so happened that one day, a young geographer who was trying to check on a detail in Dr. Calmet's Atlas made a startling discovery that no one else, dazzled as they were by the vastness of this work, had made: in this most erudite and monumental masterpiece that comprised all of geographic knowledge, Monsieur Calmet had completely forgotten to include France.

Truly yours,

Pablo

9

February 7, 2014

Martha Wilson
Brooklyn, NY

Dear Martha,

Today as I was reading the newspaper, I bumped into a quote by a political analyst that is not that special, yet got me thinking. "It is impossible to separate politics from policy." It's a fact that most of us who have been around for a while know: you may have a vision, but to implement it you have to compromise all the time through politics. It is clear how this happens in government, but we rarely discuss how this happens with art. Don't you think someone should one day write an art history of what artists actually wanted to do and what they end up doing? I imagine you may say that intentions may not be relevant to know, and what matters is what happened not what was supposed to happen. But I am an artist and while fully aware about this reality I want to still know what was the original impulse behind an idea.

In any case, it seems to me that the public tends to romanticize the vision of artists, implicitly supporting the idea that we have a vision and we simply make it happen until the world comes around to recognize it (or not). It is rarely discussed how the art work is a direct result of the clash of what the artist wants (their policy) and the maneuverings they need to engage with to make it happen.

It would be helpful for us to publicly debate how this process takes place. It would allow us to understand the dilemmas we face. For example, we hate to see art smeared by the dirt of politics and business—we reject it as opportunism. And yet it is undeniable that some of the most successful artists have managed to negotiate their work by showing a great political and business instinct. And we all do tolerate in artists a certain degree of that mixture of politics and policy. But we all have limits of course.

I will pose, as example, a particularly unfortunate case that both you and I know well.

We both are familiar with Madame Fitzgerald. Obviously I am not using her real name, but I won't have to.

Mme. Fitzgerald was truly a revolutionary artist. She made works that questioned every convention that could be had about art. Most art she made challenged the audience; she could be hostile and irritating at times, but also seductive and passionate. She completely shunned the art market and she risked her life constantly in pursuit of her work. More than an artist she seemed sometimes like a kamikaze operator, always throwing herself into unpredictable situations with great courage and integrity.

Her dedication paid off. Generations of young artists were moved and influenced by her work. She attained fame and became a key reference in art history books. But then, as the decades went by and Mme. Fitzgerald was no longer young, some of these younger artists she had inspired started making works that, while clearly benefitting from her legacy and the roads she had opened to them, were not necessarily against the art market or even traditional aesthetics. Moreover, theirs were also compelling works that started attracting audiences on their own. She saw, in a combination of puzzlement and jealousy, how these artists deftly satisfied the material demands of museums and collectors while still retaining a foot in the conceptual radicality that she espoused. These artists started becoming very wealthy and influential in their own right, while Mme. Fitzgerald who remained a moral authority, was struggling financially.

The last straw came when she saw that a car company was imitating one of her images as part of a commercial. Not much later, a perfume ad showed an image that was very close to her work as well.

This was when she decided to take matters into her own hands. And she did it in the only way she knew how to do things: with extreme radicality, in a no-hostage taken approach. She moved to New York, as she calculated that this was the city where she would have a more global presence; she lobbied to do large exhibitions in large museums—and succeeded. But at the same time, she decided to embrace the art market more fully than ever, monetizing those conceptual art works that had been symbols of her rebellion to the status quo. Many artists of her generation refused to take that step, as they saw it as a breach to their integrity; but for Mme. Fitzgerald, this was an inevitable and necessary step.

She did not stop there. Her pursuit of a legacy over the years turned into a full-fledged campaign that included attending social events, befriending celebrities and powerful collectors, producing works for benefits, and producing a myriad of collectable objects. Her fan base felt now more like a cult, while the artists that once admired and respected her started to question her judgment. Her permanent obsession with herself—which is natural for an artist—became so extreme that it verged on the self-parody. In her attempt to claim her rightful role in art, she had overreached and in the process compromised the most important thing an artist can have: the integrity of their work.

Once that was gone, there was no turning back. She had already taken a course that had merged strategy and aesthetics to an extent that it all looked, well, like strategy. And one day Madame Fitzgerald woke up and she was a has-been, while other artists of her generation, who had suffered in silence while the art world had ignored them and become fascinated with Mme. Fitzgerald, now were receiving a new appreciation as those who never sold out, who had not made the effort to translate themselves to the present.

Yours truly,

Pablo

10

February 8, 2014

Jacqueline Mabey
Brooklyn, NY

Dear Jaqueline,

You may wonder why I am choosing to write you letters when there are so many more expedient ways to communicate. One reason I use this form is for the fact that when one writes a letter, one has to be more thoughtful of what is necessary to include, and what is irrelevant. Further, when one reads a letter, one tends to read the entire piece, and if they so desire, one can go back to re-read it. If well constructed, a letter contains a coherent, whole message. This is less true of email, which tends to be quick and fragmentary, or even live speaking, which loses structure and focus in its improvisation. Finally, I feel I communicate best when I write because it is when I can think things through, and not be distracted by the intensity of physical interactions in live conversation.

Through living in the art world for years, I have become weary of our incapacity to set irrelevant conversation aside from meaningful conversation. I believe we are facing an intellectual bankruptcy, mainly as a result of ceaselessly talking and scarcely listening.

One of the most important experiences I had as a young adult was in 1995, when I had the privilege to bring the Mexican poet Octavio Paz to Chicago to read his poetry. Paz was a giant in the universe of my upbringing, an almost untouchable being—he had won the Nobel Prize a few years before. I saw him as one of the only connectors between the literary tradition I had been brought up with, and the new conceptual art tradition I was beginning to understand—he had been friends with Cage and Duchamp. My job was to be his chaperone in Chicago for five days or so, taking him around the city. Waiting for him at the airport I recall the extreme nervousness, intimidation and excitement that I felt about meeting someone I saw as an "immortal".

Yet Paz was a most reasonable and disarming individual. He was very formal. But most interestingly, he was intensely focused on individuals. As we were in the car being taken toward the hotel, he started asking me questions. How could a giant like him be possibly interested in a meaningless young kid? He wanted to know what I did. When I replied that I did performance art, he asked: "I never understood what performance art is. What is it?"

Over the years I have played the role of public programmer in museums, seeing thousands of people in art and culture go onstage, famous and unknown. Of those experiences I learned that the truly great ones are the most humble, and also the best listeners.

The true danger lies not in those who don't know how to listen—those are easily dismissed. But, on those who used to listen, and are then rewarded with positions of power, and once in power they lose those abilities. It is easy to recognize a false ability to listen—it is basically condescendence, although wrapped in a beautiful package of caring.

So what is it that really allows us to listen, and what is it that prevents us from it?

I think about this in the context of someone we both know. Let's call her Rosamond Elfland to spare her from the embarrassment—although as you will read on, you will understand that there is no way she will ever realize that we are talking about her.

The (real) name of Rosamond Elfland is held in high regard in the art world. She is credited with having brought a revolution in exhibition-making and museums. She broke new ground in many respects and created a culture of self-introspection that served well the period under which museums were looking to change their institutional practices.

Often, individuals who become successful at some point in their careers soon forget about the struggle that brought them there in the first place. Success brings a certain degree of comfort that results in making one believe that any further progress one makes can, and should, be painless. One could argue that this was the case of Mrs. Elfland. Other theories are that she achieved such an overblown renown that anything she would do after her initial successes would not have possibly prevented the perception of her eventual decline. Most likely, she became unable to discern the meaningful from the meaningless, the collective from the personal—something so hard to learn to do, and so easy to lose.

She certainly thought of herself as the greatest listener, and while she didn't promote herself that way, everything else she did and every action she took throughout her life insinuated that conviction.

Mrs. Elfland had a moment where she could have called it quits, but she then took on one of the highest positions in the art world—let's say a major museum directorship—perhaps thinking that it was the right step for her. But career moves, the more ambitious they are, start functioning like a risky gamble in a casino; if one overestimates oneself, one can lose everything one has gained.

And so it happened that Mrs. Elfland tried to test her magical listening abilities with those around her. But her instinctive hearing was in decline. Unfortunately, at that time, the experiences she had were so powerful that they rendered unable to listen to, or see, the changed world around her.

Young, energetic and talented professionals working under her, inspired by her past work, would come to her with their hopeful projects. At first she appeared encouraging, but at best she was noncommittal. Foundations threw money at her, hoping she would do something magical with the money as she had done in the past. She held meetings with these loyal young curators to come up with new and transformative ideas. But of all that was said and presented, she could only hear herself talk. Because her voice was the only one that she would listen to, she would not realize that it was only hers. So at the end of every meeting she would come to certain conclusions, thinking that she had successfully shepherded her mentees toward new and radical ideas; while they had simply sat there taking notes and wondering how they would accomplish her bewildering and random thoughts.

Millions of dollars were spent in projects to make her ideas work. When even pulling all those resources failed, she blamed it on her assistants, and on the people around her. She started looking disheveled at meetings; her once more carefully worded caring phrases now sounded outright condescending. She lost her careful sense of composure. She would complain that no one would inform her of things when in fact dozens of people around her were briefing her all the time. She usually appeared confused at meetings, not quite understanding what the discussions were about. The world started looking incomprehensible to her. And for those poor people around her—they rolled their eyes in puzzlement and confusion, wondering what to do. Although this may feel like a forced comparison, the best way to explain it is that there were moments where Mrs. Elfland appeared to look like Hitler in his final hours in his bunker, giving orders and moving fictional armies around a map when everyone around him knew the war was lost but were afraid to disclose the news.

The truth was that absolutely no one would be willing to tell Mrs. Elfland the truth. It was not worth it: by then she had completely lost the ability to listen. She would only have reacted angrily, and no one wanted to suffer her irrational wrath.

Slowly, the museum started building systems to circumvent her madness, under an unspoken understanding that there were the orders she was giving and the real order of the day that the rest of the staff would arrive at by consensus.

Finally, one morning, Mrs. Elfland was found standing in the galleries, in sweat pants, talking to the paintings. She could no longer recognize her employees.

This was more than ten years ago. By most accounts, she has not realized that she is no longer the director of the museum. The museum board, too afraid of letting her go, of creating the public relations nightmare that the ousting of Mrs. Elfland would carry, decided to build a new office exclusively for her, where she makes phone calls and writes letters, conducting imaginary conversations and concocting all sort of exhibition ideas. Officially she has an emeritus title, and when interview requests come, the PR department answers the interviews in writing on her behalf, afraid that the art world would know the truth and then it would reflect poorly on the museum for its poor judgment in hiring her in the first place.

The larger portion of the day, Mrs. Elfland spends it dictating to a secretary what she describes as exhibition essays.

I believe you would enjoy them. Most of those texts read like a play by Gertrude Stein.

Yours truly,

Pablo

11

February 12, 2014

Carlos Gutiérrez
New York, NY

Dear Carlos,

As you well know, I am interested in education. Education wasn't always an interest of mine, but it arose out of necessity after I entered into the world of museums. Over the years, when one takes pride in his work, this pride translates into enthusiasm and ownership of what one does. So in any case, I am interested in education. And as part of this interest—and I suspect we both share this—one of the ongoing questions I think we all contend with on a daily basis is what is there to be learned, or taught about art.

I have felt for a long time that we have consistently answered this question completely wrong; mainly, because it is the formulation of the question that is misguided.

The best way to try to convey what I mean is by telling you a story.

Once upon a time there was a civilization. It was sophisticated in every respect, advanced in science, philosophy and with a complex and functioning social system in place that created orderly and peaceful cities.

One day, unannounced, a particular kind of animal started appearing in the streets. It did not appear to fit any particular species known by this civilization. At first people were deeply confounded, because the descriptions of this animal varied widely. It was thought in fact that there were many different kinds of animals out there. But when they all were rounded up, they kind of started looking the same. This led the scientists to conclude that all these animals did indeed belong to the same species.

Every time one of these animals would appear they would be rounded up by the citizens and presented to the scientists to see if the animals were worth studying. On a regular basis those that were deemed of most interest were brought into spaces where they were put on exhibit for the scientists to study and for the public to look at. The acquisition of some of these specimens started becoming a lucrative business. In captivity, these beings would appear dead most of the time; it started to seem impossible to discern in fact if they were dead or alive. But it was considered an unavoidable fact that this was the only way in which they could be brought to the public for the enjoyment and education of all.

Scientists spent decades and decades studying these animals. Generations of professionals were formed with the specific specialty of becoming experts on every small variation of these beings. Thousands of pages were written on each one of them, as well as thousands of pages in response to the thousands of pages that interpreted and explained these animals. Whole universities were built to further the understanding of this species, and a private market of ownership of these beasts became standard practice amongst the wealthier members of this civilization.

Then one day word came that, once again, there was a new animal in existence out in the world. These however were fierce animals on remote islands, untamable, and impossible to capture by the scientists, as they had the ability to become invisible and ethereal, like ghosts, upon capture. It was unclear how these animals were linked to the known species in their exhibition spaces. Ultimately those scientists, who claimed to know everything there was to know about their captive animals, dismissed this new species as uninteresting and not even worth studying. Because they couldn't use their scholarship on them, because they could not capture or exhibit them, these beasts offered no real value to the scientific community and their study centers. Because they could not be purchased and sold, there was no interest amongst the business community to bother with them either. And because no one could bring them to the general public, the public was not aware of them. Some scientists didn't even believe these beings were real. As a result, the reports of their existence and what they did, which sounded extraordinary, were largely ignored.

It was only one of those scientists who once presented a paper at a conference discussing his findings about these new, mysterious, animals. He had conducted research for many years that he had spent on one of those remote islands. Not only were those animals the direct descendants of those in captivity, he argued, but they exhibited the same qualities that were recorded of their ancestors when they were young and before their capture. These new animals, however, had developed a new resistance to captivity as an evolutionary measure—thus their ability to disappear and become ethereal when necessary.

As the species, along with all its genealogy, still did not have a proper name after all these years, this scientist proposed to assign a name for them.

He said: "I propose we call them art."

Sincerely yours,

Pablo

12

February 15, 2014

Jaime Permuth
New York, NY

Dear Jaime,

We all know that if one is serious about being an artist, they must accept that one's entire career and production may be ignored or dismissed by the tastemakers, and the art world at large. To accept the world's indifferent reaction to what one does is probably the most difficult test that an artist can survive. Despite how social we are, how much family we have, we artists exist in solitude. The decisions that we have to make about our work against that solitude—particularly when we are faced by indifference—can be extremely difficult and painful.

In contrast, it is easy to be a beloved artist: feeling desired by everyone, seeing how all line up to experience one's work, receiving compliments and adulation. That also usually translates into financial success, and financial resources to produce even more desirable works.

For that reason, we should perhaps rethink the kind of considerations that we take when we critique the work of an artist. To what extent should we be more demanding of the work of the beloved and successful artist, and take into consideration the vast resources, love and emotional support that has made him or her able to produce work? To what extent should we consider the degree of struggle that an abandoned artist has had as mitigating factor—to make work against all odds?

I once heard about a psychologist who took this concern as a central issue to study. This psychologist—let's name him Xavier Ross—worked for many years in creating an experiment that became very controversial because of the way in which it affected others and its dubious ethical choices, as I shall explain.

Dr. Ross wanted to prove that the socioeconomic and critical environment under which an artist works is the real determining factor on whether the work that these artist produce is actually relevant. For that purpose, he identified two artists who were at a point in their career that they were no longer emerging artists but also had not reached full maturity—the mid-career stage, let's say—for his experiment. Both artists had similar and evolving careers, and were each at a juncture wherein they could still get a big break, or slowly stop growing.

He chose one of the artists—let's call him Hipolitus—and in indirect and secret ways started giving him powerful motivators, without Hipolitus ever knowing that he was the subject of an experiment. He maneuvered for him to receive a large art grant. By becoming a trustee of a powerful museum he managed to get Hipolitus an exhibition there. He hired an actress to "fall in love" with him and become his girlfriend; he hired critics to write positively about his work, and had dozens of people email him, write to him and stop him in the street to constantly reinforce his importance and inspiration to others.

The incredible wave of good fortune in Hipolitus' career most definitely had an effect on him. His work actually improved; by being more motivated he took more risks, produced much more work, and gained a confidence and energy that he did not have before. There was happiness in him that made his work strong, energetic, and far-reaching. Real opportunities then flew to him. As other curators started noticing him, he started getting more invitations and became an ubiquitous figure in the art market.

The other artist, by contrast—let's call him Claude—became the unfortunate subject of Dr. Ross to enact on him his "failed artist" plan. Claude obviously didn't know about this. Dr. Ross ensured that many hired hands would constantly criticize Claude's works; he actively interfered with any opportunity that would come Claude's ways, becoming very good at blocking them. He introduced negative elements in his life, also with an attractive actress, who drew him into a toxic relationship with lots of alcohol and drugs.

Within months, Claude was going through a depression. He had completely lost faith in himself. Before the end of the year, he had stopped making art altogether and was starting to consider suicide.

Dr. Ross was exhilarated—he was certain that his experiment had been successful. He now needed to reverse the course of both of these artists' career in order to prove that it was the controlled conditions—and not the artists themselves—that ultimately determined who would become a better artist.

But the process of reversal proved difficult. Hipolitus' career had taken off by now, and so many curators, collectors, and supporters had become so invested in his work that they actively advocated for him. Hipolitus' success stretched beyond Dr. Ross' capabilities to create the conditions under which Hipolitus would lose enough support and confidence. Even the actress that at first had signed up to seduced Hipolitus had really fallen in love with him.

Dr. Ross started to panic. Although he had helped Hipolitus attain his true goals, he knew that he had simultaneously ruined Claude's life. It now seemed almost impossible to cure the spiral of addiction, violence and self-hatred that Claude had fallen into. Dr. Ross was terrified that Claude would commit suicide. He then decided to come forward and meet with Claude to confess everything to him. He told Claude that he had been the author of his demise; and that Claude's failure had been scientifically manufactured as part of an experiment. Dr. Ross tried to present it as good news, suggesting that any sense of failure was only in Claude's mind.

All we know is that Dr. Ross was severely hurt that night, thrown out of a balcony. He died a few days later at a hospital, in physical and deep emotional pain. Claude was charged with murder and is now serving time in a federal prison.

You may be better able than me to surmise any meaning from the story above. I, for one, can't help but wonder how would it be possible to know if each of us has a secret Dr. Ross behind us, subtly manipulating our artistic destiny, and if so, what kind of plan he may have for our success or our demise in the world of art.

All yours,
Pablo

13

February 17, 2014

Charmaine Picard
New York, NY

Dear Charmaine,

I know that you, like me, believe in the power of education. And also like me, I sense that you struggle to solve the seemingly unsolvable problem of what is it that aspiring artists should be taught—what tools can we give them so that they might achieve their goals.

After much thinking about it, I believe I now have the answer. I will pose it to you by narrating a simple story.

There are three aspiring artist friends. Let's call them Armando, Lionel, and Timothy. Their goal is to triumph in the art world, achieve world recognition, and be able to reap the benefits of that recognition. Let's say they all have talent, and have comparable qualities as creative minds.

Armando is an idealist—he believes in the value of full dedication. As such, he becomes close to a monk in his creative approach, spending endless hours exploring his interior, struggling in the studio, and producing endless amounts of works. His focus is to find that inner authenticity that makes every artwork great.

Lionel is eminently social. He frequents bars and cafes, openings and panel discussions, biennials and art fairs. He gets himself known and ensures that he is in tune with what colleagues of his generation think and feel. He develops a sense for what kind of art can speak to the present moment.

Timothy is more of a pragmatist. He decides to study something else so that he can pay his bills and make art on the side. He chooses to study law as he is good at arguing and figures he can make a decent living.

Armando struggles all his life. His work in the end is undeniably authentic, but it is such the result of such an inner dialogue that ultimately is too hermetic and nonsensical to the public at large. While it generates certain interest and curiosity, ultimately it is dismissed as an overly self-absorbed body of work and is ultimately discarded.

Lionel is successful at first. His work attracts attention amongst his peers and indeed, as he planned, becomes representative of his time, even admired for its capacity to synthesize that moment. The problem becomes that, with the passing of the years, the attributes of the work start feeling dull, commonplace. It becomes apparent that his work falls somewhere in the middle of a whole range of similar artistic ideas, within which this artist is neither the first nor the best exponent. As a result, these works go to a second or third tier and are eventually forgotten.

Timothy has studied law and become very successful at it. He becomes a partner at his firm. He realizes that legal departments at museums ultimately control a lot of the most important decisions; the larger the institution is, the more paranoid it is about issues of security and copyright. He thus sees the benefit in creating "legal" art.

With that in mind, in collaboration with his law firm Timothy initiates a series of lawsuits that expose museum's abuses, unethical collecting practices and its bullying attitude toward artist's copyright. This artist's lawsuits attract a great deal of attention and become a PR sensation. He helps influence legislation to regulate the art market in more favorable terms to artists. Artists recognize the importance of having legal representation and some even go to law school to learn how to best protect their interests. As museum legal fees accumulate, this brings a collapse in the museum system as we knew it.

At first museums argue that having artists develop legal skills is bad for the art world at large, and would prevent anyone from collecting and preserving art in the future. But in reality, new systems are developed and put into place, with cooperative models that have the benefit of the public in mind, eliminating the excessive influence of wealthy collectors in public institutions.

Timothy becomes a hero amongst artists and is hailed as a true revolutionary.

I hope you may now appreciate the benefit to merge art schools with law schools.

Yours truly,

Pablo

14

February 19, 2014

Anne Pasternak
New York, NY

Dear Anne,

There are certain questions about the art world that have bothered me over the years, some of which are so basic and yet so troubling that I am shocked that they are never discussed—and sometimes concerned that I may be descending into madness.

One of them is the degree to which art should really be made available to the public. You may wonder how I, an art educator for 25 years, could possibly utter such profanity. But please hear me out first.

Lets think about this through a story about a country in particular—I will call it Rosaura.

About a half and century ago, Rosaura had a cultural golden age. These golden ages, as we know already from history, happen to be a combination of a rise in financial wealth, education and spare time of citizens. This was the case of Rosaura, which up to that point had been on the receiving end of culture. But this new generation of citizens produced both original artists and wealthy philanthropists. These artists were fueled by a profound sense of purpose in their work; they believed that what they were doing was urgent and necessary, that it carried a message that needed to be shared with all. It all was linked to the birth of a collective consciousness that they felt they needed to help generate.

The philanthropists, moved by these artists and their artworks, generously built museums where these artists could exhibit, and the public saw the work and was moved by it. These philanthropists had no other interest in mind but to contribute back to the society that had given them so much.

And, as imagined by the artist, there was a collective communion between that public and those artists, successfully brokered by those museums. Those art works became valuable and collected; those artists as they aged became rich and successful. The works they produced later, while great, no longer carried that urgency, as their primary purpose in life was achieved.

Within this context, the following generation of artists arrived to find the museums were built, the careers of those artists had already mostly taken place, and there was a collective understanding of how the art they had made was important to Rosaura. It was a hard act to follow. As a result these artists felt they had no choice but to make art that was not about the original subject of the previous generation, but that commented on that previous generation's art. That was also what happened with the generation that followed, and the generation that followed. To make sense of how all this internal commentary worked, museums created the role of curators, who were trained to maintain this conversation.

The public was increasingly baffled by how this incrementally hermetic conversation started evolving. While they recognized that something important was being discussed they didn't understand what that conversation was and why it was, in fact, important. Curators, whose specialty was to understand the art and not the public, thought the public was stupid and could not care less about their opinions. Yet Rosaura's museums were built on a dependency on the public, either because they functioned with public funds or because they needed the attendance revenue from visitors to keep purchasing and exhibiting art. They created education departments that would help those visitors make sense of that art, and for a while that helped Rosaura's museums to be more inviting places. But as time went by, the disconnect continued, and audiences instinctively felt that they were mere witnesses of a conversation of which they had nothing to contribute.

A few artists started to show concerns about this disconnect, and started making art specifically for those publics. One would think that this would have been a positive development for museums, but in fact curators, who now ran these institutions, didn't like it, as it displaced and sometimes altogether eliminated their role as curators. Instead they continued collecting and presenting artwork by artists who primarily were interested in talking to themselves and to previous art.

As publics dwindled, museums entered into a crisis. While they publicly continued to state their original mission, their priority stopped being to carry the urgent message contained in art, and it turned into meeting budgetary goals to keep the institution alive. They were forced to offer art as mere entertainment—art that nobody believed in, but that brought easy money to allow them, ostensibly, to do the "real exhibitions" they wanted to make.

But then Rosaura's museums turned into a strange mixture of, on the one hand, mindless spectacles that brought in a lot of people combined with hermetic exhibitions that no one understood or visited. All this while the remaining artists that were truly connecting with the public were doing so in small places and contexts, which were ironically similar to the small museums that were initially built in Rosaura during its golden age. But those were difficult to sustain, as the selfless philanthropists of old times had now passed away, and their descendants were more interested in their own private collections and in building their own personal reputation through their own pet projects.

What came next is easy to imagine. Rosaura's museums came finally to a point where they had to compete with the entertainment and tourism industry, a battle that they were not designed to fight. One day, a successful media entertainment corporation approached one of these museums to merge. Slowly, every museum started becoming absorbed by an entertainment company, becoming something similar to a culture channel for for-profit ventures.

It was also recognized that it was not necessary to depend on artists to create artworks. In any case, artists presented a wide range of problems, starting from their annoying insistence of maintaining the copyright of their works, of having a say on how their works would be reproduced and exhibited, etc. Museums started contracts with cultural experience design firms that produced studies relating to what audiences wanted and made art works responding to those interests. This allowed museums much more flexibility and ultimately it was seen as advantageous for museums to exist within an entertainment complex that might include such things as a convention center, commercial movie theaters, shopping centers, spas, five star restaurants, hotels, and casinos. One even had a brothel (prostitution is legal in Rosaura).

If you visit Rosaura's capital today, you can get packages that will include tickets to those museum complexes along with all the other previously described amenities. If you are curious, I have heard that if you take a taxi to the outskirts of the city you will find a small community where a few artists still make art in the old-fashioned way, holding out the archaic, romantic notion that art is an urgent communication; that art is a one-to-one conversation.

Yours,

Pablo

15

February 20, 2014
Brooklyn, Maybelle's Café

Ezequiel Jiménez
Bronx, NY

Dear Ezequiel,

This Saturday morning as I was walking through my neighborhood toward this café to write, I thought about the conversations that some of us involved in art tend to have regarding our disappointment about the way certain things get valued over others, the excessive importance that is placed on the market, and the spurious art that suddenly arises when the truly substantial art is largely ignored—mainly because it requires people to give it brains and dedication.

All this of course makes one wonder why this is the case. Is it a problem with art, or is it a problem with those who today make art?

I can perhaps offer a small story that may help reflect on that topic.

A long time ago, in the ancient world, word came that there was a city, Elzaia, where its citizens had developed the ability to communicate with birds. It had apparently started with a wise man who had studied birds all his life and had an immense love for them. This love triggered his desire to communicate with the feathered creatures. Over the years, he had taught this difficult art to others, who in turn also had disciples. At some point, communication with these animals became a central aspect of the culture of Elzaia. Every citizen of this city was a bird communicator. As such, many other cities became curious and interested to know how this rare art was done.

Some Elzaians started to travel to make demonstrations of their abilities. Because the public was eager to see these demonstrations, the Elzaians started to charge sums of money. Tourism poured into Elzaia, where theaters were built to make more and more spectacular demonstrations. A neighboring city, Islaya, built its own theater and promoted its spectacles in competition with Elzaia. Other cities followed. Elzaians took a more aggressive approach by creating a school for bird communicators that everyone around the ancient world joined to learn the bird language. The art started being used in battle, as it was recognized that one could send coded messages through birds. After a few decades, the art of bird communication had fully developed for war and for spectacle. Communicating with birds had stopped being a labor of love; it now was a profession and a business career. So those who joined this practice were those who had money and success in mind, in the case of the business oriented; and in the case of the military students, the destruction of the enemy fueled their interest in learning.

But it so happened that the more this practice became spread out and turned into different methods, the more limited the communication with these beings appeared to be. Birds seemed more and more reluctant to communicate now with these humans. It was almost as if those birds began to find humans boring.

The city of Elzaia began a slow decline. The elders complained that love for birds was now gone; they were now treated like instruments. The few of those who shared the love of birds of their grandparents didn't like the option of a military or business path, so they mostly left for other cities to pursue other endeavors.

But as it happens with elders, no one ever pays attention to what they are saying, dismissing them as senile or intolerant.

Finally came the day when bird communication was so ineffective that it could no longer support any kind of reliable show-business or military activity. As a result, schools started closing, armies developed more effective weapons and communication strategies, and cities redirected their efforts to attract tourism revenue.

A generation later, Elzaia was reduced to a few scattered huts, and a generation later, it no longer existed as a city.

To this day, nobody knows how to communicate with the birds.

All yours

Pablo

16

February 25, 2014

Coco Fusco
Brooklyn, NY

Dear Coco,

At this very moment it is 5:35pm on a Saturday. I am in my bedroom, during a rare moment of calm, writing. The window is open, and this is exactly the hour when the late evening is turning into night, that undefined state of the day that is, as we say in Mexico, *entre azul y buenas noches.* There is the noise of a saw heard somewhere far away, as well as the passing of cars. This sound immediately takes me to the street where I grew up in the colonia Nápoles in Mexico City, where all day, but especially in the evenings at this exact hour, when I was at the house doing homework, I would hear the saw of the carpenter and the frame-maker who were just across the street.

There is a subject that I rarely talk about to others, even though it is a reality that I contend with every single day of my life. It is also a subject that many people like us think about all the time. I am speaking of my condition of self-imposed exile.

To leave one's country voluntarily, as I did when I was young, being able to return to it if so desired, is most definitely not comparable to the condition of those who cannot return, due to political reasons. I can't even imagine the great pain and profound sense of void that they must feel. I also am not one of those immigrants who left their country in search of a better economic situation. My situation is far more rarified.

Over the years, I have become victim to the effects of exile. I have over-romanticized my country of origin, my family, my high-school crushes, my city, my street. I have spoken with ghosts (and often feel I continue to do so). I also suspect that I have developed a worldview that is rooted on remnants of that romanticism.

We all know of those cases where an artist, away from his or her place of origin, develops their work almost entirely on that world. James Joyce writing in Trieste, Ana Mendieta thinking about Cuba in Iowa, Chagall painting in New York. It's clear that making art is a way to deal with the profound sense of loss created by exile. But come to think of it, this is not too different from how we use art to symbolically restore time.

My childhood friend Jordi Sod said it to me the other day: we all are exiled from our own past. What I guess I am trying to say is that to understand how artists transform experiences of exile into art is only one way to understand the many ways in which we attempt to manifest our various experiences of alienation from times and places.

But I am not interested in talking about myself, or offering a self-indulgent confessional. Perhaps this is why the subject is difficult for me to discuss. What has become more important to me is to understand the kind of traps that exile poses to art making.

Maybe the best way I could pose the complexities and contradictions of exile is through the following example.

I once knew an artist couple. I will call them Domingo Thiers and Dorothy Ursten.

There was always a strange relationship between them, despite or precisely because of the kind of people they were. Both were professors at a small university town in the middle of nowhere. Domingo, a Central-American exile, arrived there for the job, while Dorothy had always lived there, studying in the same university where she eventually became professor. Because of that fact, she was an escapist.

I knew them from art conferences that they would attend. While he always yearned for the original, the real, she yearned always to go to fictional and unreal places. They were very much aware of their condition and spoke about it openly. They both went to therapy together. I had no doubt that Domingo suffered from the effects of having been away from his country for thirty years and with the prospect of never returning; and it was also clear that Dorothy always yearned to go away.

Their work, as they themselves described it publicly, was a reflection of their respective conditions of exile and local. Domingo would write extensive essays on the exiled creative mind, and Dorothy would present papers on how her condition of growing in an average American town pushed her to aggressively pursue very different realities.

I confess I had never seen their work myself; only knew about their writings on the subject. One time I was invited by them to lecture in their college and, as those visits usually go, I had dinner with both of them at their house, which was combined with an obligatory visit to their studios. At this point I had been very curious to see the actual work. Dorothy's career-long project was the construction of a fictional country; Domingo's was based, he said, on the accurate reconstruction of his hometown, which I happened to know fairly well for work reasons. I had developed, as it usually happens, elaborate images of what the work would look like; thinking of Guillermo Cabrera Infante's exhaustive reconstruction of Havana in the 1950s; or in the case of Dorothy, a wildly fanciful, imaginary world in the vein of the Lord of the Rings.

But as I walked into Domingo's studio, I thought it was Dorothy's. The work consisted of paintings of a place that appeared to be completely imaginary. I could not recognize his hometown in it. He had constructed a heavily idealized world that had no relationship with that city. A person from that town must have been puzzled to see most of the images and references he used.

As for Dorothy, she later brought me into her studio, which contained a series of scale models of that fictional country that her work was recreating. They looked exactly like the only place she had ever known—that average, impersonal college town.

Yours truly,

Pablo

17

March 1, 2014

Claire Bishop
New York NY

Dear Claire,

I have found that in writing I feel more free to communicate questions that arise from very vulnerable aspects of myself. I am not interested in using this medium to create any kind of self-therapy—in a way, I could not be less interested in talking about myself. Yet I find this introspective search to be the only recourse to arrive at issues that I believe are truly important and that I hope are common concerns.

One of these vulnerabilities that I have is the place of routine in my life and its relationship to art making. I struggle with routine and believe it points to an important issue. On a personal level, I yearn for it, and I want things to remain exactly the same forever. Yet, as an artist, I know I can't remain what I am by sitting still inside a room, doing exactly the same thing every day.

But could one create a work that is pure routine and still make it meaningful? I so wish I could be like certain outside artists for whom this is not a concern. Some of them sit every day and simply make art without thinking of the external world. In contrast, those of us who belong to a deeply self-conscious tradition of conceptual art can't be granted that simple gift of sitting around, creating. We have to consider the entire context of where and when something is made, and if others will think what we want them to think. I suppose that I wonder if there is any way I can ever aspire to obtain a certain sense of stability within that constant push of self-examination and change.

In other words, the more we become involved in knowing art, the more we appear to be locked into the demand for constant change. Now, you may argue that it is a kind of routine. But I would say that it is instead the worst combination of two kinds of life: the monotonous aspect of a predictable life without the calm that this predictability offers, and the anxiety of constant change, without the thrill that change offers.

I am going to pose an example of this:

Isaac Chisholm—I am using a fictional name to prevent distractions—was a famous artist. From very early on, when he was in his early twenties, his work came to prominence through a number of very popular exhibitions that launched his generation. Chisholm's work was energetic, imaginative, and with a dimension of *enfant terrible* that was particularly seductive to curators and critics.

Chisholm produced great work for a few years. The attention that he received for his work translated into a myriad of invitations around the world to participate in exhibitions, biennials, residencies, and artist talks. Over time, he was in a non-stop travel schedule where in a given month he could be in six or seven different cities realizing different projects. He rarely had a chance to be at the studio. His assistants mostly received his orders from wherever he was at the time. When he started as an artist, ideas for his projects were usually the result of conversations in bars and parties with his friends, over tequila or beer. Now he was forced to prepare and submit project ideas from the enclosure of an impersonal hotel room in a random city, late at night, after exhausting days of travel and socializing, or during idle hours of waiting at airports. His life became, seemingly, a permanent wait at an airport. In addition, because of his successful sales, his galleries wanted him to produce more and he started having to satisfy a high overhead of assistants, studio, and the high level production of work.

As a result of all this, Chisholm started feeling trapped in a never-ending cycle of supply and demand upon which he was increasingly more dependent. He had the desire to start again, to make something completely new, but that was impossible. It felt out of character. Also, he was no longer young, and his *enfant terrible* attitude now felt out of place. He was no longer cool. He knew he would not be able to significantly change his work again without losing the support of his collectors and other supporters, but he also knew that he could not continue producing truly innovative works.

That was when, just about when he was reaching a breaking point, he decided to become two artists.

I don't mean to say that he invented a pseudonym. He went much further. Chisholm hired a young woman actor who would perform the role of an artist that he had completely conceptualized. He named this artist "Eva Aarons," scripted her entire background and trained her to play the role of her lifetime—an entire artist's career. Chisholm, by now knowledgeable about the art world, knew what it likes and dislikes. He even chose a last name with double "a" because he knew that alphabetical order of artists lists always give more visibility to those with "a" (Abramovic, Acconci). The woman actor was talented and extremely attractive, and soon drew attention. Chisholm made her work with renewed energy and passion, the one that he had already lost making his own work. He was like a combination of a coach, a theater director, and an artist altogether. Eva Aarons became a hot name in the art circles in New York; she started to exhibit in top tier galleries, and got into biennials as well. In the meantime, Chisholm's "original" work was already being considered in decline, and critics derided him as a "has been." He didn't care: he was convinced that when people found out that he was Eva Aarons there would be a renewed admiration for his work.

But the fiction started to prove hard to sustain. The actress started to suffer the pressure of acting all the time after being thrown into all kinds of stressful social situations that made it very hard for her to keep appearances. More and more she wanted to quit, and Chisholm spent enormous energies trying to convince her to keep on, offering more money and reassurances. Toward the end, Chisholm was almost bankrupt despite the fact that Aaron's work had started to sell.

In the end, the actress did unexpectedly collapse at a public event where she told the truth to the audience. The entire art world knew that she had been a fabrication by Chisholm. Taken by surprise—it seems shocking that he would not have prepared better for this moment—Chisholm sent out an announcement effectively declaring the creation of Eva Aarons as an art project.

But the response was not what Chisholm would have expected. Those who had supported Chisholm's work, were puzzled by his apparent rejection of his past work; those who were not his fans in the first place found this to be an arrogant move. As to those who had supported the fictional Eva Aarons, they were outraged at having been led to collect, support and/or fund someone who didn't exist, and wondered whether the works indeed could be considered real art works or just props. Feminists attacked Chisholm ferociously. Overall everyone felt betrayed.

Chisholm never knew how to deal with such a response—it was beyond what he could have possibly anticipated. The reaction made him realize two things: one, that he was no longer interested in making his own work, but only Aaron's, and second, that after what happened no one would believe that Aarons' work was a truthful artistic exploration for him.

That was about the time when he took a teaching position at a wealthy American university in a small town—in one of those places far away from the center where reputations from New York artists loom large and where the details about controversies rarely arrive. He secured a tenured position, and never returned to New York. And as it happens in this city, the moment you leave you are automatically forgotten.

I honestly don't know if to this day he has continued making his work. But someone told me he has a house with two dogs and has become primarily interested in sailing.

Yours truly,

Pablo

18

March 3, 2014

Eugenie Tsai
New York, NY

Dear Eugenie,

As I write this to you, I am on a plane, traveling to do an artist talk. As you know, travel has become inevitable for any art professional today; to not do so would be anathema to all the ideas that we have to do with how we become visible and how travel experiences enrich us.

But sometimes I have serious questions about that. I have now come to abhor travel. I am serious about this: I particularly want to differentiate myself from those people who commiserate about their punishing travel schedules, their endless connecting flights and globetrotting, when what they are really doing is showing off and being vane; this is because in our culture, someone who is busy traveling everywhere is seen as being sought after, desirable to others.

I sometimes really wish I could stop going places; I am tired of not seeing my daughter, taking her to the zoo on Saturdays, and not having the chance to sit at my dining table late at night to write or make collages. These things have become most important to me now. If there was something I could eliminate from my life, it would be the overwhelming anxiety and the solitude connected to travel. Yet I am torn, as I know that travel is simply part of what I have to do at this time.

The question that comes to my mind in this context is why do we continue to praise globetrotters so much today? I don't mean to question those true travelers, who move to another country and engage with a different reality at a deep level; those are the exceptions. It appears to me that traveling has become so predictable, specifically the cultural tourism circuits through which we tend to travel in the art world, that it doesn't add that much to our experience. Certainly you have to wonder about those people who travel to Venice or Basel or Miami to meet all of the same exact people, only against a different stage set.

I would like to look at the problem with you through a small story:

There once was a wealthy traveler. He loved the idea of seeing every city, every river, every natural and man-made construction of note in the world. He would travel ceaselessly, in a way that felt like an addiction.

During one of those trips, as he climbed a mountain, he encountered a hermit. They started a conversation and the traveler inquired, "How could you enjoy being alone on this mountain forever? Don't you want to see the world"? To which the hermit replied: "I have read everything there is to know about the world. I have all the books written about it here in my cave and I spend every day learning about it."

They both argued that one knew more than the other about the world. In the end, they placed a bet: each would write a book about their experiences, and a group of learned judges would decide what view of the world was most comprehensive and accurate. They gave themselves a year.

During that year, the traveler traveled even more incessantly, taking notes, pictures, film, and recordings, as he traveled by boat, plane and buses down the least traveled parts of the world. The hermit went into deep study, taking notes from his hundreds of thousands of books.

Finally the year's deadline came and both men finally came together before the panel of judges. They both looked defeated. Both had many scribbled papers that described various places in the world but none of them amounted to any coherent narrative. The traveler couldn't make sense of all his lived experiences, and the hermit was unable to summarize all that knowledge into a single compendium of his own. Weeping and embracing each other, they acknowledged that both knew nothing about the world.

Yours,

Pablo

19

March 5, 2014

Caitlin Cahill
Brooklyn, NY

Dear Caitlin,

I am writing this letter as I am on the subway, going to work. As I look at the other passengers, I notice how many wear clothes and carry bags with fashionable or witty statements that ostensibly represent what they are thinking and what they believe in.

Perhaps I am aware of these things because as someone who constantly presents himself to the public through performances and other public events, I don't feel the constant urge to "express myself" through statements in clothes, bumper stickers, or tote bag phrases. I become keenly aware of this on Halloween, when suddenly everyone "explores" their inner performance artist.

Which brings me to the real question that I ponder right now: what lies behind the way that we publicly present ourselves? And what happens when we lose track of that public presentation and what may be considered the truer, private self that we may not want to share?

This reminds me of a story that I would like to share with you.

Several years ago I met a writer—I will call him Rigoberto Semprún. He had a privileged mind and, I would say, a true literary talent. He was passionate about writing and was always involved in large literary projects. At the same time, he was personable and able to connect with others. He had just moved to New York, which in my mind revealed that he was also professionally ambitious. But it would have been hard to say that of him at first.

At some point, he became involved with Hannah Roberts, an artist from within our social circles (I am also using a fictional name for her sake). No one really thought much about her work, but she was tenacious, efficient, disciplined, and relentless in her self-promotion—an attitude that served her well in getting a good gallery and her work seen around.

Rigoberto appeared to enjoy the lifestyle that they created together. They had many friends. He started organizing readings in his house, which led to creating a small magazine of which he became the editor, and which allowed him to invite friends to contribute. This, in turn, created a lot of good will—or perhaps unpaid favors—that put both Hannah and Rigoberto in the position of receiving favors and support from those who they always so generously hosted.

One day I was invited to dinner at their house. They would host Saturday night dinner parties every week. For all her abilities and social prowess, Hannah could sometimes be so transparent that she would betray a certain naiveté. As we were having cocktails before dinner, and I asked if they really did these dinners every week she said, "yes, every Saturday," and then casually: "we sometimes wish we could go out of town over the weekend instead. But, we have to do a lot of dinner parties because I really need to get into the Whitney Biennial." I thought at first it was a joke, but soon realized she was serious.

At dinner I sat to the right of a woman who was on the board of a powerful arts organization. She had writing aspirations, and talked extensively about her latest poems, which she read to us. Rigoberto and Hannah applauded and complimented her in such an effusive way that it felt obviously forced, as well as beyond the common courtesy that a host would show at such an occasion. They went out of their way to celebrate the poems. In particular, Rigoberto's compliments—someone who I had known to be so rigorous and intelligently critical of some of the best literature—surprised me.

My other dinner mate was a retired ambassador who had singing aspirations but who was much more passionate about skiing. As for me, I started having aspirations to be elsewhere that evening.

I believe Rigoberto, who is after all very observant, noticed my puzzlement, because he sat me aside at some point and talked to me with his old familiar voice, saying that he wasn't fan of those dinner parties but that Hannah insisted on having them.

As time went by, I frequented Hannah and Rigoberto less. It was the kind of distancing of a friendship that one never plans deliberately, but that instead happens gradually, and out of mutual disinterest. I suspect I was not the most promising prospect to deliver exciting professional opportunities, and perhaps also not the most lively dinner guest.

Not too long ago I ran into Rigoberto at a social event. He came to me and embraced me effusively, wanting to know what I was up to. I immediately recognized that familiar expression of excessive interest that I had seen in him years back when he complimented that woman poet at dinner. Only that now, aside from directing that expression at me, it appeared that it was his permanent state. He seemed to truly have become that person who had feigned interest in others, reaching that point that some politicians reach, where it becomes impossible to be sure if they are truly sincere about what they say or, even more troubling, if they even know what they sincerely believe.

Rigoberto is now the editor in chief of a major literary magazine. Someone who knows him told me that the magazine is so demanding of his time that he has stopped writing.

Truly yours,

Pablo

20

March 22, 2014

Elaine Tin Nyo
New York, NY

Dear Elaine,

When one studies art, there is a general expectation that one should explore his or her interior voice. "Be yourself," they say; "speak about what you know." It is unfortunate that these series of counsels reinforce a perception of the artist as someone primarily charged with exploring their inner world—an obsession that has been pretty much a constant in modernism. As a result, most of those who come to study art today are narcissists, and in art schools we feed their narcissism by encouraging them to explore themselves. It doesn't help much that studying art is a class privilege. Only those who have enough money can spend time thinking about themselves and their problems, and art often becomes a way to validate an essentially selfish activity.

I believe you know that for many years I have advocated for a very different kind of artist education. While I am not against exploring our respective eccentricities, I believe that we should primarily teach how to see and listen and be affected by what one sees and hears. But I also know that obsession with altruism can have its own dangers, and at times can be equally misplaced as a purely self-centered practice. Great and bad art results from self-obsession, but that is true also of public art—while it can be great and meaningful to all, it can also be tedious, lame, and colorless.

So where does that put us, just to say that art can be either good or bad regardless of whether you are selfish or not? Sounds like I didn't really contribute anything to this reflection, right?

True. But what this previous non-conclusion may bring us is the idea that maybe the parameters to measure *who* should make art should change. For example, what if we had a rule that only interesting people could make art? Believe me, sometimes these thoughts cross my mind when I am doing studio visits to young art students who come from very privileged backgrounds—who have no idea or real interest about the outside world, and who are mostly concerned by their own personal issues that are typical of a life of privilege.

If you will allow, I would like to share with you a story that may illustrate this problem.

There once was a country with a dictatorship—let's call the country Cyrus. Cyrus had been a mostly democratic country, with a failing economy when a socialist party took over. This led to a right-wing military coup to seize power, after which the country was held under severe restrictions of freedom of expression. It was determined by the military junta of Cyrus that art was a danger to society, and only certain individuals would be allowed to study it—mainly, individuals who would make art works that were decorative and non-threatening to the ideology of this dictatorship. Inevitably, this spurred an underground group of individuals who wanted to be artists, but were instead forced to go into other areas that felt less threatening to the regime's ideology, like architecture or commercial design. Regardless, these artists started to make incredibly imaginative and conceptual art about the dictatorship, bringing forth a golden age of art with an urgent message.

Over the years, the dictatorship of Cyrus started faltering, and the happy day came when the regime came down and the people were able to achieve democracy again. A new democratic president was sworn in, and the country, while not perfect, initiated a period of stability and relative financial growth. The artists who belonged to that underground period became heroes, and received a myriad of exhibitions and tributes. Entire museums were built dedicated to displaying their works.

As they aged, some of these artists continued making the same kind of art works they used to make, while others were attempting new forms. None were as successful as the works produced during those underground years; their newer works lacked the edge, and the urgency of the message of their initial works.

Art schools were formed, and now everyone could study to be an artist. But the art students had a hard time following the act of those grand masters who had fought the dictatorship with their art. There was not much to make art about in a country like Cyrus, which now had a boring president and an average society. As a result, the art spheres increasingly started veering toward architecture and commercial design.

Recently, at a panel discussion, an art critic from Cyrus lamented the decline of the art practice in his country, reminiscing of the greatness of the art made then, reminding everyone that those who became the best artists were precisely those who had been denied the possibility to study art in the first place.

"If we ever want to produce great art again," he declared, "Cyrus should consider having a second dictatorship."

All yours,

Pablo

21

March 23, 2014

Gabriela Rangel
New York, NY

Dear Gabriela,

I am often bothered by a particular question that, if asked aloud, wouldn't be taken seriously. This is why I like to write letters: they allow us to ask questions that can be difficult to elaborate on within everyday conversation.

In this case the question is: is there too much art in the world?

You've probably heard this question from people in primarily two contexts. One is by art professionals who exhibit exhaustion from being permanently on top of things, and so complain that there are too many biennials and art fairs in the world. The other is by struggling artists who, in moments of self-doubt, ask things like: "why add more objects to a world with so many objects?" or, "what new do I have to contribute to art when everything has already been done?"

I would like to move beyond these rather cliché comments, which, if you think about it, are less about the true concern for there being too much art out there in the world, and more about how we feel displaced by all this overwhelming excess of art, by not being able to comprehend it and dominate it all, and/or by not being seen as a participant in this professional ocean.

Yet, while the previously described feelings (that there are too many biennials and that there may not be much to say in art anymore) are commonly expressed and felt, no one has ever seemed to question the importance of expanding art everywhere; the idea that every single person in the world should have the inalienable right to experience and make art. The irony is that Joseph Beuys and Andy Warhol ended up making this right pretty much mandatory, to the point that no one in his or her right mind can possibly forbid anyone else to make art

As a result, we now live in a world where we have effectively eliminated the construct of "art" that effectively outlined any sort of distinction between what art described, and the outside world. Now, art *is* the outside world: it is everything in it, and as a result everyone in it is an artist. In that sense, the term "art" became meaningless a long time ago.

This of course doesn't mean that we have now discarded the term. On the contrary, we kind of continue using it in ways that are closer to the 1950s. That necessity, I would say, has mainly to do with the art market. Otherwise, how can one distinguish the good art from the bad art? The important question to ask these days is not whether something is art, but whether something is "relevant" art to me and you. It is mainly about how each of us, collectively or individually, relate to that art personally. But this is hard to do, given that there is so much to choose from and make sense of. And we know the basic rules of economics of supply and demand. The more there is out there, the less it is worth.

To return to my question: Is there too much art in the world? Perhaps it is a poorly phrased question. Maybe the more pertinent question is the opposite: isn't there too much world for each artwork?

Allow me to extrapolate on this for a moment. For that I will you need to imagine a story—a story of someone who I will call sister Alison Parr.

Sister Alison was a Shaker, and lived pretty much her entire life in New Lebanon, New York, where her family converted to the Shaker faith when she was seven. Born around 1816, her life paralleled the rise of the Shaker faith. It was sometime in the 1830s when the Shakers experienced something called the Era of Manifestations, a wave of spiritual revival that appeared in the from of strong visions amongst a few Shakers. It mainly affected young women of the community, and sister Alison was amongst them. One morning, after her daily milking duties (she worked in the Shaker dairy farm), she collapsed on the ground. While she was being assisted by other Shakers, her body started to experience violent convulsions. She was in bed for three weeks, during which she had high fevers; at night she experienced powerful visions, some of which lasted hours.

After this period, Sister Alison produced several drawings that described those elaborate visions—including ornamented representations of angels, trees and birds. These drawings, along with many others that were made by other Shakers with similar experiences, are called gift drawings.

Now, the Shakers did not accept the notion of art in the conventional way. For example, art in Shaker faith could not be without a purpose; as every action, as it is a tribute to God, needs to be purposeful and for that matter, useful. Pure aesthetic pleasure, it seems, would not count. Art could also not be purchased or displayed. In 1845, the Shaker Laws ruled that "no maps, charts, and no pictures or paintings, shall ever be hung up in your dwelling-rooms, shops or office. And no pictures of paintings set in frames, with glass before them, shall ever be among you." It is known that the Shaker leadership, while excited about all the powerful visions that came during the Era of Manifestations, were also perplexed, and possibly jealous, of the fact that these visions were coming only to young women in the community, and not for them, which may have been a reason for leaders to prohibit their display. It is known, nonetheless, that those drawings were often given amongst Shakers and then kept privately.

Sister Alison Parr passed away in the late 1800s. Apparently she had kept many of her gift drawings to herself, not knowing who to give them to, or rather, believing that she had not yet met the person that they belonged to.

Sometime in the 1920s, as the numbers of the Shaker community in New Lebanon started to decline, one of the Shaker buildings was sold and its contents vacated. Boxes of books and hymnals were sent to a local library. There, the daughter of the librarian in New Lebanon, who while assisting her father in opening the boxes that contained several of the Shaker books, encountered one of sister

Alison's drawings. It is said that she was immediately fascinated by the drawing and secretly took it home, staring at it for several hours that same night. It is also said that the following day she woke up with high fever and experiencing convulsions in her body, speaking in tongues, while embracing that drawing. Her father tried to take the drawing away from her, generating loud protests, cries, and desperate pleas from the daughter. Eventually she was allowed to keep the drawing.

When hearing the news, the elder Shakers knew that sister Alison's gift drawing had found its true owner. It was believed that the drawing would not create the same reaction in anyone else; as the piece was specifically created to address one individual. As far as we know, no one since that time has experienced the same reaction.

It is unclear what became of the librarian's daughter, but some say that she never recovered from the experience. There are rumors that she joined a religious order in later years.

It is said that the rest of sister Alison Parr's drawings are kept in a restricted archive only for scholars to study. There is a warning particularly for young women to look at these drawings at their own risk.

Truly yours,

Pablo

22

March 30, 2014

Christian Viveros-Faune
New York, NY

Dear Christian,

There is a question that I have been pondering more and more over the years: why do we constantly punish ourselves by forcibly trying to find a direct descendant of Andy Warhol?

You may have noticed that in both the mainstream and in the art press, the phrase "the next Andy Warhol" eagerly recurs. If we were to make a list of all the artists who have been called that, we could probably create a lineup of individuals that would resemble an Elvis impersonator convention in Vegas. Why is it that we don't read much about "the next Duchamp" or "the next Broodthaers"? My suspicion is that it is because it is very hard to even imagine what the next act of Duchamp and Broodthaers could be—that is, anything that is neither a logical development of the ideas that they initially presented, nor a complete rejection of them. But, the next chapter of Warhol can only be another Warhol, and another after that—repetitious as his screen prints. Furthermore, Warhol created a persona that was so plainly cynical and noncommittal that it is the easiest in the book to play. If you are a young artist you can be ignorant, incurious, imitative, and self-serving as much as you want and you can still play the Warhol prototype credibly. Which makes me wonder if Warhol's true genius resides in creating the impression that everyone could be him for fifteen minutes.

The downsides of this process are transparent and too often we all have been the pained witnesses of it.

I think often of the unfortunate story of a group of artists who unwittingly followed this path and how it led to another unwitting—if otherwise brilliant—curator who sealed their fate. Just to keep a fig leaf of decency, I will refer to both with invented names.

The Carpetbaggers were a group of young artists who started generating a certain buzz in the art scene. They were often referred to as the true inheritors of Warhol, and they calculated their presentation accordingly. They dressed like students, never washed their hair, and showed a remarkable ability to pretend not to care what anyone thought about them.

To their credit, I doubt they ever suspected how successful this pose would turn out to be—or as I will show, how it would trigger a brief mirage of success.

Their efforts were primarily oriented toward creating works that appeared to reflect a complicated thought process, when they in fact were just slightly more elaborate than a fart joke. They played hard to get—a strategy also from the Warhol book that still works surprisingly well with some curators, especially for those who suffer from an anxiety of not feeling up-to-date with the most current art. Amidst the fascination of encountering something seemingly authentic and reminiscent of the golden years of the city's art world, these curators go back to their offices and animatedly discuss the special moments that they experienced in those magical environments. The Carpetbaggers would then act barely interested when the curators would come to them with offers for major exhibitions and opportunities, talking to them in a condescending way, almost as if they were granting the curators a big favor.

When I first visited the Carpetbaggers' studio, my first image was of the movie *The Sting*, which was my dad's favorite film. In it, Robert Redford and Paul Newman play two drifters who create a fake betting parlor to con a wealthy mob boss. The Carpetbaggers' space had every necessary smell, look and appearance of an inheritor of the Factory, yet there was nothing behind it. Local artists looked in puzzlement at each other as they saw a growing parade of curators and wealthy supporters visiting them and giving them a variety of opportunities.

The more cynical they were in their attitude, the more desirable they were. I remember thinking that it was only matter of time before their "Sting" operation would find a good curatorial victim to truly bring them to the top.

Enter Rosamond Rivendell. Rivendell was a legendary curator who had made a name by creating landmark exhibitions and introducing young artists who went on to develop significant careers. She had risen higher and higher in the upper echelons of museums and biennials, and had reached a position of great power. She nonetheless found herself in a difficult situation at this later, august stage of her life. Precisely because of the greater position she now had, her daily life had become more about petty internal politics, administrative headaches and fundraising than about truly looking at art and keeping track of what was out there. Rivendell increasingly felt pressured to make her next major discovery, but with little time and mindset to find it. She would ask herself: have I lost my edge?

Then one day she found The Carpetbaggers online.

To fully understand this story, we need to remember a secret fact about the curatorial universe that I am sure you are aware of. It is that a curator must always feel that they were the ones who discovered the artist and that they were not cued-in by another curator. This discovery has to happen in a way that has not been forced by overt self-promotion by the artist.

And so it happened that Rosamond came, unannounced, to the Carpetbaggers' studio on one of their "open house" events. Right away they all knew exactly who she was, but pretended to having never heard of her. At the same time, they made her feel at home, and engaged her in an animated discussion. It was an immediate match. Rosamond relived the times when she had made similar artistic discoveries in her youth. She decided she would take a chance, and offered them a major exhibition.

And so The Carpetbaggers started what we could term as the "art world stardom ride." It usually lasts three or four years. The first year—its gestation—the artist starts becoming a word of mouth treasure. After their first major show, a deluge of invitations pour in, and those artists, usually insatiable and in love with their new-found celebrity status, accept every single one, believing they can outsmart the system. As the second, third and fourth exhibition come, in their second year, it starts becoming evident that there is no "there" actually there. The third year usually becomes a confirmation of this suspicion, and it is the time when the artist tries to cash in as much as possible on their status. In the fourth year the fever has broken, and a new group of younger artists have come to replace the previous ones.

The Carpetbaggers' ride, fueled primarily by Rivendell's initial and powerful advocacy, was a textbook example. One aspect of it is that it is almost over by the time it starts; mainly it reached its highest point of acclaim when they announced their first major exhibition. Once it opened, and the product was dubious and the reviews mixed, it all went downhill from there. Rivendell in fact, experienced curator as she was, knew almost from the moment she offered them their first opportunity that she had made a mistake. But it was too late: she had created the monster, and the usual invitations from other museums and biennials followed. It all would play out predictably, and inevitably.

After four years, the Carpetbaggers' art student look and irreverence were impossible to feign as authentic. On their fifth year, they had dismantled their studio and broken up as a collective. Rivendell did not ever mention this group again after the major exhibition she offered them.

The only difference with the movie *The Sting* is that it was unclear what benefit the members of the Carpetbaggers had gotten from that experiment. They had indeed reached notoriety, but not of the best kind. In fact, both supporters and the Carpetbagger members prefer not to think anymore of those years, as if it had been a night of binge drinking where everyone said and did things too embarrassing to recall.

In summary, one could say that this was a situation where all participants were both perpetrators and victims.

Rivendell has since retired, and it is said confidentially that it would have been better if she had done so a while ago. I recently saw one of the ex-Carpetbaggers—the only one who managed to continue an art career of relative stability. His work is nothing to write home about, but it is smart, engaged with the issues of the moment, and totally devoid of the adolescent humor of The-Collective-Of-Which-He-Dare-Not-Speak-Its-Name. He was wearing designer clothes, had become soft-spoken, and his hair was impeccably washed.

Truly yours,

Pablo

23

April 1, 2014

Helen Stoilas
New York, NY

Dear Helen,

I clearly remember the first time I read that famous phrase, "Art is a lie that unveils the truth." It is in a 1923 interview between Picasso and Marius de Zayas, a Mexican artist and critic. The actual quote is this:

> *"When I paint, my object is to show what I have found and not what I am looking for. In art intentions are not sufficient and, as we say in Spanish: love must be proved by facts and not by reasons. What one does is what counts and not what one had the intention of doing.*
>
> *We all know that Art is not truth. Art is a lie that makes us realize truth, at least the truth that is given us to understand. The artist must know the manner whereby to convince others of the truthfulness of his lies. If he only shows in his work that he has searched, and re-searched, for the way to put over lies, he would never accomplish anything."*

This quote is perhaps one of the most disseminated in XXth century art; often taught to art students, and often uncontested. When I think about my own art career I know that it has influenced me greatly. I have always been motivated by the ability of art to create fictions that unveil different truths.

The question is on whether, nearly one hundred years later, the day has come to finally contest this statement, as well as the various responses it has received.

By religiously following this tenet we have created a wedge between art and life. Life is always authentic by definition, while art lacks such authenticity because, in Picasso's mind, it is always a representation of life. So by force art has to be a lie, something unnatural that when it is successful it reveals the natural world.

What would be the alternative?

Let's think about this: abstract artists, for example, essentially said: art is a truth onto itself. It doesn't affirm or deny the outside world. Conceptual artists in the Duchamp tradition, nonetheless, said, in a competing fashion, that anything in life could be art. But they didn't go further enough to deny that art still depends of its own construct to exist separate from regular life. It no longer is an issue of truth vs. lie, but of truth vs. truth. We have spent an equally inordinate amount of time to make Duchamp's competing dictum work for us, trying to make art equal to life. Ultimately, though, we can't resolve the problem that arises when you make two things equal: you have no real way to differentiate them. If art is life, then art doesn't really have a purpose.

What has been happening recently has been an attempt at combining both the Duchampian and Picasso schools, doing something like: art is a lie, like life is a lie, but art still helps us to see truth in life.

The problem is that art is struggling everyday to justify its existence as a savior of life. Think about socially engaged art. The main criticism to it is—it is great that you make art that helps people, but why do you have to call it art?

So if we have exhausted these three XXth century approaches to art (art is a lie that tells truth, art is a truth onto itself regardless of life, art and life are the same) what is left?

I think I have reached my own conclusion about the matter. Although, it is very difficult to articulate in a brief letter without turning it into an academic essay. I also don't want to impose my opinion on you, so I think it would be best to express it through a brief story. And furthermore, because the history of art has always been told with no small degree of drama, I thought I would make the story mawkishly sentimental. For it I will recur to the style of Paulo Coehlo:

A long time ago, in a far and distant land that was suffering a terrible war, there was a learned man named Omar El-Sistasi.

Since his childhood, Omar believed that there was something to the world that needed to be discovered in order to save humanity, and he spent many years meditating and studying in order to find this aspect of the world. He finally spent five years wandering in the desert to find the answer to this question. When he returned to his troubled city, plagued by famine and misery, he declared to his fellow citizens that he had found the truth. This truth consisted that in the world all things had an inverted double attached to them, and that in this world that we know, he explained, you can only see half of each thing but its double is invisible. Omar had learned to see that invisible, inverted half on each thing. It was like learning a complex and difficult foreign language with many rules, but through years of persistence it was possible to attain this new vision, and with it, make a much better world possible for others.

But a few people following his instructions joined him in a monastery to pursue this new kind of vision. Indeed, slowly all his disciples started to attain this rare ability. It allowed them to see the world in a new dimension, to see the intentions and ulterior motives of others, and sometimes even to predict what would happen. A golden age of knowledge and wisdom ensued. Omar's teachings proliferated, and upon his death, he had many followers.

It so happened that Omar's disciples chose to use this knowledge not to simply attain wisdom, but to use it to their advantage, and gain wealth and power. Witnessing this particular potential of Omar's discovery, many men and women started joining this practice. Soon it came to the point that there were more people practicing this skill than not. Though no one at the time realized that the more people practiced it, the less effective it was to have advantage over others. It eventually became an arduous thing to learn that did not provide that many benefits. After two or three generations this practice had become unable to change the world anymore, and its number of followers dwindled down to practically none.

At that time, some descendants of the first generation of disciples of Omar El-Sistasi got together. They believed that this practice needed to be preserved, and that there was something that El-Sistasi's infinite wisdom had found that they could still extract from. They created a temple for El-Sistasi and made it their cause to continue teaching El-Sistasi's ideas. Now they themselves became a doubled inversion of their own history: they used the world to save El-Sistasi's ideas, and not as he originally had envisioned it. The disciples never saw the great irony in their taking the responsibility for saving El-Sistasi's legacy through the memory and documentation of his work, with the vague hopes that one day another great prophet would arrive and teach everyone of yet another new way to come and improve their world.

All yours,

Pablo

24

April 5, 2014

Jenn Nielsen
Brooklyn, NY

Dear Jenn,

In the last few years I have been giving a lot of thought to the time divide that exists between artists and audiences.

When an artist makes an art work, this happens in a concrete time and place that has a defining influence upon it. If I produced an artwork in New York in the 1960s, it probably was influenced by the other art being made and/or praised or rejected at the time; if I had been working in Mexico City in the 1940s, my work would probably have been very different from the one that I am making now. Similarly, we instinctively think of our audiences as those who are immediately around us; that is more or less what we would describe as contemporary art. It is our natural instinct as artists that whatever we make is in dialogue with each other. Those who choose to make art that dialogues with the past we in the contemporary art scene usually dismiss as overly romantic, afraid of change, and naïve.

But what about those of us who make art specifically thinking about the audiences of the future, those audiences that don't exist as of yet? At first, the thought may sound strange. Why would we make art for a world that as of yet is only hypothetical? Shouldn't we simply content ourselves with what we know?

And yet, when you look at a museum's collection, it is all populated with remnants of the past—a string of collections of "presentness", engaging with their time in various ways. As spectators, we have to take for granted that these works were not specifically made for ourselves—that is, Picasso was probably thinking of the Parisian public and his friends; Rauschenberg was thinking perhaps of the people who would show up to his gallery opening, etc. This is an obvious generalization, as we mostly will never know what specifically each artist was thinking. But when I look at those artworks made 50, 100 years ago, I do ask myself whether these artists ever imagined that their works would be in the museum of the future, with someone like me wondering what they were thinking.

This, granted, is not the artist's problem. If I were to poll most of my artist friends, my sense is that most of them would say that they couldn't care less about future audiences; what matters are the ones that we have in our lifetime. But at the same time every artist has the desire, whether vague or explicit, of posterity—of becoming a Picasso or Rauschenberg, whose pieces have entered into a canon of art that will theoretically be preserved for the ages.

So what if we as artists really made it our problem to seriously think about the audiences of the future? What if we made works that are permanently evolving, responding to the shifts of social and cultural context of every place?

Perhaps the best way I could play out some of the issues connected to this scenario is through a brief story. Sometime in the 1820s, a German archeologist by the name of Mattheus Eisenacher made an expedition to what is now northern Iraq. It was in the south where most of the important discoveries of the Babylonian civilization had been made, but his research had led him to conclude that he would make a significant discovery there.

After spending four punishing years in the desert, withstanding the attacks of thieves, various sicknesses and dust storms, his findings had been slim. It could be said that Eisenacher's expedition was mostly a failure, had it not been for a key discovery he made. Toward the end of the expedition, as he and his assistants excavated near one particular sacred site, Eisenacher uncovered a structure that appeared to be a tomb. When they opened it, they encountered a large number of cuneiform tablets.

Eisenacher took all the materials back to Germany to study, announcing that he had uncovered a large library of ancient texts.

At the time, the understanding of cuneiform writing was in its beginnings, and there was much to be learned. Professor Christian Lassen of Bonn, a pioneer orientalist and knowledgeable of the cuneiform writing who was a mentor of Eisenacher, helped him initially in his decipherment efforts.

Oriental scholars who examined the tablets dismissed them as having little historical value, arguing that they mainly included repetitive words and phrases. Eisenacher, they argued, had uncovered a scribe school. But Eisenacher dismissed their opinion as he got himself immersed in the study of these tablets.

It was in particular one of these series of tablets that appeared different from others. It was clearly made by the same hand, and it appeared to be made with much greater care and dedication than the others. It took many years for Eisenacher to decode it. Finding it so valuable, he decided not to show it to anyone.

After two or so years, Eisenacher concluded that the text was not a public record or a historical account, but something rather that read like a letter—a completely unusual method of address. Mainly, the letter seemed to be written to someone in the distant future.

These tablets became an obsession. Eisenacher became more and more involved with them, spending practically every night in a private room of his house with the tablets, at candlelight, studying every mark and every word. Slowly, a thread of thoughts started emerging—coming from a scribe who suspected that someone in the distant future would find his writings, and wanting to communicate with that hypothetical individual. The letter was passionate, full of doubts and questions about the end of the world, questions about God and the future of his own civilization, pleading to that future reader, Eisenacher, to be understanding and forgiving of the mistakes his people had made. At times, Eisenacher felt he was the best friend of this anonymous scribe, his confidant, and sometimes his deity.

Eisenacher fell into madness at some point, one night coming out of his room, yelling uncontrollably and covered with blood, having attempted suicide. His servants subdued him with great difficulty—he was a large man and strong, even in his old age. The next day he was placed in a madhouse, from which he never left. The local doctors, unaware of the historical value of the tablets, ordered them destroyed in front of Eisenacher as they thought it was necessary to eliminate the source of fixation of the patient. Seeing the tablets destroyed generated unspeakable pain to Eisenacher who cried and yelled violently as he saw the objects he had spent a lifetime decoding being destroyed. No one will know what message the tablets contained, but if one is to trust Eisenacher after his collapse, he continuously described, with painstaking detail (and as someone who had grown so obsessed with a text that he was able to quote it literally) how the scribe had described with great clarity each and every one of Eisenacher's vices and virtues, his fears and hopes, his condemnation for having uncovered and read those tablets, and how in the end his own madness would be both his curse and his reward.

Truly yours,

Pablo

25

April 6, 2014

Karina Skvirksy
New York, NY

Dear Karina,

I often wonder about those great, monumental artists that emerge very rarely in history—say, once in a generation. We know that these truly great minds seldom emerge out of nowhere: an auspicious cultural and family environment is necessary for their gestation. But if biographers and historians spend a great deal of time studying the social and cultural circumstances of the period that produced their subjects, very little is studied of the complicated environment that they leave behind them. Many times it can be like a supernova that can outshine everything else around it for a long time.

Let me present an example using fictional names in order not to hurt even more those who have already been hurt enough by the episode I am about to narrate.

The city of Ostinka always had a reputation of being a cultural capital in the world, despite the fact that for most of its history its country has been poor and shortchanged by history. Art making has always been one of its greatest prides. There was a time in particular, in the XXth century, when the country's fortunes appeared to look brighter. During that time, a remarkable generation of artists and writers emerged. That was the context of the apparition of Ostinka's greatest writer, Salomon Fiberi. Descendant of diplomats and intellectuals, Fiberi showed his talent from a very early age. He founded an influential literary magazine in his teenage years.

Shortly afterward, he moved to Paris where he befriended André Breton and Marcel Duchamp, who both took him under their wings. Influenced by Surrealism but wanting to create a national movement of his own as well as finding his own voice, Fiberi went back to Ostinka to do just that. He proved to be not only an unprecedented literary talent but also a great connector and broker of conversations. He turned Ostinka into a must-visit place for the international literary elite of the time. These constant visits by artists and writers had, in turn, a great effect on the local arts scene.

Fiberi's reputation and stature only grew in time. He quickly became the most influential and powerful individual in the arts of his country, and it appeared that no significant decision by any government about the arts could be made without his input.

Fiberi seemed interested from his youth in having a legacy. From very early on he started to actively mentor very young writers—trying, perhaps, to find in others that 16-year-old precocious youth that he once was. He was actively looking for literary children. That young generation of writers he groomed appeared indeed to be extremely precocious, smart and erudite, and, at least at face value, they appeared to represent a multiplied version of Fiberi himself.

Fiberi received the Nobel Prize of literature toward the end of his life. This recognition was the ultimate amplification of his influence and cemented once and for all the monumental contributions that he had made to Ostinka and to world literature. As he aged, he continued to work on his legacy, mainly through the creation of a literary magazine and a publishing company where he supported his young writers. No one appeared to notice at the time, that this new generation of writers was very different from Fiberi in that most of their interests and vast knowledge was very much tied to the literary references and period that belonged to Fiberi himself, and not really to what was happening in literature in other parts of the world.

Fiberi's passing was a watershed in the history of Ostinka's culture. No one could remember another instance in its history when such a large gap had been left by one single individual. Fiberi had lived a long and productive life, and his time came at a ripe old age, so his absence should not have been felt as such a surprise to all. But the years that followed his passing, it almost felt as if he had not died at all, as so many recorded lectures, TV programs, posthumous publications, letters and other writings kept emerging and circulating as result of tributes, research, and homages. Fiberi had been a polymath, and one of the overwhelming aspects about him was that he had appeared to have commented on practically every subject of human experience in one way or another; as such, his writings, his references and his weighty opinions on almost everything were inescapable.

At the same time, the public and the critics looked incessantly for the true inheritor of Fiberi's legacy, or at least a stand-in to be the commenter of the issues of the day.

It was then that the effects of such a prodigious passing started to become evident.

At first, the focus was on the writers of Fiberi's generation, many of whom were still around, all of whom had stoically, but not without resentment, existed being shadowed through their lifetimes by their more famous colleague. But when the time came for them to be in the limelight, not one of them could really rise to the occasion. So many years of being in obscurity had turned them into recluses, curmudgeons, or hermetic philosophers who could not really play the role of the public intellectual and international diplomat of culture that Fiberi once played.

So the next group to look to was, of course, those young writers who Fiberi had groomed—most of which, by this time, were not so young anymore, getting close to their fourth decade. Of this group, there was no evident heir. One of them had opted for politics, another, the most precocious of all, had only published one book of poetry and had not managed to produce another in thirteen years; one more was running Fiberi's magazine but appeared more involved in editorial than in creative work.

It was thought nonetheless that Fiberi's death would bring something good in that these writers now could open up and pursue their creativity without feeling the pressure of that paternal oversight. Fiberi, after all, had held the pulse of the literary scene so firmly that many felt it could only feel freer without him.

But in fact what happened was that Fiberi's disciples felt more lost than ever. They acted as abused orphans, or rather as children who had been so used to pretend being adults that when reaching true adulthood they only knew how to perform it by acting the part of a child behaving like an adult. Mainly, they all appeared to feel enormous pressure to produce a magnum opus; keenly aware that by their age, Fiberi had already published more than ten major books and had played a key role in some of the most significant art historical movements of his time.

Some of them started drinking heavily. One became so delusional with his knowledge that he simply continued writing in a small magazine for a handful of people, truly thinking that he was doing a comparable work to the one made by his adored teacher. One abandoned Ostinka to pursue a teaching career in the United States and become a comfortable academic in a university town. Another simply abandoned writing altogether, becoming instead an environmentalist. One of them committed suicide. That promising generation of writers, once thought of as the most promising in Ostinka's history, laid in ruins. What's worse is that their capitulation also had an effect in the generation beneath them, who weren't able to find significant mentors in them, and who were presented with such a pathetic and uninspiring state of affairs that most went into other fields, taking their creativity elsewhere.

All this time, the myth of Salomon Fiberi continued growing. His image is printed on the bank notes of his country. Schools and universities are named after him. And perhaps this is a good thing after all: it may well be that only when Fiberi's name becomes so ubiquitous that it almost feels like an abstraction can a new generation of writers in Ostinka feel the freedom to write again.

Truly yours,

Pablo

26

April 7, 2014

Harley Spiller
Woodside, NY

Dear Harley,

I wonder if you share the same frustration that I do whenever you read a recurrent phrase in the press: "Questions were raised." When a public figure is caught with wrongdoing, or an individual's dubious ethics are under scrutiny, that is a common way to suggest that they fall under strong suspicion, without taking the step of accusing them of anything in particular.

This passive aggressive form of public discourse is something that I have noticed increasing over the years. With the purpose of showing professional restraint, we tend to construct forms of indirect criticism where no one is fully courageous or liable about what they say.

I find this condition particularly interesting when this strategy is imitated in art discourse—because as I am sure you are aware, art discourse does not lead in form in other fields, but instead copies and morphs itself in function of other spheres of public discourse. So for example, it is very common to read in press releases, grant applications and art reviews that an artwork "produces knowledge" or "raises questions", or "explores issues". It usually is never spelled out what kind of knowledge such artwork actually produces—and whether this knowledge was, in fact, relevant—what questions it asked and whether it helped answer them, or what issues it explored and what was, if any, the resulting discovery of such exploration.

All this always makes me think of the case of our dear Ciro Bedford.

I think we both first heard of Ciro (I am using a fictional name out of decency) a few years ago. He seemed to appear out of nowhere in the art scene, quickly being named the most important artist in his city (let's say, for the sake of argument, that this city was called Shoulderland). Shoulderland has a long history of great art, but there came a moment when it needed a large figure to symbolize its resurgence as a cultural hub. As fate would have it, Ciro came to fill that role. Ciro did not come from art originally, but realized at some point that if he were to define as artworks his various urban projects they would be supported in significant ways. He worked in what is called an "underserved" neighborhood, a place in Shoulderland that had been forsaken by the government. Ciro was very effective at engaging wealthy individuals, deftly inspiring their generosity while at the same time exploiting their collective guilt for not supporting the underserved communities of the city that had made them so guilty. Doing so through the work of a contemporary artist was a way to show magnanimity while at the same time rising in prominence in the circles of art entrepreneurs and donors internationally.

Of these people, the Reiner family, one of the wealthiest in Shoulderland, became very close to Ciro, and more and more became more directly engaged in funding his sprawling project.

But what was that project, exactly? It depended on which angle one pursued. When Ciro presented the project in urban development forums, it was presented as an artwork; when he did so at art events, he presented it as an urban project. Because at either event it was hard to find experts in the field that could ask the right questions about the project, it mostly would go down unquestioned.

Over the years, and thanks to the generous patronage of the Reiners and the influential circle of friends that they were able to attract to support Ciro, his project grew and grew in size and budget. Ciro had a large organization that now felt more like an architecture firm, as he initiated urban renewal projects in other cities.

But the inevitable time would come when finally urbanists and art insiders would come together at a major international urbanism and art conference, and Ciro's project came into the discussion. On that fateful day, which no one doubts Ciro knew would come sooner or later, "questions were raised". The urbanists saw the project as a naïve and ineffective social experiment with many flaws that to them only counted as art, while the art critics saw in it an artwork whose lacking aesthetic qualities would be compensated by its use-value. Ciro's response to the criticism was that what he was doing did not have a name yet; thus it could not be seen as either urbanism or art.

It is one of those fascinating things about art today; it is summarized by a line of a movie that I love, "Big Night", consisting in the rivalry between two Italian restaurants. Pascal, the rich owner of a vulgar and large Italian-American restaurant, competes against an idealist couple of brothers who just arrived from Italy and create a small but authentic Italian joint. After fooling them to believe they were their friends and later scheming to ruining them, one of the brothers confronts him. Pascal calmly replies: "I am a businessman. I am anything I need to be at any time."

Ciro was, in fact, like many artists today, a businessman. He was whatever he needed to be at any time. For that purpose, it would have been very inconvenient to overtly explain his intentions or be open to defining them in any way. It only so happens, as you know, that art as a business enterprise fares poorly with the passage of time, and is quickly forgotten as a passing brand. The Reiner family had been served spaghetti with meatballs all along, thinking that they were experiencing the highest expression of Italian cuisine.

Ciro left the art world a few years after the urbanist and artists conference. But his feat was done; he had built an international consulting firm and his name is now recognized around the world. He gives his name to professorships (although he doesn't need to teach) in exchange for six figure salaries, and continues to participate in Ted talks. He's active in the global speaker circuit as an inspiring voice to philanthropists and any of those in positions of power who are trying to find advice as to where to invest in underserved cities and culture and thus find some meaning in their lives.

Ciro's Shoulderland project, by the way, closed a few years ago, when he moved out to Los Angeles to work on a major film project.

The ruins of the project are now dominated by a powerful gang, so there are not many visitors these days to that part of town.

Truly yours,

Pablo

27

Wilmington, Delaware, May 11, 2014

Julia Draganovic
Osnabruck, Germany

Dear Julia,

I write as I am on a train, trying to organize my mind as to the various topics that I have been wanting to write about in a letter over the last few days, but which have proved elusive either because I can't get my mind to concentrate or because I can't find the right angle from which to start a letter on the subject.

These days I have been thinking a lot about what one would call the "higher moral ground" in art. I have found myself amidst a whole series of discussions where people critique artworks, institutions, and artists for ethical reasons. The range of those critiques include selling out to the market and accepting support from individuals, businesses or organizations that may have questionable or objectionable politics.

While I am sympathetic to those criticisms and objections, and in many occasions I have raised them myself, I gradually have less patience with critical positions that claim that higher moral ground but without proposing any viable means to change the world. In their effort to point out our various failings, they actively seek to undo whatever possible good one may be trying to accomplish. Moreover, they make their careers the parasitic dependence of the objector, seeing their lifetime work as the criticism of those who do act. You may know that I am talking about some kind of institutional critique—not the one that emerged decades ago, but rather the one that still is being practiced today without, it seems to me, having learned the lessons of the past decades.

This brings me to the case of Leopold Rubersky.

I don't know Rubersky's precise background, other than he was born and raised in Europe (let's say he was originally from Luxenbourg), amidst a cultured and economically comfortable family, and where he received a high level education. Rubersky was very sophisticated in conversation and elegant when writing. We met in New York, when we were working at a large museum many years ago, both as educators. He, like me, made a living from teaching in museums and universities, in his case always as an adjunct or a freelancer. And, also similar to me, he always saw his art practice in the first place.

One could say that Rubersky is the most loyal follower of the institutional critique generation. Rubersky used humor, poetry, and performance to ridiculize practically every major figure and institution with power in the art world, exposing the hypocrisies, manipulations, double-dealings, and opacities that benefit individuals over the public interest, if it can be said that there is a public interest in art today. He did it with panache and style, creating performances, happenings, simulations of exhibitions a la Broodthaers and publications.

When I first saw Rubersky's work I found it cunning and intelligent. We had a period where we became friends, corresponding, having dinners, exchanging books. I, too, shared similar feelings of disappointment and even indignation—which I still feel today—about how we allow the art market and, more recently, a Hollywood-obsessed culture, to dominate the art discourse. So we both shared our ironic takes and performances.

But over the years we started diverging. In all honesty, Rubersky's elegant but permanently negative and dark ramblings started becoming difficult for me to take. I was taking a road where I felt I needed to negotiate with the system to make work in the best conditions possible, whether that meant to work inside an institution or make my own independent work but with some kind of contribution—either financial or logistical—from individuals and institutions.

This, to Rubersky, was unacceptable. His position was radical, a take-no-prisoners approach. He saw culpability by implication at the fourth degree—which meant any art project supported by money from practically any source was unacceptable. He never reconciled, it seems to me, his own need to work as freelancer or adjunct during the day at institutions that he attacked and ridiculed at night. He, in the end, lived like me in New York, a city that one doesn't move to for precisely altruistic purposes.

And so, as the years went by, Rubersky sounded more and more isolated. His writings betrayed the fact that he was getting his information almost exclusively from online publications; he abstracted conclusions from incomplete or scattered facts; he saw the face of evil everywhere. He also became some kind of recluse, only to emerge to effect hostile actions against others. This included him becoming an art critic alongside his art practice, which every time felt even more hostile and grotesque, more charged with hatred.

I have often thought about the troublesome aspects of this dimension of behavior that some artists exhibit, particularly when it acquires that level of virulent hostility. It is that, in the end, these acerbic critics of what we say and do in art are also in search of some validation, or some recognition, or both. When they don't obtain it, or feel that they haven't received enough, they double down on their criticism. So their disdain for the things they see in the art world may be compounded by the frustration of not being recognized, and perhaps the unspoken or unconscious disdain that they feel toward themselves for wanting to be recognized by a community that they so profoundly abhor.

Rubersky always claimed that he would move away from New York, but he could never bring himself to take that step. He also stopped attending any exhibitions, any social event related to art and as a result he also stopped presenting his performances, which were the only face to face action that he was doing. He instead banished himself to the online world, sporadically sending his brutal and apocalyptic manifestos, physically close to all the social and artistic events that he denounced but at the same time as distant as one could ever be from those events. By choice he lived vicariously through our lives, condemning them in the strongest possible terms and yet with such an urgency and emphasis that one could swear they were as essential as oxygen to him.

Yours,

Pablo

28

May 12, 2014

Jon Hendricks
New York, NY

Dear Jon,

The following is a letter that I have to write not without certain pain, but at the same time that I feel I must write because I can no longer remain quiet on this issue.

I have been an arts administrator as well as an artist for my entire adult life. It is a difficult balance, where one feels one is not good at either of the two things, where one thing seems at times to counterbalance the other while at the same time stifle it. I have been rewarded by working with wonderful and experienced people who understand and are passionate about art, and are willing to do whatever it takes to carry out the vision of the artists we believe in.

Nonetheless, you may share with me the frustration that comes from the bureaucratization of art by people who have been administrators for so long that their primary concern is comfort, security and continuity, and not the support of new ideas—which in general prove disruptive and uncomfortable.

I don't mean to exculpate artists from any wrongdoing; I think there are a lot of issues to do with how artists treat institutions, as well. But in this letter I want to talk about art administration.

The first question is: is art administration an oxymoron to start with? How can you administer something that in and of itself doesn't like to be administered? We must start with accepting that the whole discipline may be a fraught one from the start, and the best we can expect from it cannot be very much. We can't live without it or at least have not found a way in which it would not exist to regulate and organize the infinity of art that is made everywhere.

Perhaps the best I can do to illustrate the issues regarding this is through a short anecdote.

There was once a remarkable set of fellows back in the XIXth century, Gregory O'Malley and Sigmund Prattenauer. O'Malley was a showman, who had worked in many cabarets in London and other parts of England. Prattenauer was one of the most talented lion tamers the world had ever seen. They met in Dublin some time around 1870, and together decided to put together a circus. The Sigmund and Gregory show was very successful all over Ireland, and before one could imagine, they were traveling all over Europe. O'Malley was an audacious and courageous businessman, which served their venture well. Prattenauer, a huge man, was strong and fearless, and his fearlessness was such that it projected onto the beasts, who appeared to respect and love him. Not once had a lion or tiger ever attacked Prattenauer, and the beasts performed feats beyond belief. In their height, the Sigmund and Gregory Circus attracted over a thousand people in cities like Brussels, Berlin, Paris and London. O'Malley was generous to his staff, who loved him and shared his desire to primarily put on a good show.

One day, Prattenauer was training a young tiger that had recently been sold to the circus by a group of gypsies. The animal was very fierce and had been poorly chained, and Prattenauer walked into the cage mistakenly thinking the animal was secured. He was attacked fatally by the beast.

The incident changed everything in the circus. There were many tamers who wanted to fill in Prattenauer's shoes, and for the most part did an efficient job, but no one wanted to take the chances again of their predecessor. O'Malley, devastated by the death of his friend, ceded shortly after the leadership of the circus to his son, Frank.

The circus continued to amass commercial success, and by this time they had so many requests that they had two traveling troupes and one permanent show in Paris. Frank O'Malley was more pragmatic than his father, and his main goal was to make the Sigmund and Gregory Circus a profitable enterprise. This new generation of showmen looked back at their predecessors as idealists without a sense of the real world. They didn't want to take any chances. They created great spectacles, increasing in technical precision and special effects. The beasts were heavily drugged during performances and the tamers would take many protections before engaging with them. Because the public had also changed, they continued attending those spectacles, and the Sigmund and Gregory Circus continued growing.

By this time, the taming component of the show was all but gone; all that was left was an old lion that would be paraded around the rings. The discriminating public noticed that the show had started to lack sophistication. There was no sense of true danger anymore; it had become a bland spectacle, they said.

These attacks were brushed aside by the management of the circus. They didn't need the critics anymore; they had become a tourist attraction, catering to a public that was not very knowledgeable anyway.

Decades later, toward the beginning of the XXth century, the circus had become an enormous and profitable franchise, thanks to its expert administration. Thousands of people were coming to it, and it had become a ritual to come see them.

I hear that the latest manifestation of the Sigmund and Gregory Circus exists today as a theme restaurant.

Sincerely yours

Pablo

29

May 15, 2014

Lili Herrera
Washington, DC

Dear Lili,

We often ask ourselves whether we have crossed the last threshold there is to cross in art. Nothing, other than taking a human life, seems out of bounds. But there is one important taboo left, one that is not likely to be crossed soon: anonymity.

Anonymity seems immune to the attack by artists, mainly because out of vanity practically no artist wants to remain anonymous. Definitive permanent anonymity is hard to embrace because no one wants to give up credit for what they have done. There is something strong that drives the desire for communicating.

The mystery of Elmer Ghire is perhaps such an example.

Ghire was a writer based in an important city—let's just call that place Eldridge. While he was a talented writer, his personality was not particularly attractive, and he had the unfortunate tendency to irritate friends and acquaintances by being brutally honest. He was a critic in an important publication, and he took his job seriously, being devastating when he needed to. He had no social filters, no sense of decorum in delivering his opinions to others. As a result, practically everyone around him resented his reviews and comments. He had no shortage of enemies. For that reason, he struggled to publish his creative writing; no one could overcome thinking of who he was as a critic to support him in that endeavor.

Ghire recognized that liability of being himself, and it is believed, but it has never been proved, he created a heteronym. A mysterious writer named Rosa Lavinia published a first novel in a small, self-published edition that circulated around Eldridge. The book was a nuanced and powerful narrative with complex characters, a thick plot and an unexpected ending. Everyone—including, suspiciously, Ghire, who rarely was positive—praised the book. People praised the sincerity of the book, its trenchant observations and its elegant prose. Soon the book took off and became a best-seller around the country. A few years later, a second novel by Lavinia came out, and was even more successful than the first. By this time the identity of this author caused enormous curiosity and obsession, but there were simply not enough clues to know who could have written it. It is very likely that some writers familiar with Ghire's style would have thought of him as the true author, but the animosity that all felt toward him must have prevented them from ever seriously considering that he had been the author. In reality, it would seem obvious: Ghire had no social life, and could spend months at a time writing. He was one of the only obvious candidates with enough knowledge and skill to pull off the creation of a fictional author. But no one suggested the connection and Ghire never gave even a hint that he may have written those novels.

The second novel was the last work by Lavinia. There was the rumor that a third book would come out, but that never came. It coincided with the fact that Ghire died around that time, of cancer. If he had indeed been the author we may never know. But several researchers who have studied Lavinia's prose have made the compelling case for Ghire's authorship. If true, Ghire must have experienced a complicated relationship with his anonymity. He may have reached the height of both pleasure and indignity when another critic, in a decidedly hostile review of one of his books (that is, a book actually signed by Elmer Ghire himself), wrote that "Ghire would very much benefit from reading the brilliant prose of Rosa Lavinia."

Because Ghire never confessed, and if indeed he was Lavinia, one wonders why he could have embarked in such a monumental deceit, throwing himself to anonymity. He would have successfully completed two careers—on the one hand, the one of a revered, admired author, and on the other a despised critic. One can only think that he initially did it for the secret and completely intimate pleasure of seeing the writers that so much despised him suddenly fall for a writer that he had created, making them praise and praise the works of a person who they all quickly dismissed as a nobody. But then why not confess in the end? Wouldn't it have been the ultimate redeeming act and embarrassment to his critics?

I believe the only possible reason Ghire was afraid to reveal himself as the true Rosa Lavinia was because he was afraid that his revelation, instead of redeeming him as a truly great writer, would instead have made his enemies dismiss Lavinia. He must not have wanted to give them that opportunity. He must have preferred to take his secret to his grave, knowing just for himself that for once he had created a perfect writer.

All best,

Pablo

30

May 16, 2014

Lisa Blas
New York, NY

Dear Lisa,

There are a few things that we seem to never contest: one is that everyone should share in the joy of art, and the other, which prefaces the first, is that art makes our lives better. The thing about this well-intentioned rationale is that we often don't think about whose idea of art that includes, and whether or not we should debate that before we go on to share the joy and the supposed transformative powers of it.

This usually takes me to the strange episode of the life of Jonathan Knölke.

Knölke was an unusual ethnographer. He studied in the university of Berne, a dual career of ethnography and art. He lived in Amsterdam in the late 60s, where he met many important conceptual artists and was convinced of the power of art to improve one's worldview. As part of his doctoral dissertation in ethnography, he sought to argue the idea that inserting Western contemporary notions of art into societies which lacked an understanding or practice of it would be beneficial to strengthening communication, self-introspection, and critical dialogue within those communities.

Knölke's thesis didn't go over well. His professors and peers, coming from an intellectual moment where post-colonial theory was emerging with the influence of Frantz Fanon and others, accused Knölke of attempting to reinforce colonialist ideas. But

Knölke rejected those accusations, and wanted to prove that art was not a colonial construct.

He decided to find a community that lacked the construct of art making as we know it, and show them the wonders of what it was. After much research, he decided to work with an indigenous tribe in the Amazon. Knölke brought examples of art works to the tribe, to which they reacted with fascination, but without the clear understanding that these works had been made by individuals. The idea of the single individual as an artist was not fully comprehensible to them. Most things in that community were made collectively. Knölke then realized that there was a man in the community who carved tools in a very skilled way. He used him as an example for the tribe to show that he was an artist amongst them. The craftsman was at first puzzled by the attention, but later came to like it. He started parading around the community with his head held high and started to show a certain degree of arrogance.

This singling out of by Knölke of the craftsman generated envy amongst other craftsmen, some of which started to proclaim themselves as the better craftsmen of the tribe. Knölke held then what he termed as a "critical thinking" session where he compared tools between craftsmen to show them what represented better toolmaking skill.

The next morning, Knölke's craftsman appeared downstream, apparently as a result of an anonymous attack. A number of rival craftsmen appeared at Knölke's hut to ask him to chose them as the next village craftsman. Knölke realized at that moment that his experiment had gone terribly wrong, but didn't know how to disentangle the confusion he had generated. As he refused to "appoint" a new top craftsman, this generated an internal fight amongst the tribe. This led to more violence. Knölke left a few days later, when two more craftsmen had perished in a knife fight argument over the issue.

Knölke never returned to Europe. He had caught a mysterious Amazonian sickness while with the tribe and after two weeks of virulent fever, he passed away in a hospital in Rio de Janeiro.

These days in Brazil there is a store that sells "indigenous arts and crafts" inspired by this Amazonian tribe. The actual tribe unfortunately declined and ultimately disappeared sometime in the 1980s.

All yours,

Pablo

31

May 16, 2014

Mara McGinnis
Brooklyn, NY

Dear Mara,

Ed Koch, the recently deceased mayor of New York City, was a colorful character. My favorite comeback line from him was, "I can explain it to you; but I can't comprehend it for you."

I often think of this in terms of art. As you may know, a good portion of my professional life as an art educator has to do precisely with helping people experience art in a meaningful way. I confess that I often verge on desperation, as people can be so closed and incapable of letting themselves venture into engaging with an art work. But that is, in the end, what educators are for. As my uncle Billy used to say, truly talented people don't really need teachers. Still, I often wonder what it would be like if we could devise a way in which we could, as Koch suggests, "comprehend" things for people. And this leads me to the story of Justiniano Quiles.

I will never forget Justiniano, who I had met in art school in Chicago back in the early 90s. He was a cheerful painter from Lima, Peru, with a thick amount of black hair. He was a painter, as well as an art educator in a local children's art program. He was older than me, having finished a clinical psychology degree before coming to art. I also recall that he was a fervent reader of John Dewey (long before he became fashionable in the art world) and was very interested in figuring out what he, somewhat cryptically, described as the "holy grail of communication."

One day over coffee in Belmont Avenue, Justiniano explained

his theory of art interpretation to me. As I recall, it went like this: art interpretation, he argued, is a flawed concept. It is not useful to share an interpretation of an artwork with others, as what you are transmitting is nothing related to the actual artwork but only your own ideas. Art experiencing, Justiniano argued, could only happen from the educated art professional who is deeply engaged with art, and who could form experiences that are unique and specific to the self. So what to do with the masses of people who are not art experts? Are they destined to never truly experience art in the true sense? I said this to him.

"I have a solution for that", Justiniano said. "Over the years I have developed a technique of art experiencing."

Responding to my puzzlement, Justiniano explained what he meant. Instead of wasting time in trying to teach someone how to experience art, he would experience it for them. First he would interview the individual, getting a sense of his or her interests and passions, gathering a complete psychological profile of them. Afterward he would go to experience art on their behalf, literally becoming a surrogate viewer. He had done some initial experiments and he was very excited about its potential. He wanted me to join him.

I was curious about his proposal but I never took him up on his offer. The project seemed too elaborate and I had too much going on in any case.

Years later, I saw Justiniano again. He not only had continued pursuing his art experiencing project, but he had turned it into a business. Modeled after the model of art consulting, Justiniano's art experiencing business was primarily geared at rich individuals who wanted to be part of the glamour of the art world but didn't have the time, or quite honestly, the interest, to spend their lives looking at exhibitions, reading books, or even watching films. (Somehow seemingly to justify himself, Justiniano explained that he also had a non-profit branch, and that the rich clients would help him offer these services to the less fortunate.) He was thinking of copyrighting this method of art experiencing. I believe he wanted to call it "VAE—Visual Art Experiencing."

The next time I saw Justiniano, at some non-profit arts

organization benefit, I hardly recognized him. He seemed to be twenty years older, almost frail. He told me that he had continued with his art experiencing business, and it was still going strong. "The only problem," he told me, "Is that it is very taxing, physically and emotionally."

Justiniano was like a Dorian Gray in reverse: he was absorbing all the anxieties, fears and hopes of his clients, and using art to sublimate those experiences. His sessions with his clients could be very emotional, and as he referred his experiences to them many times he would collapse in tears.

Here I must clarify that Justiniano was a supremely talented educator and individual. I never doubted that he must have delivered exceptional experiences to those who hired him. I also doubt any regular artist or educator would have been capable of doing so. But Justiniano was entering into an uncharted territory. It is also a fact of life that artists usually are trained to communicate to others about how they experience their own feelings, but we are poorly prepared to empathize with others.

The last time I saw Justiniano he looked drastically better. He was remarkably slim and fit. Yet he looked a bit strange: his hair was somewhat ridiculously styled as if he were a teenage idol. He told me that he had left the art world as well as his art education theories. He had a new relationship with a man down in Miami, a successful wine exporter. He didn't have to work anymore. I asked him at some point why he decided to leave his work with art experiencing. What he told me stuck to me ever since:

"I have discovered the joys of selfishness."

All yours,

Pablo

32

May 17, 2014

Maria Damon
Brooklyn, NY

Dear Maria,

I am doing a great deal of writing these days. Come to think of it, I have done a great deal of writing over the last ten or so years, to the point where I often wonder if I am still a visual artist. I am not proud of it, as I find the description of "writer amongst artists" a sort of demotion to being an artist, mainly because I remember what was said once of a Mexican intellectual who did both poetry and philosophy: "poet amongst philosophers and philosopher amongst poets"—which was just a way of saying that he wouldn't be taken seriously as either a poet or a philosopher.

In any case, and regardless of the value of it, one does what one is compelled to do. So, I write. But the larger problem that I face is that my act of writing may be a lost cause, mainly because the primary audience that I am addressing—that is, the art world—doesn't like to read.

Certainly there is an argument that we may be reading and writing more than ever before, because of the online world, which I also share. But that is not the kind of writing and reading I am interested in. Thus this letter project, which I confess is a desperate attempt to have what I consider real communication with others.

But I have observed over the years that in the visual arts there is a minority of people who read, and that the uses of text in the visual arts are mainly ornamental. For example, how many people do you think actually read exhibition essays? We all are, seemingly, too busy to read anything more than tweets or status updates.

Which brings me to the extraordinary case of Dr. Athanasius Delaware, which I am sure you have heard of (although I have changed his name just as basic courtesy to him).

Athanasius Delaware was an art historian with a degree in psychology from the University of Chicago. His art historical writing, which drew a lot from his psychology background, was not well received by other art historians. You may know that the art history community tends to keep to itself; anyone who enters with a slightly different take on things is often regarded with great suspicion, not unlike the way one would look at someone with eccentric sexual deviations. Delaware was, as you can imagine, disappointed by how his ideas failed to gain traction. Then, he was the victim of a fascinating incident. It turned out that a magazine, just by chance, had hired a reputable writer to review Delaware's latest book. The review was lukewarm, but what Delaware realized after reading and rereading the review was that, 1. The writer had obviously written that review in haste, ostensibly, he thought, for the money. 2. He had not actually read past page 38 of Delaware's book, and had skimmed just enough of chapters 4 and 6 to provide a few examples of what Delaware was arguing. And most importantly, 3. The writer had somehow gotten a hold of a summary that Delaware himself had written about his book and passed around to his graduate class to help them discuss some of the ideas in it. Delaware had made that summary also in haste, and in some cases the descriptions did not quite fit the original book. He found in the review, sometimes verbatim, quotes from that summary.

In sum, Delaware believed that because it was highly unlikely for any art theory critic to ever dedicate the time and patience to a book of several thousand pages, they would instead focus on the first 36 or so pages of the book as well as the beginning or summaries of a few chapters. By providing a just enough solid text in those parts of the book, and making sure to make available online a good amount of anonymous and detailed summaries of the rest of the book, he could get away with filling the rest of the book with mostly nonsense or spurious theories. He would write, in fact, the *Finnegans Wake* of contemporary art theory.

And so he put himself to work. Even though the final work was going to be spurious, it still took him seven years to complete it. In the end, the book comprised 5,900 pages, 2,600 of which were footnotes and references. It was the dream of every art historian and art theorist, the landmark book of books of XXIst century art ideas.

The sheer size and weight of the tome, when it came out, overwhelmed everyone in the art world: no one had seen such a monumental book ever come out from the field. We need to remember, by the way, that we are visual people, so appearances are, in most cases, more important than the reality.

Delaware made another series of skillful moves to coincide with the book's launch: under a variety of false names, he wrote a Wikipedia summary of the book as well as a number of reviews in online sites, all positive of course, and written in admiration of many of his sometimes bewildering ideas.

When the (real) reviews came out, they all were positive. No one would dare confess that they hadn't been able to read the whole book—a gargantuan task that would have taken several years of the life of any reviewer. As Delaware planned, no one was able to get past chapter I, and the rest of their opinions were derived from those online sites and the Wikipedia review he had created. He had artificially formed a buzz for his own writing, but in such a way in which it was not off-putting to reviewers and discreet enough that those who jumped on the bandwagon to celebrate his writing felt they were doing so out of their own accord and consistent with their own sophistication as thinkers.

Delaware thus became somewhat of a celebrity. He made sure to keep his public appearances to the minimum, knowing that a lot of exposure would wear out the desirability of his presence and would generate a great risk of having to reply to specific ideas in his book. He mainly accepted high profile speaking engagements with audiences that were more fixated in saying they had heard the great Athanasius Delaware speak than in actually listening to what he had to say.

His second book, produced a few years later with the help of many assistants, and even more extensive than the previous one, was another great success. By now he was receiving honorary doctorates from various universities and had joined the celebrity speaker league, charging around $30,000 per lecture.

But all this kind of fraud was weighing heavily on Delaware. He himself could not have imagined how successful his deception would become, and he found himself carrying a growing, intolerable guilt. At some point, Delaware decided it was time to confess, whatever the consequences. He published a short article where he explained what his social experiment in art had been about, profusely apologizing to the academic community.

But then an unexpected thing happened: no one took him seriously. They all celebrated his "confession" as a great satire, in the style of Swift or Ambrose Bierce, interpreting it as a critique of "those pseudo-academics" who cut and paste their essays and research. Delaware had constructed a fiction so effective that it was, seemingly, impossible to disentangle. It had also inspired scholarship by other art historians and theorists who had also become influential.

Delaware didn't know what to do. But in the face of such rejection to his lies, he somewhat felt he had been excused of continuing to argue for his guilt. He thought: if they want to believe it, let them.

A close acquaintance and ex-student who keeps in touch with him (Delaware now lives in retirement in Florida) told me that he knows that he made a pact with the devil; that one day a dedicated student from the Courtauld Institute or Columbia or the Institute of Fine Arts may finally take on the reading of his entire oeuvre, wasting most of his or her life in navigating the labyrinth of irresponsible references and misplaced quotes, and conclude that his work is a fraud.

His student added: "He only hopes that by that time he will be long gone from this world."

All yours,

Pablo

33

May 20, 2014

Ana Janevski
New York, NY

Dear Ana,

As a fellow New Yorker, I am sure you are more than familiar with the neurosis of the average New Yorker—of which we all suffer to some degree, I suspect. Also familiar to you and me is another, perhaps more virulent variation, which is the New York art world neurosis. I was particularly exposed to it years before I moved to New York, and found it scary. But as I moved here and lived it on a daily basis, like anything else to which we get overexposed for a long time, I became used to it, with intermittent moments of awareness when I encountered particularly serious cases along the way.

My constant fear, and I wonder if you also share it as well, is to do with whether I am succumbing—or have already succumbed—to this same neurosis. More specifically, my greatest fear is becoming Viktor Haddock.

You know Viktor well (although I am not using his real name). I can't remember how or when I first met him; I did know of him before meeting him, as his writing resonated in the art world. Viktor was a well-known critic, whose fame—and complicated personality—preceded him. He was a meticulous researcher and reader, which served him well when writing essays and reviews. But he was at the same time the kind of person who would spend an inordinate amount of time looking at the menu of a restaurant, quizzing the waiter exhaustively about every single ingredient of every dish, and complaining through the meal about every single possible topic. Moreover, he had a habit of commenting on what one ordered and even on what one ate from their dish, providing ample lectures about nutrition and health. Still, as long as one didn't have to travel or spend too much time with Viktor, one would be able to overlook his extreme neurosis.

Viktor had made a name for himself by becoming a critic of dubious ethics in art. It is a topic that, as you know, generates great debate: when we face an artist whose work is socially engaged but then "sells out" to the market; or when an artist seems to be taking advantage of a community to make a work that will primarily raise their reputation but with dubious benefit to that community. Viktor was always the primary attack dog to those kind of self-serving projects, and everyone (with, of course, those to whom those criticisms were directed at) was happy that at least someone would hold the perpetrators accountable for their actions.

Things became slightly more challenging for everyone when Viktor joined Facebook. Social media gave him a platform for observing everyone up close and commenting on the propriety of what everyone said, did, or liked. He became something like a moral police, constantly complaining or objecting about the jokes people posted, or the comments people would make about exhibitions and other artists. It was like having Viktor seated at everyone's living room or studio permanently, as a judge of our every move. In his defense, his role as bastion of morality, of course, was only acceptable when he was not questioning *one's own* morality. But it was extreme all the same, and hard for anyone to put up with.

Slowly, everyone started to distance themselves from Viktor, subtly blocking him from their accounts and avoiding him in person at social occasions. As this happened, Viktor's obsession with becoming the bastion of morality in art only worsened. He became even more vitriolic and intolerant, writing long diatribes of several paragraphs that puzzled most people. He published a giant book that I hear expounds on these frustrations, but as far as I know no one has read it.

He reached the point where his indignation was more entertaining than irritating. A group of young artists realized that there was value in provoking Viktor, and started to make works that specifically had him in mind, as cheese in a trap for the unsuspecting mouse. This, of course, produced great results. It was an effect similar to the one occasionally produced by the Catholic Church when it forbids certain books or movies: immediately afterward, everyone goes to read and watch them, if only out of curiosity. So, unbeknownst to himself, Viktor Haddock has now reached a dubious honor, as the main indirect promoter of all the artists he publicly abhors. It is a dirty job that no one had to do, but that he accidentally is doing, and will likely cause him to be remembered by future generations to come.

I do hope that you and I don't fall into such unfortunate circumstances, and if we do, that we make a pact to help each other to overcome our own judgment.

All yours,

Pablo

34

May 22, 2014

Lauren Bierly
New York, NY

Dear Lauren,

As years go by, and as we get older, the set of concerns that we have about life understandably changes. I am not surprised that now that I am in my 40s I feel a certain urgency to produce lasting works that I did not feel in my 20s, when I didn't feel that time was so precious. But one thing that I did not expect to think about at this stage in my life is how the choices that I make as an artist will affect my daughter.

This obviously is a problem only for those artists who have children. In any case, when you look at the history of the direct descendants of famous artists, it usually is a story of dysfunction, madness, neglect, and social devastation. A perfect example is the documentary "My Architect", the story of Louis Kahn's children and ex-wives, produced and narrated by Kahn's youngest son. Watching that movie gives one little hope that one can become a great artist without substantially destroying all the loved ones around you.

This is, you may think, a somewhat narcissistic concern: this presupposes that we consider ourselves great artists, and the damage we may do to our progeny is directly proportional to our success or lack of it. But I have reason to believe that it is not just the children of the artists that reach world-wide celebrity status who suffer, but also those children who have to withstand the eccentricities of their artist parents who push them to a life of difference when they would have perhaps preferred a life of conformity.

This always makes me think of the heartbreaking case of Turner Condon. Condon (I am sorry that I can't use his real name here, but I feel the need to conceal it to protect his family) is perhaps not an artist that you would have heard of, mainly because he was of great renown in his own country, but it was a renown that didn't go much beyond that place or beyond his time for reasons that I will soon explain. Still, Condon received a huge variety of honors, bestowed by the government and the main art institutions around him. Condon, It must be said, was always a very good politician, and managed to position himself well with the political and cultural elite. He was a hard-core communist while young, but as he matured and started to get higher positions in universities and the ministry of culture (to which he eventually ascended to the helm) he became much more diplomatic in his approach.

In terms of the work itself, for all his oversize personality, Condon's work was about depicting the invisible. He spent most of his career attempting to portray disappearance. The best work, he once wrote, was the one that the viewer didn't know was there in the first place.

It is not an understatement to say that Condon was an egomaniac. It is a quality not difficult to find in most politicians and artists, only that in the best of them it goes undetected at a first glance. For these individuals, this attribute mostly becomes a mere irritant in their social relations and can become a great quality when they make art if they remain single. Unfortunately in the case of Condon, he had five children from four different marriages.

In most of these cases, like in Kahn's, the children mainly grow up amidst neglect and a paternal vacuum, with their father mostly absent from their lives like some kind of ghost who barely, if ever, gives them any attention or thought. But the additional misfortune was that Condon wanted to be a hands-on parent: over the years, he tried his various theories of society, education and politics on his kids. This meant that Jonah, the oldest, was home-schooled; Tina, the second, was sent to school in a developing country to experience "otherness", Charles, the third, was not taught to read until ten, nor allowed access to pop culture until he was a teenager; Robert was given every liberty to do whatever he wanted from the day of his birth, and Ursula, the youngest, was put through the most grueling education, with activities every hour of every day—as if to compensate for the laxity of education that Condon had imposed on the others.

All this social engineering at the Condon family was somewhat suspected, but no one other than his wives—who he also managed to manipulate in various ways—knew the extent of it. I won't get into the details of just how extreme Condon's interference was into his children's lives. I will only say that Condon didn't seem to see the difference between the creation of his work and the raising of his children. They were, in effect, an extension of his own work.

Toward the end of his life, Condon had become a commercially successful artist, and if not a legendary one, at least respected enough in art circles. He had left nonetheless and as it is more or less typical, a pathetic parental legacy behind: his youngest daughter, Ursula, threw herself from a building, tortured by feelings of inappropriateness caused by years of trying to meet impossible academic demands. Robert had passed away from a drug overdose, and Tina had disappeared with the Zapatistas in Chiapas without being heard of ever again. It was Jonah and Charles who, with deep resentment toward their father and deeply pained by what had happened to Ursula, decided to take the matter into their own hands. Condon had become frail and sick, and without anyone who would take care of him, Charles brought him to his own house. There they kept him locked in a room, with barely enough to eat. It is believed during this time, and as Condon descended into dementia, that the brothers made him sign a series of legal papers that sealed his fate.

When Condon died, the children raised the prices of his best works to exorbitant levels. When they had made all the money they could, the brothers created a foundation in their father's name where they effectively prohibited the reproduction of his father's works to anyone. This unheard of action was taken with disbelief by the art world, but no one could do anything about it as Condon's children held the entire legal copyright of the works. Finally they produced a piece of paper, signed (coercively, one may surmise) by Condon himself, where he demanded for none of his works to ever be conserved and to be destroyed upon his death. Those collectors of Condon's work who refused to obey "the artist's wishes", were fiercely pursued by the brothers in the courts. This resulted in many of the works being destroyed, and those who weren't, confiscated by the court. Finally, in what became the last straw of this sad tale, the vault where all the works were gathered during the litigation suspiciously caught fire during an "electrical malfunction".

That was the end of the work of Turner Condon. As things stand today, no work of Condon can ever be seen in print or online, because of the copyright prohibition.

I wonder what Turner Condon would have thought of it all. Clearly, one can only imagine his dismay. But perhaps in a most perverse way, one could also think that he may have thought of this as a brilliant act of disappearance that he had pursued in his art all his life, one that had never happened in art: where the art work—that is, the children—has taken upon itself the task of erasing its own maker from the earth.

Truly yours,

Pablo

35

May 24, 2014

Samantha Hunt
Tivoli, NY

Dear Samantha,

We recently learned that a local Miami artist entered an Ai Wei Wei exhibition at the Perez Art Museum and destroyed one of Ai's vases, worth one million dollars, in protest of the museum's policy of only showing international art.

It's a fascinating story. It does make me wonder why, in contrast, there aren't more protests about regional art—that art that so offends the educated eye at every airport and public plaza, promoting aesthetics that make us all look like we all live alike. Should Picasso have never been allowed to leave Málaga, would he have just made realist paintings of Spanish majas? Or, alternatively, if Joyce had never left Dublin would he have written substandard imaginary stories about Trieste? We'll never know.

But perhaps this artist has a point.

Let's play out an alternative art historical scenario:

Sometime ago, nationalism took hold on country X. The leaders of this country found it essential to reject international influences and instead support local artists exclusively as the true representatives of their country.

The question became, however, who would represent each region of the country. Local regions wanted to have their own artists represent them. So regional artists were selected. This caused protests from various cities who wanted their artists to represent them as well. So each city created its own process to select their representative artists.

Yet this created another conflict, given that within each city there were competing artists from different neighborhoods who wanted to represent their own constituents. When neighborhood artists were selected, the conflict continued, coming down to street representatives. But this was not specific enough: Neighbors on the north side of the street complained that they were being represented by someone from the south. Representation then came down to every Household. But even then, there were more protests: what about the households that had more than one artist?

This originated the idea of single artist representation. When this country went on to organize a biennial, it had to include every citizen of their country, resulting in an exhibition of millions. They had to build spaces equivalent to the size of ten stadiums to fit it all. The cost of the biennial nearly bankrupted the nation, so the exhibition was stopped in the end.

The poor economic situation led the best artists of that country to move to London and New York and develop international careers. They weren't allowed to exhibit again in their homeland, as they were seen as traitors, but they didn't miss engaging in their native art system. They became "festivalists"—artists who frequent the international biennial circuit. As "dissident artists" of their country they were even more admired and celebrated by the outside world. They had been liberated from the local public.

But then they encountered another reality about the international arena. Pretty much all the video installations looked the same, the post-colonial rhetoric repetitive, and the strategies similar.

Furthermore, the audience was pretty much the same globetrotting crowd of collectors, curators, and critics.

Without realizing, by wanting to escape the yoke of the local, they had landed on the most provincial arena of all: the international art scene.

All yours,

Pablo

36

May 27, 2014

Claire Barliant
New York, NY

Dear Claire,

Here I am once again, at the airport, having a breakfast sandwich as I wait for my plane. This time at least I was able to wake up with my daughter, but most days I am not so lucky. Usually, I wake up at 3am to make the 6am flight and then try to get the earliest flight back home the following morning. Tonight I probably won't have more than three or so hours of sleep.

It has become some kind of badge of honor amongst art professionals to be constantly traveling and constantly at airports. It is one of those things that seemingly symbolizes success, desirability, and, of course, an international career. I remember when I first started seeking—and getting—these opportunities. It was something quite thrilling to arrive in another city or country and do an art project there. But over the years the endless string of impersonal hotels, rude treatment at airports, constant anxiety for being late or not making a connection, and distancing from our home has really wore me down. It feels inappropriate or pretentious to complain, because when we hear others complain there is no small degree of vanity in it. "Look how sought after I am", it appears to signal. But the reality is that traveling all the time has pretty much lost even the luster of desirability. Everyone does it. The question is, for what purpose and to what effect?

It reminds me of the case of someone I used to know named Héloise Bingen. I of course am not using her real name.

Héloise was a wonderful, charming person. She was generous with her friends and passionate with her work. I never inquired about her financial status, but it is clear that she didn't need to work, nor did she ever express the anxiety that most of us usually talk about at times about the cost of life or the need to have a daytime job. In any case, whatever her situation, it allowed her to pursue her artwork. Which, I am afraid to say, was never extraordinary. It feels wrong to judge the work of others and it pains me to write it, but there is a difference between the art work of an artist who you may dislike but still respect for the rigor and consistency of his or her art, and then the art work of the artist who is simply not aware of his or her contemporary context, has poor attention to detail, an arbitrary conceptual approach, and is overall visually irritating in an intentional way. This was the case of Héloise.

Because of this fact, as much as she tried to promote her work to curators and galleries, she found few takers. It must have been very frustrating for her to constantly experience this lack of enthusiasm. To another person in this situation, this would have meant to abandonment of their art career to turn their attention toward other endeavors.

But not Héloise. Her response was to travel to unusual places where no artists go.

She went to Timbuktu, Asunción, and Transylvania to install solo exhibitions—I assume at her own cost. In these cities, where practically no international artists goes, she was received with open arms. She continued doing exhibitions in Tibet, Bhutan, and at some point even Greenland. Wherever there were people, she would go to present exhibitions. And at every one of those places, she encountered audiences who were curious, who had the desire to engage. One thing led to the other, and as we all know, one invitation usually results in new invitations. She became an unlikely kind of international artist: the kind that serves the communities that the high-profile, blue chip artists have dismissed. We think that the art world is international, but when you look at it closely, it is rather a closed circuit of large cities that produce and mediate the art discourse, with members all over the world whose lives, despite where they live, still function in dialogue with those centers.

Héloise had bypassed that entire system. She became, and she is still now, an artist who found her public. Maybe it is not the public she wanted; maybe what she wanted, like many of us, is the respect of her peers. At the least, I know she earned mine. I now reflect, as I am sitting at this airport with my microwaved, now rubbery, inedible breakfast sandwich: what exactly is the audience I am in pursuit of?

Truly yours,

Pablo

37

May 29th, 2014

Jennifer Miller
Brooklyn, NY

Dear Jennifer,

I have been learning quite a lot about myself through the simple act of writing letters. Somewhat surprisingly to me, I realized that it is very difficult to write in this format without becoming very personal, and, at times, confessional—a word that I always have feared when it comes to art. So I have been thinking these days about what I would term as the "art as confessional" problem.

First: why would being overly generous about displaying our most intimate hopes and fears to the public be problematic? The answer would be, I think, that it is not the personal revelation that becomes problematic, but the rather narcissistic expectation, first, that these hopes and fears are relevant to others, and moreover, that they deserve to be elevated to the realm of art. And we all know that when it comes to evaluating the importance of our personal issues, objectivity seems impossible.

It was a cliché in art school—and I think that it still holds true today—for a student to develop work about their childhood traumas, their sexual issues, or their ethnic, religious or racial backgrounds. Most of us who have been to art school are familiar with the scenario: sitting and standing around while a student goes on and on talking about himself or herself in ways that feel more like group therapy. The confessional impulse, it seems to me now that I think of it, may be a defense mechanism to the normal scrutiny and critique that comes with making art. If the work is based on a deeply intimate and fragile emotional experience, it becomes very hard to critique tactfully. I remember once at a critique panel, before we even started, the exhibiting student broke down in tears, without anyone yet having uttered a word.

Let me tell you a story that may perhaps help illustrate some of these issues.

Fray Bartolomeu Balcells had joined the Benedictine Monastery of Montserrat, in the vicinity of Barcelona. In his youth he had studied art but his religious calling pulled him in to join the order. He always thought of art nonetheless, writing personal notes to himself about its potential as a means for communication.

Fray Bartolomeu was also a superb listener, which made him an excellent confessor. Everyone, it seemed, wanted to be confessed by him. He had the fame of being a wise advisor. He started writing and thinking a lot about the practice of confessing, lamenting to himself that monks didn't really know how to confess their sins. He then, arguing that a monastery is "a school in the service of the lord", proposed the creation of a confessional program inside the monastery. The prior was intrigued by Fray Bartolomeu's proposal and after a while of reflecting on it, gave his blessing to him to pursue the endeavor.

Fray Bartolomeu based his confessional program around art classes, starting with painting and then expanding to photography, video and performance art, which Fray Bartolomeu found particularly conducive to confessing deep and troubled experiences.

The beginning of Fray Bartolomeu's confessional school was very successful. Many monks from other monasteries joined and became very involved in creating their confessions. Here I should point out that Fray Bartolomeu was adamant that this was a religious school, a place of faith and reflection, not an art school, but it attracted art-inclined monks all the same, especially after the school's reputation started to spread through the region.

But every enterprise runs the risk of falling victim to its own success.

As much as Fray Bartolomeu opposed the idea of the monks to exhibit their art publicly, many of these stated doing so, usually under pseudonyms, exhibiting and performing in local galleries. The leadership of the monastery started looking at Fray Bartolomeu's experiment with trepidation, but Fray Bartolomeu convinced them that the project was bringing very positive results.

Things, however, got more complicated when a fellow monk who had joined the sessions had the poor judgment to show a 2-channel video installation with strong sexual overtones, and involving young children, at a local alternative space. The piece triggered an investigation that proved that this monk had been abusing minors over a period of several years, with the full knowledge of the prior. The monk went to prison and the prior was removed and sent to Algeciras.

As you may imagine, this was the end of Fray Bartolomeu's school. It did produce a couple of artists of certain local renown. One of them became a monologuist in the style of Spaulding Gray. Another monk, who left the order shortly after, became known for exploring nudity and sex in public spaces as part of his work.

Fray Bartolomeu himself left as well and never returned to Spain. I heard that he now lives in San Francisco, where he runs a local arts healing program.

Yours,

Pablo

38

June 1, 2014

Marisa Jahn
New York, NY

Dear Marisa,

I often wonder about an apparently simple question: should we treat art making as a profession?

I don't regard it a cynical question, in case you may be wondering. I imagine that most of us who engage in art making would instinctively reply that a life dedicated to art requires a degree of knowledge and expertise, and those of us who actively work as artists in the field and constantly travel, develop and present projects and exhibitions, rightfully feel that we should be treated like professionals, instead of being asked at times whether we have a "real job". But at the same time we tend to be of two minds when the whole topic of professionalization comes up. We roll our eyes at artists who get PhDs, and look with suspicion at the entire apparatus of for-profit art schools along with the implicit sense that investing in a professional art degree means becoming an artist. You and I know, furthermore, that if art is a profession, it is not one that you typically retire from, because its practice is so intimately linked to life itself.

Perhaps the following story may sound familiar.

Some time ago Eliot M. Robeson (I am using a fictional name for his sake) founded an art school to create truly professional artists. He was a wealthy industrialist who believed in art education, and along with a group of wealthy friends and supporters he was able to build an important institution. He did not want it to be the traditional arts school: he wanted his students to see their trade as a transformative force in the world. The Robeson University for the Arts produced many generations of important artists over the years and attained a reputation for being a leading higher education institution.

This reputable University, however, needed a new leader. It was agreed that it needed to be someone with new ideas and an understanding of how to bring the organization into the XXIst century.

Frank Tourneau was selected to be the next director of the Robeson University of the Arts. His impressive resume included having been CEO of an important Silicon Valley company and he was known for energizing and inspiring his staff. Tourneau immediately implemented a new teaching philosophy, and the results were visible right away. To start, he initiated a new recruitment culture, looking for highly self-confident students. "I want overachievers, go-getters", he would say. He renewed the teacher pool to include specialists in career counseling and marketing; economists and business school veterans. Non-active artists were eased out of the main programs, to teach in more tangential ones. He did not want to create a traditional school, but a radically different learning institution: he wanted art students to see their field as a small business or private enterprise. They received training by corporate career gurus, courses in branding and long term value based marketing, public relations, basic investment economics, and image consulting. They were trained to do elevator pitches about their work, and there was a "future career planning" class where the students were encouraged to plan big in a shameless way. No plan was too ambitious: how to get a solo show at MoMA, how to get into the next Documenta, how to become a blue chip artist.

Tourneau organized an annual conference to showcase the work of the students and some alumni, where high profile curators, festival organizers and other tastemakers would gather to look at the work of the students. These showcases often resulted in opportunities and in the advancement of the student's career. Critics described Tourneau as some kind of cult figure. It also was pointed out that the students were not even spending time in the studio anymore; making art had become an afterthought, while self-promotion and career development were in overdrive. The art the students were making all looked more or less similar, with wonderful presentation but suspiciously lacking of substance beneath. But no one could deny that Tourneau had modernized the art profession.

One day, one of Tourneau's favorite students was found dead in her apartment. She had left a note with a message apologizing, saying something to the effect that she felt she was incapable of succeeding in the way she was expected to.

The PR department of the Robeson school handled the matter with great finesse and expertise. They spread the rumor that this student had a history of depression.

Still, the incident is said to have generated a lot of soul searching amidst the faculty regarding their academic goals and their approach. The fact is that the following year, the school made some adjustments to their curriculum. They recognized that students should be able to realize their shortcomings. One of the new classes in the current sessions was "how to extract success from failure."

Yours,

Pablo

39

June 3, 2014

Mary Jane Jacob
Chicago, IL

Dear Mary Jane,

If there is something that defines the lives of most people around us, it is the feeling of being permanently overscheduled. This is certainly true for me, where I feel that every hour of my life has to be accounted for. Which makes me wonder: in such a state of mind, how can one give enough time to art?

I think about that question when I observe certain visitors at the museum, most of them more focused on looking at *all* the art as if it was a job, or a checklist to cover; often taking pictures of every artwork and contemplating their own phone screens for most of their visits.

I understand them. I am also not the contemplative kind. It makes me think about the fact that we continue exhibiting artworks in a lineup format, in this chronological, Cartesian fashion. It translates to the sensation that we are in a production line of experience, and we become factory workers of perception.

Once I heard a story from a museum researcher whose name I have forgotten; I will call her Francesca Walton. Francesca, for many years, studied museum visitors in galleries. As you may suspect, visitor behavior in museums is fairly predictable: we generally know how long they will linger, what they will spend more time looking at, what they may miss altogether. But there was one visitor in particular that this researcher encountered where the results were particularly unique. Let's call him Takeshi Hikari.

Mr. Hikari was a successful retired doctor with a great passion for art. He was not a collector per se—that is, he did not collect actual artworks. He collected pictures that he himself took of them. His goal in life was to see every art museum in the world and to take pictures—with or without permission—of whatever the museum had on display. He was remarkably skilled at this task—so much so that even the most suspicious and alert museum guard would be fooled by his tactics. He went to the lengths of having secret cameras installed on a lapel pin and on a cane he walked around with. His impeccably discreet demeanor, and the fact that he was quite a distinguished-looking gentleman, made him practically undetectable. It could take him a few minutes to go through an entire small museum. When he could, he would also videotape the galleries.

Walton ran into him at a gallery where photographing was actually allowed. In those cases, Dr. Hikari would take a regular camera and photograph every single artwork, spending two or three seconds on each, moving swiftly to the next. She followed him until he had photographed every single art work.

Then she approached him. Dr. Hikari was surprised and one would say scared. When he learned that she was not a museum employee, he then relaxed. He proved reluctant at first to speak, but Francesca was an expert interviewer and very personable, someone that makes people easily at ease. He agreed to be interviewed for her study.

At some point, Dr. Hikari invited Francesca to his apartment in the Upper West Side. As she recounted the experience of entering that site, she would struggle to find the words to describe what she saw.

Dr. Hikari's apartment was packed with disks, video tapes, and various other forms of documentation of art works in museums, as well as every kind of museum souvenir imaginable: snow globes, posters, catalogues. It was impossible to even walk through the apartment without kicking or bumping into a pile of objects. By his own calculation, he had visited 7,300 museums in his lifetime, and photographed all artworks on view in every single one of them. To him, the Holy Grail was the collection that was never on view; this caused him a great deal of grief, like the mountaineer who dreamt all his life of climbing that inaccessible peak.

And what did he do with all that material? Francesca asked him: Did he look at it? Dr. Hikari would never give a straight answer. But it was apparent that, like a regular pack rat, the thrill was in owning the thing, not in looking at it or experiencing it later.

Francesca and Dr. Hikari stayed in touch. From my perspective, I don't discard the notion that given that Dr. Hikari was a lonely older man and Francesca, an attractive young woman, he would have fantasized about having scored a romantic relationship, a fantasy that I highly doubt she ever shared. The fact of the matter is that when he passed away, he left in his will his entire collection of images to Francesca. It was an overwhelming behest; it took five large crates to empty the entire apartment. Francesca tried to find a place to donate this incredible wealth of material to—some kind of library or foundation. But once it was examined, it was clear that it would be useless for any purpose. The surreptitiously taken photographs were of poor quality; none of them were labeled, which made it a practically impossible task to identify them; many of them were in formats that were difficult to transfer, and others were already corrupted or unreadable. In the end, Francesca had no choice but to dispose of it all, through a Staten Island waste management company that took it to a landfill. And in a matter of a few hours, Francesca saw that entire collection be taken away—a lifetime of chasing artworks all over the world, millions of images documenting one viewer's journey through all imaginable museums, all pointless, all of them never opened or seen by a human eye.

Yours,

Pablo

40

June 5, 2014

Micaela Giovanotti
Brooklyn, NY

Dear Micaela,

I wonder if you have ever asked yourself, as I have done for many years, the reason why in newspapers there is a section titled "Arts and Entertainment." Why couldn't it be called "Quantum Physics and Entertainment" or "The Middle East Conflict and Entertainment?" I concede that perhaps I am being a bit too facetious in my question. I know very well that art traditionally brings us joy and pleasure in ways that reading about the Syrian conflict does not. But I can't help but notice that such a pairing of categories denotes a particular perception about the role of art in our lives, which is to provide some form of pleasure. I am sure that you, like me, are interested in a kind of art that does give us a certain intellectual pleasure, and it may do so by putting us in uncomfortable places, mentally or physically. I wouldn't call it masochism because the pain itself is not the ultimate goal, but a necessary step to gain a greater insight into a particular issue, so we willingly subject ourselves to the kind of art that, while difficult and challenging at times, ultimately offers us a greater insight.

There are extreme positions on the subject. It must have been Aristotle who said that learning comes from pain; from there must have derived the cliché that all great art comes from pain, and the retort from other artists that art instead should be a celebration of life.

It also makes me think of the example set by the city of Corolaria.

Corolaria was a city that emerged many centuries ago, led through the wisdom of a great monarch and religious leader. Before the rise of this monarch, the city was poor and its people experienced great hardship. Yet they were known for their resilience and, mainly, their art. Artists made poems, paintings and songs about love and nature. Art was seen as a means to help the people forget their hard lives and struggles.

This monarch led the city to prosperity; he expanded its commerce and wrought a new era of wealth that no one had experienced before. Everyone was exceedingly happy. The city became hedonistic; the old and the sick were sent to another part of town so that they wouldn't be seen and spoil the appearance of youthfulness and happiness in the city.

This all led to a sense of selfishness in that society. Empathy started to vanish. This troubled the monarch; he knew that this kind of contentment was not a good thing in the long term.

He then had the idea of bringing all the artists of the city together to discuss the problem. He gave them a mission: they should make art that served as a warning about contentment and complacency. Artists thus started making poetry, art and songs about death, illness, injustice, and sadness, apocalyptic visions of the world.

The public embraced these works with enthusiasm. Seeing all that evil in art works reminded them of just how lucky they were in their lives. Seeing the privation of others made them feel great and relieved about their own privileged condition.

Yours,

Pablo

41

June 6, 2014

Mara McGiniss
Brooklyn, NY

Dear Mara,

When one is a young art student, one feels very vulnerable to the world. Reading my own diaries from those years I recall those feelings of being overwhelmed and awed by looking at so much great art, and asking myself whether I could ever produce anything that could match the greatness of what I saw in art history books. And yet I admit that, at the same time, I had a naïve arrogance, thinking that I could be one of those artists. If I hadn't, though, I think I would have stopped making art at some point. Becoming an artist is a complicated process of balancing a strong self-confidence or arrogance with the humility needed to recognize that we are just one more drop in the ocean of art.

I had a friend who never displayed such humility. Let's call him Jonathan. When we were young, and in college, he would tell others that he would be the next Ingmar Bergman, or the next Fellini. No other outcome was acceptable to him.

Jonathan was awkward socially. He yearned to have a relationship with someone, but his ice-cold personality and extreme withdrawal into himself made any meaningful relationship with another person impossible. Later I realized that his idea of a romantic partner was equally demanding to his idea of the kind of artist he wanted to be. So, nothing short of a professional model, with vast intelligence, wealth and talent, would be acceptable to him.

As other film colleagues of his started to land low-level gigs and unpaid internships at the very bottom echelon of the film industry, Jonathan made fun of them. He would never be subjected to those hierarchies; he was convinced that he would be discovered by a studio and would be able to make his great opera prima, a full feature film that would establish him as the leading filmmaker of his generation. He thus continued on in school, getting master's degrees and PhDs, as he prepared himself for that great moment.

Years went by. Jonathan's colleagues eventually started getting better opportunities, having paid their dues through years of unpaid or poorly paid labor; one of them got to shoot a commercial; another became assistant director in a successful movie. But Jonathan still looked down at them. They were conventional careerists, he said; they will forever be understudies or assistants. He saw himself differently; because he was truly exceptional he would be found by that studio or producer and be given finally that opportunity to produce that first major work.

More than twenty years have gone by now. My generation is in their forties. Many of us have children; some of us have started to lose our hair. Some have had greater success than others, and some have changed professions more than once. We are perhaps in the most important moment of our professional lives, on that threshold when we may still have enough energy to undertake certain ambitious endeavors, with enough experience to carry them through; but with an ever greater awareness that time is not eternal, bearing the weight of our family commitments and other pressures. We become more pragmatic and accepting of the fact that all those options that seemed unlimited in our 20s have been reduced; it is too late to realistically launch into a new career or to take a dramatic turn in our course. My family does not have a particularly great record of longevity, so I bare no illusions of having an extra long life, or at least not one with the retained lucidity and energy that would make it worth living.

But Jonathan is still out there, in some city connected to the film industry, waiting to be discovered. We lost touch a long time ago. I did make some efforts to reconnect, but they were not reciprocated. I don't think he wanted to maintain the old friendships from the past, perhaps, I assume, because he doesn't want to know what came of our respective professional lives. But I do confess that I often seek him out online; it is not an obsession, but a burning desire to know what came of him. Almost every time, on that social media site that we all are too aware of, I can see his profile. He always posts pictures of himself posing with drop-dead gorgeous actresses. When you examine the picture though, it is always set in the context of what appears to be public events with hundreds of fans lining up to get themselves photographed with the actors.

Jonathan has not yet made his master opus. But we may all be surprised; it may happen at the end of his life. I think the agony of it all, for him and for anyone in that situation, is that one never knows.

Yours truly,

Pablo

42

June 8, 2014

Milagros de la Torre
New York, NY

Dear Milagros,

Perhaps in every one of us who is inclined to reflect on our own work there lingers the question of what is the most significant thing you've done in your life. It is perhaps a question that one may have at the end of their life, but one can also have it in the form of a projection: what do I want to contribute to humanity in my lifetime? With artists, the question usually translates to: what is the best work I have ever made? It can be characterized in some way as the pursuit of the masterpiece.

But what is that construct, "a masterpiece"? I honestly feel ridiculous thinking of my work in those terms. And that word, in and of itself, feels overly romantic. It conjures up Balzac's character, Frenhofer, killing himself after failing to achieve his masterpiece. But perhaps in a more banal way and for the Hollywood-versed audiences, one would think of Kirk Douglas in the film "Lust for Life", slicing his ear. Saying something is a masterpiece has a degree of grandstanding and exaggeration, and it doesn't say much about the work itself. I admit it works well with classical works, like *The Well Tempered Clavier*, or *Las Meninas*. But when we use it in contemporary art it feels inappropriate. Perhaps that is because something can only be considered truly a masterpiece by people many generations later. But here is another thought: what if the notion of a masterpiece is now defunct entirely?

I know that this supposition seems absurd at first glance. But before you throw away this letter as I suspect you may be very much inclined to do at this point, I would urge you to let me describe to you a thought scenario:

Let's imagine four different alternative realities. In one of them, there are a handful of remarkable artists, living at a time where most other artists lack the same level of brilliance. Most works they create are considered masterpieces.

Now let's imagine that in the second world there are no geniuses, but only artists who work at exactly the same level.

In the third world, all these artists are geniuses, and produce magnificent art works, one as brilliant as the next.

In the fourth world, there are hundreds of millions of artists, good and bad, and there are so many art works emerging all the time that no one can dedicate more than a few seconds to each.

It seems clear that the residents of the second imaginary reality have no hopes of ever knowing what a masterpiece is, if all the works are equally mediocre. But most importantly, how can the residents of the third world recognize a masterpiece since there is no bad art to contrast it with? What follows is the rather obvious conclusion that masterpieces can only exist as long as there are bad artists. So far so good.

But then we go to the fourth world, where the fact that there are new artworks emerging every second means that there is no time to see or reflect on, or discuss any particular art work for a long time. Regardless of whether those works are great or not, there would be no way to know it, since there is no time to look at them and conduct a collective discussion. There is no time for the importance of any single artwork to take effect on someone, as it is so quickly replaced by another one.

Coming to think of it, there is a more relevant question from this story aside from the one regarding masterpieces. But I will let you ponder it on your own.

Yours truly,

Pablo

43

June 9, 2014

Steve White
Norwalk, CT

Dear Steve,

The art world has always had a certain fascination with Hollywood—from artists like Warhol who simply wanted to share the same degree of media attention and project the same kind of glamour, to artists who have actually made the step to create movies in Hollywood (with great results, actually). But it has mostly been an unrequited love, as Hollywood has generally looked at contemporary art in puzzlement, and whenever it has depicted it, it has done so in parodic and usually condescending ways.

But now as you may have noticed we are witnessing an interesting phenomenon: Hollywood stars who want to be conceptual artists. Suddenly, perhaps courtesy of the visibility that Marina Abramovic gave to performance art, actors now want to dignify their careers by describing themselves as artists.

So I want to imagine what the world would be like if this tectonic shift in high and popular culture comes to some kind of completion. Let's imagine the future, told in an art historical narrative.

In 2015, a radical group of Hollywood actors proclaimed the end of art making as it was known. The "Hollywood Manifesto", signed by a number of actors of significant name recognition, rejected art making as an intellectual endeavor, arguing that it needed to become democratized. This manifesto marked the beginning of the transformation of the art gallery; dealers became agents. It also marked the effective end of the unique artwork: production by actor-artists, to keep up with the distribution of their films, usually was done in the hundreds of thousands. Movie theaters opened galleries with some of the works by these actor-artists. Acting schools replaced old art schools, including performance art "method" acting. The Academy Awards introduced, in 2017, Oscars for installation and conceptual art.

The most significant notion introduced by Hollywood into the visual arts is the one of the "remake".

Truly yours,

Pablo

44

June 11, 2014

Deborah Fisher
New York, NY

Dear Deborah,

It is in an artist's character to cross thresholds of every kind; to break conventions, to erase boundaries, to do what no one else can do. Yet there is one threshold that is particularly difficult to cross: leaving art altogether.

There are certainly those people who practice art for a while and, after being unsuccessful in their efforts, eventually stop making art and continue their lives doing something else. They, I would argue, were never artists in the first place, so that type of parting of ways with art is not what I am referring to when I refer to leaving art. It is the moment when a true artist decides that he or she will stop making art; when, as they find themselves at the top of their creative energies and at the pinnacle of their careers, they decide to call it quits.

I think, of course, of Lygia Clark. I think of Rimbaud, who when he died in his thirties had not written for ten years.

That renunciation makes these artists, in a way, eternally young, like Greta Garbo who went out of her way to not be seen in her old age. But the simple desire to cultivate the myth of an enigmatic and elusive figure could not be a strong enough reason to truly make that final divorce from one's art. It has to be something much stronger—a complex combination of wanting to be left alone and having found true satisfaction in being with oneself. Fray Luis de León once wrote:

Vivir quiero conmigo,
Gozar quiero del bien que debo al cielo,
A solas, sin testigo,
Libre de amor, de celo
De odio de esperanza, de recelo.

(Alone I want to live with myself,
I want to enjoy the good that I owe to heaven,
Alone, unwitnessed,
Free of love, of jealousy,
Of hatred, of hope, of apprehension.)

It makes me wonder if the greatest artist is the one who overcomes the need to find an audience. But the question is whether that is even in our power as artists, in the same sense that we have no control of what may happen of our art works once they have left our hands.

I will share with you a brief story.

There was a conceptual artist named Conrado Sorellana. He was one of the most remarkable artists of his generation. He was bothered by the attention of being an artist, and as brilliant as he was, he was convinced that he needed to leave art making to focus on other concerns of his. So one day, to the surprise of everyone, he announced that he would never make any further art works. The news was so shocking to everyone that no one, at first, believed that he was serious. But as he truly stopped making any further works, the art scene realized that something had changed. A critic that had followed his career then published an article arguing that Sorellana's self-imposed departure from art was nothing but a strategy to call even more attention to himself and should be seen as a conceptual gesture. This irritated Sorellana to no end, who responded with another article arguing that he, indeed, had left art without any question, and was no longer interested in making or thinking about art works ever again in his life.

But Sorellana's response was interpreted by everyone as an artwork itself. Someone even framed the article and exhibited it in a gallery as part of a group show. Sorellana, who by the way was famous for having a short fuse, was so irritated by that curator's action that he one day walked into the gallery where that article was displayed, ripped the frame from the wall and smashed it to the floor.

This action delighted Sorellana's fans. They saw in it the greatest conceptual art action of his career.

Sorellana fell into a deep depression. He became even more reclusive and hostile to people. He drank heavily and exhibited an unpredictable behavior whenever he was seen in public. Always this was interpreted by his public as another experiment in the context of his work.

He committed suicide a few years later, leaving a message on his worktable, which read: "I lived in a world where I found art to be a lie, a disappointment. I tried to leave art and go to the other side, not realizing that art was also waiting for me on that other side."

His supporters attended his funeral in the thousands. To them, with his self-inflicted death in rejection of art, he had accomplished the final and most daring conceptual act of any artist.

Yours truly,

Pablo

45

June 15, 2014

Prerana Reddy
Queens, NY

Dear Prerana,

What compels an artist to continue making art? Why are we never satisfied with making one work and then walking away to do something else? It is not easy to respond to this question. It is easy, perhaps, if you describe art making as an addiction. But it is not an addiction. Rather, I believe it is the constant pursuit of trying to forever resolve an essentially permanent unresolved emotional attachment.

Let me frame it for you through an example.

Celestino Magi was an artist. He always recalled his becoming an artist in his early school days, when he must have been around ten years old. He always looked forward to the art class for various reasons. The first one was because he was naturally inclined to drawing and he was good at it; he also enjoyed going to the art classroom, which was in a sunny part of the school, with beautiful blue tables and a big window through which a lot of fresh air and sun came in, and one could see the trees and other houses. (He envied the people who walked down the street, thinking about what it would be like to be an adult and have the freedom to walk around. He didn't know that we never truly attain freedom, either as children, adults, or artists).

But the main reason he loved art class was because there was a girl in it who he was deeply in love with. He ached for her blue eyes and blonde hair. She was the best student in the class, and was quiet and discreet. At night, Celestino would hug the pillow, dreaming of her. Art class was the time when he would get to see her more closely, as the best artists of the class would sit at the same table, and that included her and him.

He never confessed his love to her. But one day, a bully who wanted to make fun of Celestino took his lunch box away. When Celestino tried to recover it, this bully and his friends, who had noticed Celestino's fixation with the blonde girl, dared him to ask her to be his girlfriend, saying that otherwise they would not return his things to him. And Celestino, who was weak and somewhat naïve, went ahead and did so. He went toward her in front of everyone at the table and asked her "do you want to be my girlfriend?" Everyone laughed.

The blond girl turned red. At that moment, Celestino realized that he had made a terrible mistake. He had embarrassed the girl he loved most in the world, and had ruined his remotest hope to truly be with her.

But then what was worse, was that the girl told him: "I will consult this with my pillow."

He never thought that she would say that.

The next day, Celestino did not dare bringing up the matter again with the girl, not ever again. They grew up, and at some point the girl transferred to another school. Celestino left his country to study art and become a professional artist.

Celestino was never satisfied with his work. He continued exhibiting throughout his life and achieved not a small degree of success, but regardless of the endless amounts of people and places he visited, he never encountered satisfaction. He also was unusual in that he refused to sell most of his works, including his best pieces, because he had the conviction that he needed to feel certain that he had found the right owner.

Then one night, toward the end of his life, Celestino had a revelatory dream that came to him unannounced.

He spent the rest of his years looking for that girl, and working on a project in a secret location. These were the two tasks that consumed him for the rest of his life.

A year or so after Celestino had passed away, his old classmate, now a grandmother herself, received a letter from one of Celestino's loyal assistants, who had promised to find her. The letter contained a key and an address in another city and country, with a plane ticket to visit it. She remembered Celestino, and readily agreed to travel.

As she arrived at the designated address, in the outskirts of the city, she encountered a large building. The building contained an entire museum, inside of which there were hundreds of artworks made by Celestino, including all of his best pieces—his entire personal collection.

At the entrance, there was a note addressed to her. It was very brief.

It simply said:

> "All these art works are yours. It took me a lifetime to realize that you were the only audience member I ever wanted to make art for."

Yours,

Pablo

46

June 18, 2014

Regine Basha
Brooklyn, NY

Dear Regine,

As I write this letter, it is Sunday morning. I remember that for many years, I found Sundays depressing, especially in the brief period when I was a student living by myself in Spain. It was because on these days I confronted my loneliness in a more direct way than ever, and I had a difficult time being with myself.

I confess that I have a certain admiration for those who are capable of being alone with themselves and finding solitary fulfillment in what they do. It is an attribute of most eccentrics: they are generally happy in their work, and don't need the validation of others to pursue it.

I wonder if you, like me, have encountered people through life who, in order to vanquish loneliness, turn their lives into an extended "state of exception." I don't mean that term in the legal or political sense of Agamben. Instead, I use the term for lack of a better way to refer to this strategy in our lives where we create parentheses of routine—these include holidays, special occasions where we go out to celebrate, vacations, and for those who are not professionals in the arts, going to see or experience art, amongst other things.

There was someone I knew who carried out this state of exception in her life in a most poignant way. I will refer to her as Hildegard Spleen.

It is not important to describe how I knew Ms. Spleen, but let's just say that she was close to my parents. I had known her since I was a child. She was an extraordinary woman in many ways. She had studied abroad at a time and place when it was difficult for women to become professionals; she had a remarkable career as scholar and was an authority in her field. This allowed her to obtain a well-remunerated job as the director of a research institute. She always dressed impeccably and was fond of elegant clothes and jewelry.

Ms. Spleen's great sorrow, however, was that she never married. She had a great attachment to her parents and had lived with them until far into her adult age. Honestly speaking, she was unattractive, but mainly she spent her youth focusing on her travels and excelling in her work to an extent that the thought of encountering a relationship with others didn't fit her interest. But when her parents passed away, she found herself facing an unbearable loneliness.

Thus Ms. Spleen started organizing parties and dinners. She was an expert host, and made herself, as she always did, the best at the thing in which she was interested. She lived comfortably in a large apartment that allowed for parties of 20 or so without a problem. She had round the clock maids and cooks that she would direct. It was those parties that carried her through her loneliness. They lasted incredibly long hours; preparations would start the night before; the first guests would arrive sometime around noon, and appetizers would start around that time until practically 4pm. The meal would be served around that time, and the dinner would last for another four hours at least. Then listening to music and drinking took over, and the guests would remain in the house until 2 or 3am. It was not unheard of at Ms. Spleen's parties for the guests to stay until the next morning.

As one may expect, Ms. Spleen loved to travel. Travel was a long state of exception, like a long party. She spared no expense in these experiences, and she had a particularly demanding taste. In New York, where I used to see her when she visited, she insisted in going to the most expensive restaurants—a luxury that any of us New Yorkers would find excessive. But she always treated, which landed me often in some of the most sumptuous establishments in the city. She would wake up late every morning, do some shopping, and then arrive at the restaurant where she would spend approximately six hours. By dessert, it was time to go to the opera.

Opera was the ultimate state of exception for Ms. Spleen. Not only did she thoroughly enjoy this art form, but its inordinate length (in particular Wagnerian operas) suited her very well. On the days when, at home, she didn't manage to entertain, she would invite at least one or two people to watch opera on TV, drinking and eating elegantly of course. As one may imagine, this sedentary life of exception did no good for her health, and her health problems increased on a steady basis through the years.

This behavior, all things considered, was not out of the ordinary. But as the years went by, and as Ms. Spleen aged and especially when she finally retired from the directorship of the research institute, loneliness became truly unbearable. Her strategy was then to turn her life into a permanent state of exception, turning every single day into a huge dinner or party. She spent her entire life savings on sustaining this degree of entertaining. Due to the number of parties and dinners she was throwing, this exhausted her friends; even the heavy partiers wouldn't be able to do these parties every single day. So she became an avid pursuer of new friends and people; she would invite the friends of friends and the friends of friends of friends. I hear there were occasions when she was throwing dinner parties at her home for people who she had barely met. Her house became some sort of free restaurant, and all sorts of random people gravitated to it. Sadly, at some point the guests at her parties downgraded to alcoholics and freeloaders who themselves had little idea or interest in Ms. Spleen.

With all this partying, Ms. Spleen's already poor health deteriorated even further, and rapidly. She was instructed not to over-eat and particularly to stop drinking, but this was out of the scheme of possibilities for her.

She was found by her maid one morning, in her bed, with her eyes wide open. There was an expression of surprise in her. She looked like the character of Olympia, the mechanical doll that seduces the poet Hoffmann in *The Tales of Hoffmann*.

I think of Ms. Spleen often. I sense her spirit whenever I listen to opera, whenever I see or walk by one of those luxurious restaurants or happen to taste unaffordable champagne. I don't believe in God, but for some reason I always want to imagine Ms. Spleen finally content, in a better place, in a permanent banquet with great friends, tasting the most glorious food and listening to the most heavenly arias in opera, overjoyed, in a state of permanent ecstasy.

Yours,

Pablo

47

June 20, 2014

Russet Lederman
New York, NY

Dear Russet,

I am interested in how history may explain and shed light on our current issues. I have had a nostalgic bent all my life. An anecdote that my older sister Batiz usually tells about me is that back when I was a 4-year-old, I once said: "I love this music; it reminds me of my childhood." So as someone that is preternaturally inclined to nostalgia, it is not lost on me that there may be a certain contradiction in making contemporary art: art that, at least in theory, is about the *new*.

I think you may guess where my question is leading in this letter. Is there something inherently nostalgic in the notion of newness?

The idea that always comes to mind when I bring this up is the idea of the "tradition of rupture" that I first read about when reading Octavio Paz's understanding of modernism—the idea that the avant-garde's inherent contradiction is to create a system that, in creating innovation, also is creating a predictable, and ultimately conservative pattern. So when we think we are being radical and disruptive we are simply furthering a predictable pattern of actions.

I would like to bring to your attention a story that perhaps may resonate in regards to this issue.

In the city of Osteland things always moved rather quickly. The arts in the city were no exception. Osteland experienced an avant-garde movement that broke with all the aesthetic ideas of the past. It had a huge influence, and changed the way everyone looked at art.

But in a matter of a few years, a group of artists rebelled against this avant-garde movement by creating their own movement. This movement consisted in mostly reinstating the aesthetics of the previous generation, who became revalued as their true inspiration.

A few years later, another, younger group of artists came with their own movement, which reinstated the first generation of avant-garde artists. And a few years later, another generation reinstated the old aesthetic again.

Finally there was a generation of pragmatic artists, who noticed the patterns taking place on a recurring basis in Osteland. So they devised an avant-garde movement that would break every pattern by stating that whatever happened was supposed to happen; that aesthetic breakthroughs would not happen intentionally, and that art should not believe in any special or unique aesthetics.

This is the movement that still predominates in Osteland.

Yours,

Pablo

48

June 21, 2014

Sandy Lipsman
New York, NY

Dear Sandy,

Over the last few weeks, I have written a lot of letters to friends, with no particular primary objective in mind other than to share what was on my mind. I realized, not without certain sadness, that pretty much anything I felt I could meaningfully write about, and start a conversation about, is ultimately to do with the nature of art and our relationship with it. I often feel that I write in monotone, while at the same time confess that I am sort of surprised that not more people concern themselves with these topics. I am not sure what it is about myself that almost immediately makes me think of the large philosophical topics: What is art for? What does it mean to make art these days? How do we value it? And so forth.

Perhaps this natural impulse has to do with my late older brother, who was a philosophy student when I was still a child. He would read me Sartre and Camus, would try to explain to me Xeno and Heraclitus, Kant and Marx. I think from very early on I understood art not as simply an act of communication but rather as something that had to be rooted in a complex view of the world.

But I am also aware of the difficulties of attaching philosophical thought to artistic expression. I have images of art students reading Lacan or Lyotard and basically trying to make works that illustrated quotes by them. The results were like unintentional self-parodies. Probably the only artist who has managed to do this properly has been Saul Steinberg, when he drew cartoons of philosophical words, such as a giant word "who" pushing against another leaning, edifice-like "did", pressing onto the word "it" and with an interrogation mark at the end.

We all agree that philosophy and art are intimately related, but the problem is that we can't ever seem to find a good enough philosopher who can also understand the artistic practice, nor an artist who can be well-versed enough in philosophy to either explain how they work in their practice or understand enough philosophy to successfully employ them in their art. At best we can say that the relationship between art and philosophy acts in mysterious ways.

Let me present you with a small, imaginary example.

About a century ago, in Vienna, Ernest Himmelfarb was a major philosopher of his era. Over the decades he had slowly produced a monumental series of works that focused on ethics, ontology and politics. But the most elusive part for him was the development of an aesthetic theory that would fit with his complex philosophy. After many years, he encountered the work of Sylvia Thorn, a young and rather unknown artist at the time, and he was fascinated by it. Every aspect of her work, he thought, exemplified in a perfect way the issues in aesthetics that he thought were defining of that time.

Himmelfarb then approached Thorn about writing a theoretical book based on her work. She was delighted and proud of receiving attention from such a major figure of philosophy. So Himmelfarb initiated a series of visits to her studio, taking copious notes of her form of working, conducting lengthy interviews, and interviewing close collaborators of hers.

Himmelfarb's book on Thorn came out, and it had an enormous impact. Himmelfarb's observations on art were brilliant and lucid, and prompted a wide variety of debates amongst artists and critics in cafés throughout Vienna, and later, throughout Europe. Newspapers discussed the book; someone even made a theater work based on Himmelfarb's ideas. The book became an obligatory reference in philosophy circles.

However, no one could quite understand why Himmelfarb had seen Thorne as such a great example of his theories. Her work, most art experts thought, was plain, uninteresting and devoid of any of the attributes or ideas that Himmelfarb saw in it.

Many years passed, and the influence of Himmelfarb's book started to wane in philosophy circles. Many more books and thinkers appeared bringing new ideas. Finally, some younger philosophers took on Himmelfarb's notions and questioned their validity; almost every single idea he had argued about now proved to connect him with an outmoded aesthetic theory. He had completely missed the sea of change that the avant-garde brought a few years afterward. He became, to that generation, an example of how a philosopher should not conduct an aesthetic investigation.

But something equally interesting happened at the same time: the same generation that found Himmelfarb's arguments weak and old fashioned became very interested in Thorn's work, which to that point had all but disappeared from view and only had survived from the references that Himmelfarb had made to it in his book. Someone managed to rescue Thorn's artworks, left in the attic of some private collection in Salzburg where she had died. The works were exhibited again and she was hailed as one of the precursors of the central ideas of modernism—all of which, one by one, had been missed by Himmelfarb's writings.

Yours truly,

Pablo

49

June 25, 2014

Sara Demeuse
Brooklyn, NY

Dear Sara,

At the risk of repeating a series of clichés, I can't help myself but to remark at how quickly time goes by; how swift is the transition from being a young professional to becoming already someone that must be displaced. There is something to be said, however, for reaching a certain age where you can command a certain degree of respect from others. While I don't consider myself old at 43, I am no longer, for better or worse, an emerging artist; I am not the naïve person I was back in my 20s. At the same time, I have become more set in my ways. There are things that, in the past, I didn't have to worry about, and about which I have now started to develop certain concerns. One of those is to not develop the habit of sharing my experiences with younger artists as if I were an art history character. It mainly is because such impulse reminds me of Susannah Pesanti.

I met Susannah Pesanti (as you may gather, I am giving her a different name) sometime in the 90s. She had a reputation for being a good curator, an entrepreneur who had opened a gallery in New York in the 70s. But her career always seemed to me enigmatic: she would reach a certain important position in an institution or start a great project, then she would abruptly leave the position at some point or the project would end. The only project that I initiated with her had such fate; she unexpectedly left the organization where she was working, and consequently the project collapsed.

I remember her telling me that it was the fault of the board; that they had driven the organization to ruin.

Susannah Pesanti had an oversized personality; she was very self-assured, always speaking as if she had a secret plan to take over the world. It was almost certain that in every conversation she would bring up the gallery she once had in the 70s. She claimed to be the first one to have exhibited this or that major artist; to have introduced art and technology, video, performance and so forth. She liked to remind me at each one of those conversations that I was probably five years old when she was exhibiting someone like Sol Lewitt.

At some point, she became director of a nonprofit space in New York. An artist friend of mine from another country, who I respected and admired, had received a grant to bring a project of his in New York and, with the hopes to help him, I called Susannah to see if the space she directed would be interested in receive my friend's project. She insisted that it could only happen if I agreed to serve as curator of it, which I accepted, if somewhat reluctantly—I have never wanted to be a curator but did believe in my friend's work and wanted to support him. I said yes and we had an agreement.

We then met to discuss the logistics for the exhibition and matters of budget. My friend's grant would cover his travel and the transportation of the work, as well as other small expenses. But then Susannah presented me with a budget she had created, which included payment for the space's overhead during the time of the exhibition, which as I recall included trash removal and her own salary. I objected to this budget, which I felt was completely abusive and inappropriate; no non-profit space ever charges an artist to cover their overhead. She acted as if it was the most normal thing in the world. I argued that this was tantamount to running a vanity gallery but under the name of a nonprofit, not only unethical but probably illegal. She again replied as if she had no idea what I was talking about. I left her gallery, swearing to never wanting to have anything to do with her ever again.

But as things are in New York, I continued to run into her in various openings and exhibitions. After a brief time, she left the alternative space she directed, and became what one would term a vanity curator: someone who curated exhibitions for artists who had money and funds but whose work had not translated into any invitations to exhibit. Thus Susannah Pesanti found her place in the art scene, helping others construct myths for themselves in an impeccable way.

The last time I saw her, at a social event, she arrived with a couple of young interns that were working with her on her projects. You could see them looking at her in awe, so impressed by the heroic stories of her gallery from the 1970s, which she was relating to them. When she approached me, I was speaking to a seasoned and reputable New York curator who has also been in the art scene since the late 1960s.

He had never met her before.

All yours,

Pablo

50

June 28, 2014

Carin Kuoni
New York, NY

Dear Carin,

You may be wondering why I have chosen to write letters in this old fashioned format. There are many reasons for it, but the one I will share for the time being is this: I am feeling asphyxiated by the immediacy and spontaneity of social media. Mainly, I want the opportunity in my life not to be spontaneous. It has taken me many years to realize that I am not at my best when I have to think on my feet; mostly, I cannot think. It is the distance of time and space that allows me to articulate thoughts properly, to think about things before I express them, minimizing the possibility that I may regret them later.

Which brings me to an interesting subject to consider: spontaneity in art. More interesting to me is the question: can art be spontaneous anymore?

You may know that I like to ask questions that at first glance seem absurdly basic. But as an educator, facing visitors who ask the most basic questions every day, I know that no question about art can ever be basic. So is the problem of spontaneity in art.

We probably can think about art that comes from intuitive outbursts of creativity—let's say "accident" painting—but also from coldly calculated moves. Artists like Warhol, who acted as if they were being intuitive, most likely were being coldly calculating. The problem that I see is that there is no tangible proof that an artist who is purely intuitive would manage to create a body of work that consistently pushes the boundaries of art in a critical way.

To illustrate my point, I would like to tell you a brief story.

Carolyn Fuller was one more foreign student from the many who every year go through art schools in the United States. Before she achieved international fame due to the events that I am about to describe, her professors and classmates regarded her as a quiet, hardworking but otherwise unremarkable student. She was interested in photography and had managed to achieve a certain degree of skill taking professional photographs. Her photographs, mostly of painterly landscapes, were fairly unremarkable. It was one day when a visiting artist was looking at her work that she intimated that she was forced to make money to pay her tuition by taking photographs for the porn industry, particularly for a fetish magazine. After this visiting artist looked at her photographs, he immediately saw the potential in them, and encouraged her to exhibit this kind of work instead. It had never occurred to Carolyn to exhibit those photographs in an art context, and she was somewhat embarrassed to reveal that she was involved in such a shady line of work. But finally one day she armed herself with courage and submitted the photos for consideration for a group show.

The photographs attracted attention immediately. A curator from a major museum saw them at that exhibition and included Carolyn in a biennial she was curating. She wrote an extensive interpretation of those photographs, describing them as a social critique of human perversions. From conversations with the curator, Carolyn sensed that this curator was hoping that the photographs would be printed large (she would normally print them in small sizes) and so she obliged. When the biennial opened, Carolyn's work, hanging at the entrance of the exhibition, became the most talked about. She landed a major New York gallery shortly after, and the works started being sold for substantial amounts of money. The interest in the work appeared to be insatiable. She continued printing photos and accepting exhibition invitations. Whenever she was interviewed about her photographs, she would repeat ideas from the essay of the first curator who had "discovered" her.

After a year, galleries and curators were calling for more. "What is next?" they constantly asked her. "What are you working on now?" Carolyn wasn't sure how to continue the body of work that had taken over the art world. What compounded the situation was that the fetish industry had become aware of the notoriety of her photographs, and many of the actors and publishers were suing her for contract infringement. The lawsuits had another subtext, which was that every time these images appeared in the media, they were accompanied by an attack on the porn industry and presented Carolyn's work as a brave attempt to denounce the objectification of women in this industry. This was resented by models and publishers alike, and she thus became a persona non grata in the porn industry.

She tried to restage the fetish scenes based on what she could remember, but they never matched the original series; they only looked like a secondary product. She then tried to make altogether a completely different body of work, going back to her original interest—abstract landscapes—but the exhibition of those works was met with universal puzzlement and disapproval. Her dealer was gentle but firm in his demand: "We would like you to continue pursuing the body of work you launched your career with."

Carolyn's fetish photographs can be seen all over the world, in many collections. Twenty years later, she is still trying to figure out a way in which she can continue the brilliant series that shook the art world to its core.

Yours,

Pablo

51

July 2, 2014

Hye-Ruong Min
New York, NY

Dear Min,

Recently in the news there was a sensational story related to a celebrated deaf Japanese composer, Mamoru Samuragochi. Samuragochi's compositions have been admired all over Japan for many years, and he was praised for his talent and determination against all odds, as a modern day Beethoven. At the time of the Sochi Olympics, when a Japanese figure skater was going to use one of his compositions as background, a man by the name of Takashi Niigaki came forward to say that he had ghost-written most of Samuragochi's songs—which was confirmed by the embarrassed composer. Furthermore, it appears that Samuragochi is not even deaf, but rather pretended to be so in order to reinforce the Beethoven comparison. Both men were the authors of one of the greatest frauds in classical music.

It is a spectacular story. But aside from the juicy details, you can see how a story would be fascinating for the press, which is particularly attracted to topics like forgery and authenticity.

The reality about authorship, as I think you know, is much more complex. It is not often clear, in the age of process-based art and coproduction, where the true boundaries of authorship lie.

As an example I can tell you a bit about Victor Lovejoy. Victor (I felt the duty to give him a different name) always was a talented painter. He had a difficult childhood of many hardships and suffered great neglect from his parents. He had to grow quickly and figure out a way to do everything by himself. As he became an adult, and as a result of his hard work and natural talent, he started to receive attention for his paintings. His works started to sell for decent amounts of money and the demand for his work increased. He needed assistants, and when he finally got them he realized that he loved to delegate, to tell others what to do. It was perhaps a way to counter the difficulties that he experienced in his youth.

As the prices of his works increased, he could afford to get more talented assistants. That is when he encountered Yang Lin. Yang was from mainland China, and had come to New York to study at the Students League. He was classically trained like most Chinese artists. He had a superb drawing ability as well as a great sense of color and composition. Victor immediately realized he had struck gold.

Victor's next show, made largely by directing Yang's expert hand, won wide acclaim. It was described as his best show so far. The next and the next exhibitions were the same. By this time, Yang was pretty much taking care of the entire manufacturing of the works. While Yang had not invented Victor's aesthetics, he had become a better Victor Lovejoy than Victor Lovejoy himself, and both knew it.

One day, Yang shocked Victor by saying that he had decided to move back to China. He was tired of his job and wanted to do something else—perhaps mountaineering. Victor begged and cried to Yang. He offered him triple his salary; he implored him to reconsider. But Yang was unmoved. He had made his decision.

Victor was suicidal. But he was not the type that would actually have the courage to end his life. He also had no choice but to move on. Frenetically, he tried to find a new Yang. But after going through an endless string of new assistants, none of them would give him the same great hand and masterful brushstroke.

Yang always remained Victor's secret; practically no one ever knew that he existed. No one could figure out how Victor's work suddenly declined so quickly. But Victor continued producing, focusing mainly on the more commercial venues, with lower standards. Still, the discriminating public never forgot those paintings from Victor's golden era, which are the most sought after and which certainly will be considered the best works of his career.

Yours,

Pablo

52

July 4, 2014

Raul Zamudio
New York, NY

Dear Raul,

I often think about how being an outsider can be such an important condition to increment awareness of the world. I have lived it in various ways; as an immigrant, as someone who doesn't always look like what he is supposed to look like, and especially as an artist. Being an outsider allows you to look at the world around you as a whole; being different allows you to express that difference in contrast to the homogenized world that you see in front of you.

We tend to see this outsider condition as a burden we need to carry all our lives, as the permanently misunderstood teenager. But in reality our condition of outsider is a very fragile trait that once we lose, we lose perspective on who we are in relation to others, and risk losing our ability to look at the world as artists.

I want to bring up an interesting example of an artist that I heard of some time ago.

Marcelo Hiberman was the kind of artist that you may have encountered in the middle of Zucotti Park, actively organizing protests and mobilizing people during the Occupy Wall Street days. Marcelo's father was a sociologist and his mother had worked in government—a family legacy that produced in him the interest to become actively engaged in community organizing and public art.

At some point after his Occupy Wall Street experience, Marcelo was impatient and thirsty for effecting true and radical change in society. He concluded from the experience that if he really wanted to change the system he would need to infiltrate it completely.

He then decided to do an art project wherein he would infiltrate Wall Street with the objective to find sensitive information that he would leak to the world. However, he found it extremely hard to even land an entry-level position at an investment firm. The amount of knowledge about the markets needed even for the lowest echelon of any company was more than he could manage.

Meanwhile, he decided that he would learn espionage techniques, by working for a private investigator who specialized in cheating spouses. Marcelo thought at the time that developing investigative experience would allow him to research the dark secrets of the financial world.

Marcelo became very talented at conducting the tasks of a private detective, and as time went by he was given more and more responsibilities at the private investigator's office, particularly in online spying. The online surveillance skills he developed, which included a series of very effective methods to hack other people's computers, allowed him to secretly hack computers of global traders and other people on Wall Street. But what he found was unexceptional, usually boring, or incomprehensible—complex calculations and endless numbers and codes that he was unable to fully understand.

At some point, he couldn't resist the impulse to spy on his activist and artist friends and colleagues. What he found about them was shocking: cheating, dishonest behavior, undisclosed wealth, secret political affiliations that made him wonder whether anyone he had met was actually the person they claimed to be. Even some of his most radical, inspiring mentors had embarrassing facts in their private computers that caused great disappointment in Marcelo. He first felt indignation, thinking that most people he knew were dishonest; but then he felt embarrassed: Was he the sole naïve individual that truly believed in fairness? Part of him at that point wished he had never seen this information; but it was too late to ignore it.

Some time later, he wrote to a friend: "I have concluded that unethical people who act out their disregard for others in plain view are better than those who condemn them while being dishonest with themselves. And, as far as I can tell, the main thing we are dishonest about is that we all need money in the end."

Disappointed by the world of artist activism, Marcelo has since turned to painting. He is very happy making art works that are bought and collected by usually well-off collectors. He shows at a gallery in Paris now and has moved to Southern France.

"My life," he wrote to a friend, "has become wonderfully uncomplicated now."

Yours truly,

Pablo

53

July 5, 2014

Andrew Ginzel and Sarah Walker
Brooklyn, NY

Dear Andrew and Sarah,

Tonight I was thinking about my generation—those people who are, as someone once said, "travel companions." Those of us who are roughly the same age and who have chosen to dedicate our lives to art. For better or worse we are in it together, we will celebrate our successes and support each other at the times when we will be down, and mainly, we will grow old together.

One of the types of relationships that I find most interesting about artists who share similar age, background and array of interests is one where they become so keenly aware of each other's works that they become entangled in a web of influences, professional jealousy, and admiration.

This brings me to the story of Ingemar Short and Claude Spassky.

Short and Spassky were two renowned artists from the same town. Their families lived on the same block; they belonged to the same social background and they attended the same school. Eventually, they both became artists, and their aesthetic interests were closely related. This became a very uncomfortable situation for both as they became renowned artists internationally. It was clear that if Short was invited to an exhibition, then Spassky would not be invited, and vice versa. They simply didn't seem to fit together, and yet they were perfect replacements for one another in museums and collections. They both despised each other privately and embraced each other publicly. They were mutual nemeses.

They both secretly hoped that the other would magically disappear, while still being the first ones to visit each other's exhibitions, to see what the other was doing.

At some point, Spassky, who was fed up and a bit tired of such permanent competition and discomfort, moved to another city. This was a relief to Short who suddenly enjoyed the space he had gained, without the intromission of his rival. As for Spassky, he was also initially happy, finding a new environment in which to make art as well as a new audience to communicate with.

But then an interesting phenomenon happened: as both artists became more comfortable with their current state, their work started feeling more complacent and self-indulgent than before. First the critics noticed it, then their artist colleagues, and finally, the public. The last ones to realize it—as unfortunately happens sometimes—were the artists themselves. Both started receiving bad reviews of their exhibitions. Short noticed his sales, audiences and accolades disappear, while Spassky fell into misery in his new city, and struggled to find enough incentives to make art.

After a few years, Spassky made the decision to return to his city—the city where Short still lived. Immediately—it is a small world, after all—Short knew that Spassky was back. He greeted him warmly at an opening. Both appeared sincere.

Shortly afterward, both presented rival exhibitions around the same time, and both were greatly praised by the critics.

They probably still don't know the reason why both had suffered temporary setbacks in their careers.

There is one thing I have always wondered. When Catullus wrote:

I love and hate. Don't ask me why, but I feel it happen, and I suffer.

Could he, perhaps, be referencing the act of creating?

Yours,

Pablo

54

July 7, 2014

Chelsea Haines
Brooklyn, NY

Dear Chelsea,

I imagine you may be as familiar as I am with the rhetoric that artists use to describe their work. It is difficult to speak about one's own art; yet it is practically unavoidable for most of us. Speaking about art work is also a liability because whatever the artist says is immediately attached to the work as if it were a necessary extension. And because good makers are not always good speakers, the act of attempting a description presents the real risk of having the poor description replace the direct experience of the work. And, on the opposite end, artists who are very articulate may not be enough good makers to substantiate, in their objects, the elegant claims of their works. In short, no artist has ever managed to avoid the problem of properly balancing their making with their speaking.

With the exception, of course, of Massimo Tamagno.

Tamagno was born and raised in Bologna, a city of great erudition and hermetic tradition. His father, a book binder, was a very learned man. Tamagno grew up knowing several arte povera artists in his youth. When he became a young adult, he wanted to be an artist very badly, but early on he knew he was incapable of making any kind of interesting object. Reportedly, his few attempts were so frustrating and unsuccessful in his mind that he always destroyed the works before anyone saw them.

As he was sitting in his studio, depressed, looking at the pile of trash that was his latest attempt at making a work, he thought to himself: at least no one will ever see how terrible the work was: for all anyone knows I could describe this work as the best work ever made.

This one passing, almost accidental thought became the defining moment in his career.

Tamagno started writing feverishly, focusing on elaborate, eloquent descriptions of the most powerful and poetic works.

Then he slowly and discreetly started circulating those descriptions amongst the art world. He hired actors to bring them up at openings; he hired writers to interview him so he could describe the elaborate and stunning installations and projects he was working on, and that no one had yet seen.

Those interviews along with the bewildering descriptions caught everyone's attention. Curators started contacting Tamagno to see his pieces; dealers and collectors became interested. Tamagno ignored these requests, and continued to produce more descriptions. He instinctively knew that when you generate interest in the art world, the best strategy is, instead of satisfying this interest, to make it even harder to satisfy.

Each new description of each work was even more phenomenal than the last. It eventually created an obsession. Writers and critics started writing about these works, speculating about their attributes and influences, without having ever seen them. Younger artists started claiming that they were influenced by Tamagno. He started being mentioned as one of the leading artists of his generation.

The attention that he received was much more than what Tamagno anticipated. He found himself in the impossible situation of either revealing that none of these works ever existed, or making work that he knew would fare poorly in comparison with the descriptions he created.

One day Tamagno finally announced an exhibition of his works at an old cheese warehouse in the outskirts of Bologna. Hundreds of people—critics, artists, curators, la crème de la crème of the art world—came to see the exhibition. The doors of the building were locked and all visitors were waiting in anticipation for them to open. When they did, they entered into the huge, dark storage space, all empty with the exception of a large mound of trash in the center, which appeared to consist of destroyed canvases, frames, and other materials. Tamagno wasn't there; he had only left a parrot in a pole, to the side of the trash pile, repeating a phrase:

"The perfect art work is the one no one ever saw."

Yours,

Pablo

55

July 11, 2014

Chris Havens
Brooklyn, NY

Dear Chris,

The Greek diner near my house went out of business. I confess that I was overjoyed when it opened about two years ago: I love diners—they remain one of my favorite aspects of New York. I adore the very simple act of being able to sit down and have a cup of coffee or soup, or comfort food, knowing exactly how it is going to taste, knowing it won't be a gourmet meal, and won't break the bank.

And now I am so pained that it closed, to the point that I am surprised at my own pain. But why should I care so much and especially why should I be bothering you with this information?

I travel all the time and don't have much time to spend in my neighborhood here in Red Hook. But I think precisely because of that I have developed a great need for continuity and predictability in other aspects of my life—and particularly in the neighborhood where I live. I don't think you can sustain a life full of continuous instability, or at least not for long.

Art is about destabilizing the status quo, so if your profession is to do that, you may need some routine and even boring aspects of your life if you want to make great art. I understand completely for example, why Warhol never drank and why he lived with his mother. How else could he have run the Factory?

The greater problem is that stability is as addictive as disruption. Let me provide you with an example.

The Iron Forge Art Center was created as an art school

connected to a state university. The university president wanted an experimental, forward-looking program, and hired a young and energetic director named Sally Townsend to carry out this vision. Townsend was very connected in the art world and brought with her five or so up and coming artists of her generation to teach there.

The dynamism and excitement that the group brought into the program was palpable. These artists brought other collaborators and together they created highly imaginative seminars, performances, urban projects, multi-disciplinary research and provocative exhibitions. In a couple of years everyone was talking about what was happening at the Iron Forge. The first generation of students came from all walks of life; thanks to some generous grants, many students from working class backgrounds were able to join and pursue an artistic career.

Partially as a result of the success of the program, the demand grew and with it the pressure to accommodate more students. Townsend wanted to keep the program small, but the university insisted in the need to increment the revenue; it was agreed that a few adjuncts would be hired to cover the extra class load. In the meantime, the artists from the founding faculty were very coveted and successful, and started traveling often and requesting leaves; the adjuncts would cover for them. Townsend herself was in high demand, and as she also traveled, she delegated the day to day running of the program to her deputy director, a life-long administrator named Betsy Ives. Ives sought to regulate the program, introducing a number of report systems, evaluations and paperwork to ensure that all expenses and projects in the school were accounted for. The founding faculty artists protested at the increasing headaches that the paperwork generated; at this point, they were in high demand from biennials in museums. In time, the prospect of remaining at the Iron Forge looked less and less exciting. Even purchasing a ream of paper required what appeared to be an equal sized ream of forms with needed signatures.

Townsend was offered a curatorial position in a major museum, and she decided to take it. Ives then became acting director, a post that she held for three years, while the board could not decide on who to hire. In the meantime, the artists slowly started bowing out of the program, not without sadness, but facing the reality that their professional careers had already taken off and it was time to say goodbye. The ones who took their places were the adjuncts, who had always dutifully filled out the reams of paperwork for their classes and who Ives appreciated for their diligence. The experimental seminars, which had brought major international visiting artists were reduced for budgetary reasons and ultimately altogether eliminated; so was the performance program, which was moved to the theater department. The still-life painting class, which was favored by one of the ex-adjuncts, was introduced, as were a tempera and an etching class. The profile of the students also changed; as tuition fees were raised, only richer and whiter classes would come. With them somehow also realism came; fewer and fewer students wanted to deal with conceptual art.

Today the Iron Forge is a large and profitable art school with a generous endowment. It has now positioned itself as an academic painting school, with efficient professors who gave up on their art careers long ago so as not to conflict with their teaching loads. It functions like clockwork. At times it is compared to the early years. Whenever someone remembers the parties and the excitement, Ives, who is now the director of the school, usually replies: "That was a different time. We came to the point that we just had too much innovation."

Yours,

Pablo

56

July 14, 2014

Dannielle Tegeder
Brooklyn, NY

Dear Dannielle,

I was not too long ago at a meeting where the scholar Mieke Bal declared that she was an anti-intentionalist: she looks at art with a complete disregard for what the artist says about his or her intentions in making the work. At first, as an artist myself, I was scandalized: how can we ignore what the artist intends here in the XXIst century when so many artists' conceptual works consist mainly of declarations of intentions? I may have misunderstood. But then, thinking more carefully about that problem, I think I can understand that stance. For, how can we as artists be so sure about what our intentions are behind every work we make? Isn't it true that when you look back at a work that you make you realize that there were all sorts of things you were trying to solve at the time that you were not really aware of when you did the work?

This reminds me of the case of two actors: Conrad Sauer and Eleazar Tunnel.

Tunnel had a great personality, an attractive physique—in a classical sense—and he also had a commanding baritone voice. He started his career young, playing romantic leads, and had some success. He was known as "the voice," because of that notable trait of his, and you could tell that he enjoyed making it even more notable by projecting from his diaphragm as a singer would. He particularly impressed when he was playing angry macho or authoritarian roles, which led to him being typecast as the villain.

Sauer, by contrast, was a comedy actor. He was one of those actors whose face alone would make one laugh. He was typecast as a comedic artist, so he always got offered those kinds of goofy roles.

Tunnel and Sauer were good friends. One thing that brought them together was that both resented their being ghettoized in one particular character type (this, if you are somewhat familiar with the actor world, is not uncommon). No matter what each tried, they would only get offers for the same type—angry villains in Tunnel's case, and silly clowns in Sauer's. Tunnel wanted to make people laugh, and to be loved—not hated as the permanent villain; and Sauer wanted to be taken seriously for once in his life.

Finally, one day it happened that Tunnel and Sauer were cast in the same play—cast, once again, in their predictable roles. After a rehearsal when both went out for a drink, they were talking about their mutual frustration and lifelong desire to play something like one another's role. It occurred to them that they had an opportunity to do so now, with assistance from each other. So they secretly switched roles, following the rehearsals in their original roles, while rehearsing the other's lines after.

When opening night came, the audience—and the cast included—were shocked when Tunnel emerged on the stage playing Sauer's role, and vice versa. The experience for both actors, and for the audience, was exhilarating. Both had never felt more alive; they felt that they were finally acting, instead of simply being themselves. The surprise turned into admiration and awe; there was a standing ovation at the close of the performance. It was as if both of their careers had been reborn.

After that news-making experience, various comedic roles were offered to Tunnel and many serious roles—often antagonist—were offered to Sauer, and both accepted them all, with the hopes to finally reach new horizons in their work.

But then the surprise was that their subsequent performances were little more than mediocre. Tunnel showed no sense of comedic timing, and his jokes would almost always fall flat; while Sauer was just too funny looking to be taken seriously in a drama. So after a few attempts, this new part of their career was over, and, out of necessity or sheer desperation, both had to go back to perform their old types.

Tunnel passed away not too long ago, while Sauer still lives, albeit long retired, somewhere in upstate New York. When interviewed recently about that particular chapter of his life, a journalist politely asked Sauer why was it that the first performance when Sauer and Tunnel had switched roles had been so successful, while their subsequent attempts to perform other characters had not been well received.

Sauer was silent for a minute. But then he finally said:

"Playing comedic roles was second nature to me because it was like being myself, so what people saw wasn't a character—they just saw me as I was. But the reality is—and it took me until recently to realize this—I was never actually interested in acting a fictional character. I only really, desperately wanted to be Tunnel himself. And I believe he felt the same way about being me. And that night was the only night of our lives, I think, when we fulfilled that desire."

Yours,

Pablo

57

July 15, 2014

Kerry McCarthy
New York, NY

Dear Kerry,

I have been writing letters for several months and I am barely getting a sense of the true reasons why I am doing it. At this point, I believe one of those reasons is that I am yearning for a more grounded sense of communication with others—something that feels more concrete and tangible than everyday emails or social media. Thus, the letter. But another, perhaps more complex reason, has to do with the fear I have developed about myself and which I am hoping is unfounded; namely, that I am becoming intoxicated by negativity and by an objective outlook on the world. To write down my ideas to you forces me to confront them in a very direct way, and because I believe I am most authentic when I am writing (even when I write fiction), even I become surprised by what I end up discussing in my letters.

So, let's discuss negativity. I have never been a strong believer in happiness theories; nor do I think that we should try to be happy all the time. For a very long time I have been a strong lover of nostalgia, which I believe is a less delusional sentiment than relentless, Pollyanna-esque optimism. More importantly, in what pertains to our profession, it has been observed several times by historians ranging from Greenberg to Clark that the avant-garde has historically propelled itself through negation. Irony and critique, which are traits that modern and post-modern art embrace, are common; humor and happiness are looked down upon.

So are we condemned to coexist with the negative?

This reminds me of the interesting case of Kira Dorritt.

Dorritt was a psychologist who, in the late 1950s, precisely became interested in the way in which contemporary artists were making reactive works to existing ones, always making something by rejecting something else. After working a few years as a counselor in an art school, she became fascinated by the process of negation that sparked creativity. In her research around this phenomenon, and from notes from various sessions with students and alumni, she observed this negation was almost always accompanied by an indirect desire of the artist to be accepted by the powers-that-be of the art community (including artist peers, critics and curators).

This desire of acceptance, accompanied by the willingness and interest to create confrontational art works that reject the immediate past, made her consider a relationship between this social dynamic and the one that occurs within fraternities and their initiation rituals. In Dorritt's view, the fraternity had an inverse dynamic of shaming the novice, while the art world has a process of the novice becoming initiated by shaming the predecessors. However, both were ultimately exclusive societies with their own passcodes and rituals. When Dorritt proposed this subject as a doctoral research topic, it was rejected by her advisors; no one took her seriously.

So she decided she would secretly try out her theories in a practical way to prove the potential of understanding the art world as a fraternity. She discreetly started inviting some of the most talented art students to join a special mutual support group entitled The Ether Group (she made sure to refrain from calling it a sorority or a fraternity; in fact, the group included both genders).

Because Dorritt knew that these young artists responded to rebellion and would act against what they were told, she ensured to make her meetings not an invitation but a warning against joining this group. At individual and very surreptitious meetings, she privately explained to each potential member that she had heard that the student had been selected by the group due to the quality of their work, and that they had a chance to join a secret society that would propel their careers. After she warned them of the dangers of joining this group, she knew she had awakened the curiosity and interest of these students.

Dorritt engaged Neil Garrett—a psychologist friend and collaborator—to pose as a senior artist and followed up contacting these students to join the group. Without exception, they accepted. Garrett would meet with each individually, keeping the membership of the group a secret.

No member, each was told, was allowed to discuss the group with anyone, not even its own members; they would only communicate through their work. Each was then presented with an elaborate set of rules, vocabularies, rituals and conceptual gestures that each member would need to follow. All of them had been made up by Dorritt, and they ranged from the merely hermetic to the altogether ridiculous. She wanted to make them evident so that they would be easily detected by other members. It was guaranteed that if each artist incorporated that set of references in their work, it would be recognized by the "leadership" and it would ascend in the canon.

The experiment worked with astonishing precision. All the "members" modified their way of working and before anyone realized, the invented references and menu of conceptual mannerisms that Dorritt had assigned were easily apparent. This caused puzzlement amongst the professors, who suddenly were seeing their best students making works that didn't seem to have a particular relationship with any other known artistic school or aesthetic. They all had emerged mysteriously.

Dorritt never published her study; it was never known why. It is speculated that she was conflicted by the deceitful nature of her experiment, which had influenced and, one could say, manipulated these young artists in an unethical way, and this influence had taken on a life of its own in ways that Dorritt herself did not anticipate: non-member art students who saw these gestures also started using them, most of them, ostensibly not even knowing that they belonged to The Ether Group. Because as a rule no member was supposed to talk to another or to even acknowledge the existence of the group, it seems impossible to know who truly had been a member and who hadn't.

After Dorritt passed away, her psychology collaborator published an article in a psychology journal detailing her study and her research to others, but for the most part he wasn't taken seriously, nor is it likely that his article was ever read by any of these artists. Garrett refused to reveal the kind of gestures that Dorritt had conceived, but he did say that many of them in fact are used and quoted profusely in art today, probably by artists who have incorporated them unconsciously, trying to embrace that kind of radicality with the desire for acceptance that continues to define our art world.

Yours,

Pablo

58

July 18, 2014

Laura Lona
Long Island City, NY

Dear Laura,

We often use the phrase "being at the right place at the right time," to refer to people who were just lucky to receive a certain kind of opportunity. It also emerges in situations where one shows certain contempt or condescendence toward that individual, attributing whatever happened to this person not the result of their own effort, but of happenstance. This is certainly the case of several figures in art history who perhaps may not be so relevant but they happened, indeed, to be at the right place at the right time. Don't you often wonder what your life would have been like if you had had the chance to be at the Bauhaus during its golden years, in Paris in the teens, or at Black Mountain College in the 1950s? These suppositions are of course frustrating, because there is no way of knowing what it could have been like. But, I believe objectively speaking, there are the cases of those who were indeed, at the right place at the right time, and yet it didn't help them, and perhaps even sealed their fates in a negative way (which would then bring us to have to say that they were at the right place and time for pretty much everyone else but themselves).

I often think this was the case of Armando Solana, which now we can analyze with a certain degree of historical perspective.

When I was still an art student, working in a museum, I had the chance to meet Mr. Solana (again, I feel it necessary to give him another name), who was pretty much at the end of his career. He was gentle, apparently satisfied with his life, and full of fascinating anecdotes of art history, as he had been a enviable witness to most of the most important chapters of XXth century art. He was sort of a legend in his country, and by that time (he was in his seventies or so) he pretty much had art works of his in every major public art collection in his home country, and seemingly at least one major public sculpture in every major city of that country. I can't remember too well what I thought of his work as a young student; I certainly wasn't particularly interested in it, but I was definitely awed and impressed by his fame and the legendary artistic times he had witnessed. Basically, Mr. Solana had been some kind of boy wonder, with great drawing abilities that at the time made people compare him to young Picasso. He also came from an aristocratic family who were very involved in supporting the arts of their country, which included bringing influential artists from all over the world and helping out what became one of the most important generations of artists.

Mr. Solana grew up in an extraordinary environment, where he met some of the most important artists of the XXth century, such as Stravinsky, Breton, Eisenstein, and Buñuel, who would come visit his parents. Solana became the youngest witness of the works of a generation of artists who took him under their wing as some kind of little brother. He left to live in Paris when he was 16, where he received support of many of those who were already there, and where he ended up living for several decades.

Over time, however, the great promise that Solana had as a youth did not fully materialize. While the other artists—his "elder" artistic brothers as it were—started producing important writings, art works, and musical compositions, Solana didn't seem to ever find a very unique voice. One may dare say that his work was, at best, an efficient but boring reiteration of ideas that more significant artists had already introduced. He most certainly was dedicated and prolific, producing a vast amount of works and engaging as collaborator in many of the projects of his mentors. Poets particularly welcomed him as a collaborator, and he illustrated many of their books.

When this generation grew older, and started being more in

control of the cultural policy and decisions of their country, they all continued supporting Solana's practice, which led to him becoming one of these ubiquitous figures, and frequently commissioned by the government and exhibited in museums.

Yet the enthusiasm for Solana's works was not the same internationally. There was a certain presence of his work in France, where he had lived for so long, but otherwise, and particularly the contemporary art scene, did not consider him a predecessor or an influence as they did with other artists of his generation.

As he grew older and reached the age when I met him, the recognitions toward his work appeared to be mostly from governmental organizations, official acknowledgments that included exhibitions in embassies and awards given by regional governments, libraries named for him and even a number of realistic, soviet-style busts of him in his native town, in the hallways of a run-down school and other god-forsaken places; but even this somber kind of attention contrasted with the almost absolute silence from the art scene. Most definitely, the fact that Solana became the typical artist who would often receive recognitions by the government didn't do anything else but diminish his image even further amidst the emerging artistic intelligentsia.

I have no idea if Solana was aware of this, and if he was, what he would have made of it. Certainly many older artists who are not recognized by the young ones take it as a fact of life, arguing for instance that younger generations don't appreciate the past. But in any case, it must have been a difficult reality to confront. The passing of the slightly older generation of artists and writers that once had supported him accelerated the contrast between that official recognition that he enjoyed and the larger indifference that the younger artists, and the international art world, showed toward him. I think there was a time, toward the end of his life, that people were so used to creating tributes and naming places after him, that the reasons for doing so were not debated anymore, or even thought about.

Perhaps all these things are something both you and I may have to consider at some point in our lives (one never knows). Our native city may come to us wanting to propose a monument in our name.

I, for one, if I am still lucid, will ensure to prevent that from happening to myself, and if it happens, will be the first one to deface it.

Yours truly,

Pablo

59

July 22, 2014

Luis Enrique Perez-Oramas
New York, NY

Dear Luis,

Perhaps one of the most persistent clichés of art making is the notion that an artist is "misunderstood." We say of that of important artists whose work we praise today but who were generally rejected during their own time, or even those who were celebrated albeit for the wrong reasons. To praise an artist by saying he or she was misunderstood gives us a certain satisfaction, as if we collectively were able to rectify the unfair treatment this artist once received and vindicate the work for art history.

Yet there are various problems with this seemingly simple title, "misunderstood." For one, it assumes that the artist is very clear to himself or herself about what they are trying to achieve. For if the artist doesn't understand himself or herself well, how could any misunderstanding happen? As I think about my own practice, I often don't know why I am doing what I am doing, or if the reasons I think I have for doing it are nothing but a rationalized cover for a deeper, more unconscious reason. Do you ever experience the same uncertainty? Does operating from intuition count as understanding? And finally, how are we—and by we I mean, the collective art historians—looking at the artist from the past to say that we have "understood" that artist?

Some of these questions surround the story of Ursula Reifig. Reifig was a modern art historian based in Bern. She was precisely interested in researching artists who may have been overlooked by art history—those who were part of important artistic moments but either were overshadowed by much more powerful figures, to the point of becoming a mere footnote in the larger art history of the period.

Reifig took particular interest in a practically unknown artist who lived in Paris at the turn of the century—let's call him Leonard Pirouette. Pirouette had been overlooked by art historians of the period because few works of his had survived and those that had revealed a highly uneven artist—working on a wide variety of second-hand versions of styles that ranged from post-impressionism to cubism and futurism. Pirouette did not date his works, which made them hard to situate in the timeline of art history, but it was generally thought that he was one of the artists that usually came a bit too late to each artistic breakthrough.

Yet Reifig shocked the scholarly community when she published an article that quoted a manifesto of Pirouette's that she supposedly found in the papers of Pirouette's widow, dated 1901. In this document, Pirouette eloquently stated the intentions behind his art works. The document not only became an incredible validation of many of the aesthetic decisions behind Pirouette's work, which made everyone look at his works anew, but it established Pirouette himself as some kind of forefather of a number of key ideas of modernism, and technically the person from which Cézanne must have drawn direct inspiration to further his ideas for his 1907 exhibition in the *Salon de Autonne* that led to Picasso's and Braque's creation of Cubism.

Reifig's paper was later followed by a book that substantiated more of her thesis and produced other documents related to Pirouette. Increasingly, Pirouette started emerging as one of the giants of modernism, and possibly the true inspiration to most of the avant-garde. The implications of his sudden appearance into art history were profound.

But then, as more and more art historians became fascinated and even obsessed with Reifig's discovery and Pirouette's himself, all had a hard time finding or getting access to the documents she cited in her research. Reifig claimed that she now was the sole owner of Pirouette's widow's papers (who had since passed away) and she always demurred when a colleague wanted to have direct access to them.

The increased interest in Pirouette, in the meantime, incremented the prices of his paintings, many of which were put to auction by minor collectors who had them and wanted to capitalize on their recent renown; many of the works went to major museums and private collections. It was one of those major museums that decided to conduct lab testing of one of Pirouette's cubist paintings, which Reifig had situated at around 1909—in direct competition with Picasso for the first cubist painting. But the analysis showed that Pirouette's painting dated from 1920, as it contained art materials that without a doubt had not existed before then. The same happened with a proto-futurist work that, according to a letter from Pirouette to his mother that Reifig had published at another paper, was dated from 1909 (the year of Marinetti's Futurist Manifesto). The museum's conservation lab study concluded that the piece was made sometime between 1925 and 1927 for similar reasons connected to materials. One by one, the claims made by Reifig were debunked. Finally, the dean of her university demanded to see the supposed original papers of Pirouette's widow's archive, with the objective of publishing the facsimile version of these and thus dispel any doubts of Reifig's research (and clear the doubts surrounding the level of scholarship of his faculty). As the dean walked one morning into Reifig's office, she was standing in the middle of the office, paler than ever, with no papers on her desk. She somberly, and slowly, explained to the dean that she had falsified the existence of Pirouette's archives, first through footnotes and finally through the creation of entire documents, to the point that the lie had been overstretched for so long that it was impossible to contain.

That was the end of the brief notoriety of Ursula Reifig and her unsuspecting victim, Leonard Pirouette, who eventually descended again into historical obscurity. Perhaps the only greater indignity than being forgotten is to be recalled from oblivion only to make it clear and evident to all that you had never been worth remembering in the first place. Perhaps the only good thing for Pirouette was that this brief disgrace was posthumous, and that he did not live to see himself as the victim of the intentions of an overly eager and delusional art historian.

Yours,

Pablo

60

July 25, 2014

Jim Osman
Brooklyn, NY

Dear Jim,

I have often wondered what it must have been like to live in Central Cascadia.

Central Cascadia (a territory situated somewhere in the east) was never a democratic society per se. It had a great culture and wealth, but its leaders weren't exactly elected; it was, in fact, a caliphate.

At some point, the caliph, Omar Farif, became versed in contemporary art, and it soon became an obsession for him. He started purchasing hundreds of works—aided by his seemingly endless wealth—and created museums throughout his city.

He soon noticed that the public didn't like the works. He constantly heard the usual critiques from visitors who first encounter contemporary art: "my four year old could have done this," or "this is not art," et cetera.

He had each one of those visitors executed.

Each year, there would be a review of the degree of knowledge that each citizen possessed about contemporary art. Those who failed the exam would be "purged."

In the end, Omar Farif's caliphate was reduced to a few people, but all of them were deeply knowledgeable and informed about contemporary art. Aside from the means through which it had been achieved, it finally was an art scene freed from ignorance.

Yours,
Pablo

61

July 28, 2014

Julián Zugazagoitia
Kansas City, MO

Dear Julián,

Today, as in many other days, I think about my father. I think about him partially because I am now a father myself and am close to reaching the age that he was when I was born. I also think about his hopes and expectations for me and whether I am fulfilling them in the same way he hoped to fulfill his own father's expectations. I know I shouldn't be living my life according to my interpretation of someone else's ideas of what it should be, and especially when that person is not here anymore to bear witness (my father passed away a decade ago). But I still feel compelled to carry out that expectation, as some kind of mission that I have been assigned.

A similar question arises regarding whether or not we are fulfilling someone else's expectations when we make art. According to Thierry de Duve, who explains modern art as a paradigm shift in the dialogue with tradition, artists who can't speak to their long dead predecessors replace them with the knowledgeable public. So Modernism becomes an ongoing, frustrating attempt to maintain dialogue with someone who isn't there anymore, and instead replace it with a—perhaps also frustrating, in another way—surrogate, collective interlocutor, often faceless and anonymous.

There is at least one artist I know of who attempted to break this communication scheme. Let's call her Ivana Korshnoi.

Ivana was a painter obsessed with art history. She was the kind of artist who would travel to another country (whenever she could afford it) only to see one painting or exhibition. She made a living as a night guard in an encyclopedic museum—imagine something like the Hermitage. The graveyard shift suited her well, since she was not a people person and this allowed her to study a painting for months at a time. As primarily a landscape painter, she had a particular affinity to the work of Jean-Baptiste Camille Corot, which she obsessively studied and knew practically every detail about. She sometimes felt she shared a supernatural connection with Corot. She memorized his every painting and brush stroke. She read every piece of writing and biographical information by him or about him; she felt she was in direct dialogue with him.

At some point, Ivana became interested in the ideas of theosophy and spiritualism in the writings of Helena Blavatsky. She believed that each painting had a spiritual force contained in it.

One day she attended a lecture by a Hungarian spiritist, Georg Sulyok, which deeply affected her. Sulyok argued that artworks were uniquely positioned to be passages to the spirit world because so much of the energy of the individual had been invested in making them. She approached Sulyok and asked him to teach her his techniques so she could try them out. Sulyok agreed to work with her and they decided that they would try to summon Corot's spirit at the galleries of the museum.

As a portal to the connection with the artist they picked a painting titled *Bridge at Mantes*, a painting that Ivana had copied numerous times. They decided to conduct the séance on a Christmas Eve, when the very few guards in the museum were celebrating, distracted and drinking at another wing of the museum. Ivana and Sulyok entered the building with her painting tools. Sulyok believed that as Ivana commenced painting of the landscape, he would try to sense vibrations from the portal and thus they would ask the spirit of Corot to direct Ivana's hand onto the canvas. They brought a record player to play Gabriel Fauré's *Après un Rêve,* a song composed around the same time of the painting.

It is believed that they started the experiment toward 11pm on Christmas Eve, when Sulyok started reciting a variety of spiritist phrases that were meant to open communication with the deceased artist's spirit. Several hours later, nothing yet had happened, but closer to 2am Ivana felt a twich in her arm.

What happened later is matter of conjecture. The celebrating guards heard a noise in the Corot gallery and ran to the rescue. They bumped into Sulyok who was running down a hallway, with a terrified look in his face. He was not to be seen ever again. As they arrived at the Corot gallery they found Ivana on the floor, lifeless, still holding the brush, eyes open, with an enigmatic smile on her face. At the center of the gallery, in front of Corot's painting, was Ivana's easel with the paint set up, and a perfectly made painting, a remarkably authentic Corot landscape that served as a perfect complement to the original *Bridge at Mantes.*

Lab tests later determined that this painting had been made sometime in the 1870s, right around the time of *Bridge at Mantes.* Yet no one could explain the provenance of this work, nor how it could have made its mysterious appearance at the museum's gallery.

Yours,

Pablo

62

August 1, 2014

Liz Munsell
Boston, MA

Dear Liz,

Writing letters like this one has unexpectedly given me a chance to get a better grasp of the present. It also has allowed me to record fleeting thoughts that I usually don't pay too much attention to, but when I excavate their meaning further in writing I always encounter something larger, usually an unresolved concern.

Right now I am obsessed with a neighbor of mine, in Brooklyn. Her name is Susannah Mushatt Jones. She is, as of today, 115 years and 57 days old. She is the oldest resident of New York, the fourth oldest person in the world and only one of five remaining people in the world who were born in the XIXth century. These days I am checking on her livelihood every day, with certain trepidation, hoping she is still with us. A year ago, there were 10 people alive in the world who had been born two centuries ago, and now there are five. So for whatever it is worth, that human connection to the past is quickly drawing to a close.

I am the first to acknowledge that this is a mere symbolic fact, and perhaps it may be meaningless. You could say that all art is nothing but symbolic facts that become meaningful because we give them that meaning. So I can tell you that the fact that Ms. Jones still wakes up every day in Brooklyn like me, the fact that this morning we experienced the same weather and maybe listened to the same news, is not meaningless to me. Now the question is, why would having a XIXth century human alive be important?

I attribute this to two things. One is my simple personal obsession with the past, which I have never been able to explain completely, but which was present in me since I was four years old. The second is the experience of being an immigrant; someone who left his city and his country and, as it usually happens with immigrants, lost quite a number of things in the process: the continuity of relationships, the trauma of learning about places and people who disappear or change without us being present to see that disappearance or transformation. The anxiety of knowing that the place you left is now another can be very disorienting and produce anxiety. So for me, who is already so attached to the past, the passing of individuals who represent the human bridge to that past becomes important.

And yet it is not like I am doing much to resolve this anxiety. It is not like I work in a history museum; in fact I work in a contemporary art museum. And I tend to produce art that is extremely fragile to time; usually performances and experiences that can't be retained forever. But perhaps it is precisely these contradictions that confirm, in a wider way, a pattern that at the time neither I nor others could appreciate.

Because of these things, I often wonder if we all play a role in the way in which Madigan Proliux did.

Madigan Proliux was, one could say, an unusual artist. Some people claim he really was an inventor, as he constantly made machines and automata. For the year when he lived, which was in the 1840s, certainly no one would have ever called him an artist, but that his how he described himself. He was obsessed with the future and claimed that what he made was not meant to be understood by his contemporaries, who he despised. He was all for change, but the things that he made were meant to last forever. He was a professor of mathematics at la Sorbonne, which allowed him to work on his machines on his own time. He did not allow anyone (or at least as far as we know) to ever see these machines. Once he finished them, he would encase them in large boxes or chests, very well protected, similar to a sarcophagus. He was convinced that he would be redeemed by the future generations, who would recognize how unappreciated he had been in his time.

The chests were discovered sometime in the 1980s in an attic of a house near Brussels, where he spent his last years. The discovery caused a certain sensation; it is not often that one receives a message from the past. Inside the containers there were letters from Proliux fraternally speaking to the reader, as if to a lost friend, as if finally encountering the interlocutor he searched for his entire life.

But the language from the 1840s was hard to relate to. His assumptions of the future were completely wrong. Yet these assumptions betrayed a certain perception of the future that was in fact very representative of his time. Several historians became interested in these objects and letters and started analyzing the motivations and influences behind them, later theorizing and sharing their findings with the history community. So, in an ironic turn of fate, Madigan Proliux became not a contemporary of the generations of the future but a representative voice of a time that he was profoundly at odds with.

Truly yours,

Pablo

63

August 5, 2014

Elizabeth Hurst
Brooklyn NY

Dear Lizzie,

I think all artists can admit—even if some do so reluctantly—that they have artistically stagnant periods in their lives. Those are periods we understandably prefer to forget. Yet, I believe those times are also the most important periods of our careers, as they clearly expose our weaknesses and strengths and can reveal a lot about what may come next—or explain, in retrospect, why nothing came next. I witnessed this in particular through two artists friends of mine, who I will call Anatolia and Ivan.

Both Anatolia and Ivan were from the same town. They met when Ivan was a teenager—Anatolia was some four years older, which made her the more experienced of the two. They never had a romantic relationship, but just a close friendship. Anatolia was nostalgic for her town and would seek Ivan constantly, to the point that Ivan thought she was infatuated with him. Rather, she had a thirst for her past, which Ivan, in his more naïve and uncorrupted personality, somewhat represented to her. He was both excited and scared by Anatolia, who constantly would take him out to see exhibitions, films, and attend lectures. Both were drastically different in that sense: Ivan was a homebody and Anatolia was insatiably outgoing, inexhaustible in her desire to experience new things. Their character was related to their studio work: Ivan felt most happy and safe in his studio, closed into himself, working there all the time. Anatolia always struggled being inside, working while she listened to the radio. She would listen to all sorts of programs and constantly write on her studio table names of people, titles, dates, topics and any other idea that would catch her attention that day.

At some point, Anatolia moved her studio next door to Ivan. Ivan was again not sure what to think of this decision, but he didn't want to make a big deal out of it. But this meant that Anatolia would walk into Ivan's studio all the time to talk and tell him about the news of the day, the exhibitions she had seen, and the lectures she had attended. Ivan was at first slightly bothered, but then he came to like that Anatolia was some kind of filter of reality for him. He stopped pretty much reading, watching TV or going out; his interactions with Anatolia were enough. Somehow receiving second hand information about every subject allowed him to think of how to incorporate it into his works. These started to have a great degree of originality, depicting things that seemed familiar and at the same time removed.

Things started to get complicated when Ivan increasingly got attention for his works. He started receiving exhibition opportunities and accolades for his projects. Anatolia in contrast, with an empty studio and always working on the same, ever unresolved project, started resenting the attention directed to Ivan, mainly because he appeared to make art about the topics of his conversations with Anatolia, and she told him so. Ivan was surprised: because he only knew about the world from what Anatolia would tell him, he had no way of knowing where Anatolia ended and where "the world" started. He attributed her comment to jealousy. That was the beginning of the cooling of their relationship. After one or two arguments somewhat connected to this topic, Anatolia stopped coming altogether to Ivan's studio and eventually moved to another city.

Both continued making their work, or rather, struggling to make their work without ever finding a good resolution. Neither was successful again. Ivan always looked for an interlocutor like Anatolia; without her he thought he would simply disappear from art history. Anatolia felt similarly, but she also secretly delighted in the fact that, thanks to her absence in Ivan's life, she had effectively brought both of their careers to the same point of stillness. One day, she once thought, they would be equals again and regain their everyday conversations.

Yours,

Pablo

64

August 10, 2014

Harper Montgomery
New York, NY

Dear Harper,

Once, at a dinner party at the house of a collector in Mexico City, I was talking to someone from the business world. At some point when I was talking about how unpredictable the life of an artist can be in financial terms he said—"it seems to me that you artists just love to complain. The art world is full of free dinners and drinks. You don't have to worry about feeding yourself."

That comment is one of many I have heard throughout my life that has made me reflect on the extent of the divide between the rich class and the "creative class," for lack of a better term, that coexist, somewhat uncomfortably, in the art world. While there is usually a great deal of admiration between an artist and a collector, for instance, there are other feelings at play: certain insecure feelings from the wealthy man who wishes knew more about art or had talent to make it, and from the artist who may be uncertain how to behave and interact in upper levels of society. There is from both sides a certain envy of being the other.

There was once, however, an exception.

Walter Kousevitsky appeared in the New York art scene one day, all of a sudden. He was a wealthy Russian businessman who had made his money from a lucrative import and export business. Before anyone could remember, he had already become a household name in the New York art scene, joining various boards and supporting various non-profit arts organizations. He became a coveted guest. He particularly liked hosting parties at his penthouse on the Upper West Side—a spectacular space with a stunning collection of modern and contemporary art. Curators, museum directors, dealers and other collectors would walk around his collection during his cocktail parties, awed by what they saw. He was also unusual in his deep knowledge of art and art history—much more than what a collector would usually know.

There were only two things about his collection that seemed strange: one was that it mainly consisted of obscure or never seen before works by famous artists. The other strange fact was that Kousevitsky would never discuss where he would obtain the works. Dealers wanted to sell him work, but no one in New York could say that they had actually sold art to him. Because of this, the rumor started circulating that Kousevitsky was purchasing forged art works. But why would he do that? He certainly had the money to purchase works at the actual price, and his connoisseurship was so impressive that to think he could be fooled in buying something inauthentic seemed incongruous. Suspicions grew when an artist whose works were in Kousevitsky's collection said she had never made those works herself. In that instance, Kousevitsky was apologetic and reacted with great puzzlement, saying that he must have been duped by a dealer in Vienna who he never identified. But just around that time, the truth was discovered by a local framer with ties to the gallery scene. He was contacted by a man who said he had a very large print that needed to be framed, and asked the framer to come pick it up at a studio in Greenpoint. When the framer showed up for the pickup, he recognized Kousevitsky from a photo he had seen of him in an art magazine. He was wearing jeans and a t-shirt stained with ink.

The print felt like it had just been made.

The framer mentioned this to an art blogger he knew, who in turn became interested in the story and decided to dig deeper.

Kousevitsky, he found out, was not only a truly wealthy man, but also a very talented craftsman who had never been able to be recognized as an artist. He was a remarkable imitator, and had decided at some point to use his talent and wealth not to buy art works from others but to construct his own contemporary art collection. Initially a private fantasy, he soon realized that his forgeries were undetectable, and he relished the idea that he could show off a collection of works that were actually his in more ways than a collector can claim ownership of an art work.

When he finally had to confront his deception to others, he didn't apologize to anyone. "I never lied to anyone," he said to a reporter. "I always spoke truthfully when I described the works as belonging to me. The hypocrisy is in other collectors, who believe that the works in their collection truly belong to them."

Yours,

Pablo

65

August 18, 2014

J. Morgan Puett
Beach Lake, PA

Dear Morgan,

Tonight I am particularly tired, and somewhat emotionally drained by a lot of negativity I have experienced personally around me. When I am physically exhausted and exposed to a great deal of negative experiences or unfair treatment, these experiences tend to become amplified in my mind. I become a zero-tolerance individual, and as I age, this state, I am sad to say, feels even more hardened.

Among young artists, it appears the only ones who manage to survive are those who are capable to survive and adapt to a changing or inhospitable environment. I believe I was gifted with a particular strength from my father, both physical and mental, that allowed me to sustain physical and mental abuse with certain stoicism and self-determination. I don't consider myself particularly unique in that regard, but I know that this strength has given me the possibility to make art for 25 years professionally and at the same time find a way to sustain that practice in one way or another, always having to adapt to whatever climate I am presented with.

I would like to say a word about compromise.

No one can ever find or own the formula for the perfect conditions under which one can create the best art works. In fact, it is through that constant act of compromise where the best artists thrive; whenever you tell an artist they should not do this or that, he or she always finds the way to go around the problem and find a creative solution to it. But there is a fine line between allowing certain concessions in making a work and making a compromised work. And it is something that unfortunately is exploited by artists and curators alike.

It is something I observed in the life of Anastasio Torres.

The first time I saw Anastasio's work I was very impressed. He was a young artist then, exhibiting for the first time at an international biennial, which happened to take place in his hometown.

Anastasio stood out in the exhibition. He was of a humble background, and had become an artist with great efforts. Because of his limited financial resources he worked with recycled or cheap materials, in public spaces, using great imagination and creativity. I met him at the time, and remember a shy, soft-spoken fellow.

He received a prize at that biennial and was hailed at the time as the great new discovery of a promising career. Soon I started noticing images of his works in major art magazines.

I saw him again a couple years later, this time in Amsterdam, by chance. He was wearing a leather jacket and expensive shoes. It struck me, as I remember thinking that his finances had obviously changed and, most importantly, he wanted people to know about it. His comments and demeanor in general were very different; he still was very self-conscious, but now with the awareness that he needed to play the part of a successful artist. He had been taken under the wing of a powerful curator who had sensed this ultimate vulnerability in Anastasio. He was exhibiting the same piece I had seen him show at that biennial, but it seemed oddly adapted to a gallery space. The work didn't seem to fit a gallery; it lost completely the freshness of what I had seen it have in the public space. When I inquired about his decision of exhibiting this work in that way, he hinted to the fact that it had been the curator's idea.

As years went by, I continued seeing his work in various places, particularly galleries, art fairs, and museums. This curator had helped him a lot, and—perhaps this is perverse of me—I kept thinking of what Anastasio said in Amsterdam, and in looking at the works I could sense this curator coaching him to exhibit or make the work in this or that way.

Anastasio relaxed his style; now he was seemingly more comfortable with the globe-trotter aspect of being an international art star. The work is very efficient, and it always seems to contain a very concise conceptual explanation that makes it palatable to even a beginning student of contemporary art. I can't help, however, to return in my mind to that original work, made out of cardboard and on the street, that work that had been the product of some of the most difficult limitations imposed upon an artist. Somehow I knew that Anastasio despised that piece and that he would never go back to work in that way again.

Yours truly,

Pablo

66

August 25, 2014

Matthew Deleget and Rosanna Martinez
Brooklyn, NY

Dear Matthew and Rosanna,

This morning I was thinking of Gelsomina, the character from Fellini's *La Strada*. She is an innocent and lively young woman who is forced to go on the road with Zampanò, an evil strongman. Despite the fact that Zampanò only mistreats Gelsomina, she falls in love with him. He responds only with cruelty and abuse, and ultimately abandons her on the road. Then, years later, when he discovers that she has died, Zampanò breaks down in tears.

I often feel that I am that abusive strongman, and that my present life is Gelsomina. She comes in to engage me and, because I am involved in other matters that I consider more pressing, I brush her aside. Everyday I am ever more irritated by the interference of the present, while I also know—I know this part of myself well—that I will regret having given priority to the future instead of focusing on the now. One day I will lament the fact that my daughter is no longer a child, that I will no longer have what some people call "the old age of youth", and that many people that I care about may not be around anymore. Perhaps the fact that we as humans spend so much time preparing for the future is our ultimate paradox. And, as artists (I am sure you suspected that I would eventually bring art into the conversation) we encounter the ultimate paradox of making something that is a definitive affirmation of the present but which only makes sense to be made if it has a bearing on the future, even if it is a performance.

An artist who I will call Elie Ambrose tried to address this problem through a life-long project. She was known for doing small performative gestures, many of which were smart and entertaining. She, however, didn't consider these as her best work, and sometimes even felt irritated that people would pay attention to these small works of hers. She thus decided to make a major, monumental work that would take years to be made. She calculated a mid-point in her life—something like 43 years of age—to culminate the big event, which would be the most significant art work of her life. She spent around 15 years preparing for it. Her plan was not only to create the anticipation and excitement toward the event but, when it happened, ensure that it would be exhaustively documented and chronicled. She had read, in her youth, a story by Adolfo Bioy Casares, "The Invention of Morel", a novella about a millionaire who is obsessed with posterity and throws a party at an island that is exhaustively filmed to be reproduced, in 3-D format, at the exact places where the encounters had taken place.

When the event took place, it had the feeling of a wedding or a family reunion—an emotional ritual. There was music, food, speeches. Many photographers and videographers were hired.

But the anticipation had been such that it was hard to be entirely happy with the result. She had perhaps created too much expectation.

Years later, as her career seemed clearer in perspective, young artists and scholars were approaching her about the early works she had made, telling her about how influential they were. Curators sought her to get documentation of those spontaneous gestures. Museums were eager to collect anything related to that glorious period of hers, when, without being aware, she had made history.

Yours,

Pablo

67

August 29, 2014

Nato Thomson
Philadelphia PA

Dear Nato,

I have been attending a seminar on philosophical issues around art. While some things that are said are interesting, I am always left with the feeling that everyone is talking about the idea of art, and not art itself. In other words, one can become enamored with definitions and descriptions that have little to do with how art itself manifests and is experienced in the world. Perhaps this is an impression that I have because I am an artist and have to face the act of making on a daily basis.

Maybe there is an alternative reality where all philosophical concepts do apply to art. And that alternative reality may be the past, or the future. This was at least what the Baron Etienne Rotschild may have accidentally accomplished in his life's work.

Baron Rotschild studied philosophy at the University of Jena in the 1850s. He was influenced by Hegel's idealism. He was primarily interested in aesthetics, and spent a number of years working on an aesthetic theory of representation. He argued that art was essentially unknowable; that all that art produces is a lie. Art, Rotschild argued, can lie in as many ways as there are viewers, which was his way of solving the problem of interpretation.

This theory was dismissed by other philosophers, who asked: isn't there an indirect truth to be learned from a lie produced by art? According to this the true meaning of art could be unknown, but not unknowable.

But Rotschild dug in his heels amidst this criticism, to prove that there was no truth in art. He conceded there were facts about a work—measurements, medium, materials with which an art work was made—but that didn't amount to a truth.

He replied to these criticisms with a second, even more radical book. He argued in it that art was some kind of mirage of communication, something which resembles human connection when it only reinforces our solitude. This theory perplexed his critics even more; art, if anything, was considered by everyone as a vehicle of communication. His piece was torn apart by other philosophers.

But the Baron de Rotschild was not someone who would be intimidated by criticisms. If anything, this gave him motivation to write a third book, wherein he delved further into controversy with his theories. In it, he argued that art was not a lie and a source of solitude in mankind, but that the notion of art in itself was an impossibility: only life existed.

At this point his critics didn't even bother responding to his ideas. The Baron became a hermit—he retired from social life, and didn't publish any of his writings again.

He was only quoted to say once, as a curse: "I predict that, in the future, artists will desperately try to fuse art into life, and will fail miserably."

Yours,

Pablo

68

September 2, 2014

Paco Cao
Bronx, NY

Dear Paco,

Today I was at an intimidating seminar with a group of remarkable artists, theorists, curators and art historians, focusing on the subject of recreation and representation of art..These gatherings tend to be very charged—one really has to fight to insert a comment and rehearse what one is going to say, as I recall feeling when I was taking classes with James Elkins in Chicago in the early 90s and we were trying to make our way through *Les Mots et Les Choses.*

In the end, I am not sure how much we learned from the encounter. I was left with the feeling that everyone spoke without paying much attention to what the other was saying, and that the theorists spoke at a degree of abstraction that had little bearing to the practice. I believe the gap between theory and practice is often felt in art. The theoretician can construct a compelling argument, but his problems start when this compelling argument starts being tested against actual art works. And when the thesis precedes the practice, that is, when an artist tries to make work in accordance with a particular idea, the art work is the one that usually suffers; it feels contrived.

Let's think about a certain scenario.

Romario Beardsley had his moment in the art world. He came from a country—let's call it Romaria—where there were few competitors at the time, when the profession of criticism was still in development and where a sudden surge in great artists demanded someone to step into the role of critic, theoretician, and chronicler. So Beardsley stepped into the role. He was good at it; he was well read and had a certain ability to write. He also was soft-spoken and generally agreeable.

As the interest in Romaria grew, the big art magazines started desperately looking for someone who could write about the art from that country. Beardsley immediately appeared in the picture.

His first essay, "Romaria and the Comic" was a text making the connection between the comic book and graphic novel tradition as a major influence of Romarian artists. The essay was published as a feature article in a major magazine, and later Beardsley turned it into a book.

Another essay was entitled "Romarian Artists and the Skyscraper," wherein he uncovered unusual relationships between architecture (particularly the skyscraper) and male artists, problematizing macho attitudes in that country. The essay was used a lot by various curators and others interested in Romaria. Beardsley had a knack for finding interesting trivia about a subject and relating it to the artist. For example, he would relate an artist who made a work where the image of a lion appeared to the fountain of the lions in Alhambra, and then use that reference to tie this artist's work with Moorish architecture and culture.

But by the time his third book came out, entitled "The Romarian Doll: Artists and Toys," wherein he argued that Romarian art had a particular fascination with children's play, another Romarian critic had emerged—let's call him Stockman. Very carefully and methodically, Stockman started showing that in all his books, Beardsley had made completely arbitrary relationships between topics that he liked and local artists. Instead of observing local art and trying to draw conclusions from what he saw, he would embark from a topic that he was interested in (in this case comics, macho attitudes and toys) and then try to find artists that fit those interests. In fact, Stockman argued, there were many more important artists whose works had nothing to do with those subjects in Romaria—the vast majority in fact—who had been completely ignored by Beardsley.

Beardsley dismissed these criticisms at first, attributing them to professional jealousy. But as the field started to become professionalized, more and more critics and historians started questioning Beardsley. In the end, he became so profoundly discredited in the field, and became the object of such ridicule, that he practically went into hiding. He left Romaria.

But there was a certain silver lining to all this. Some of the artists that Beardsley had championed, who perhaps were not into the topics he associated them with, had agreed to play along and make art works about dolls, buildings, and comics. A couple of them ended up getting a good gallery and a number of exhibitions, and by the time the Beadsley fiasco was uncovered, they already had received enough professional opportunities (and taken advantage of them) to sustain a relatively stable career. And, as for Beardsley himself, he became the Romarian expert in the history department of an Ivy league university, where, as you may imagine, no one knew anything about Romaria. His last books dealt with the history of fishing in Romaria (which, as it so happens, is a landlocked country).

Yours,

Pablo

69

September 10, 2014

Adrianne Wortzel
New York, NY

Dear Adrianne,

There are very worrisome things happening in the world right now—the Russian invasion of Crimea, the increasing authoritarianism of Venezuela—that are bringing a number of very important questions to the fore regarding what we understand as the project of the left. In such an important moment, the art world seems to largely sidestep the problem, coming up with vague comments in support for liberalism or progressivism, but at the same time proceeding with its parade of biennials (including the next Manifesta in Russia, which I know you find problematic) and other art exhibitions as in business as usual. It doesn't take an expert to notice that there is a real disconnect between the institutions of the art world and what is happening in the world at large. Museums are more interested in competing with each other or in getting the better collections than in making a statement or engaging in global issues.

Is this the result the professionalism in art that has resulted in the 25 or so years after the fall of the Berlin Wall? Have we become apologists for a form of life that aspires to have the glamour of the fashion world and the celebrity status of Hollywood but with a foot on semiotext(e)?

This is, I think, the big question for our generation. The answer will define our relationship to this universe that at least I personally can't identify with anymore.

It does seem like an intractable problem to make art matter in this web of social and political issues, and at the core is the more important question: do we want to save the world using art or do we want to use the world's troubles to save art?

You may remember this famous quote by Camus when he received the Nobel prize: "Each generation doubtless feels called upon to reform the world. Mine knows that it will not reform it, but its task is perhaps even greater. It consists in preventing the world from destroying itself."

Today I ask myself, and would like to ask to you, without any irony: what do you think is the true mission of our generation?

Consider the following scenario:

There was a time of great war and destruction when a generation of writers and artists emerged. Most of them fought in those wars; most of them lived short lives. Many of them made deeply important art works that documented that experience, that admonished future generations and attempted to point in new directions to prevent the madness that they had lived through from ever happening again.

The second generation that followed these artists kept those issues in mind, but had largely inherited a world of relative peace and prosperity—as a result of what the previous generation had accomplished—that allowed them to focus on issues of aesthetics in their work. This rich reflection on aesthetics is what they left as their legacy.

When the third generation came along, they were very versed in the history of turmoil from the first generation, which now read like ancient mythology, and were highly trained on issues of aesthetics. Suddenly, the world was in chaos again. Tyranny, death and destruction devastated every country, and war emerged everywhere.

This generation was inspired by their grandparents' generation, and knew they could not repeat what their parents' generation had done before.

So they went to work and proceeded to analyze and theorize about the wars that were going on, producing beautiful and eloquent texts and art works that reflected on that reality, knowing that whoever came to see the resulting ruins of that monstrous turmoil, would at least find masterpieces that rose to the occasion.

Yours,
Pablo

70

September 14, 2014

Alanna Corbett
Brooklyn, NY

Dear Alanna,

The act of writing a letter has forced me to slow down somewhat. It makes the act of communicating with another a real commitment and a real investment, not a seemingly effortless stroke of a few keys on a computer or phone that gets sent immediately. Forms of communication become markers of the passage of time, and when communication is slow, it seems to me, not only does it force us to deepen our awareness of that passage of time but it also makes us value every step of the exchange even more.

My ultimate concern, as you may imagine, is not how to figure out how to create a slow correspondence, but to generate the conditions under which an art work, in this day and age of immediate gratification, can still pull away a bit, not giving itself immediately, gradually giving. I am not sure if this gradual process of unveiling is in and of itself meaningful—probably not—but I am certain that when things get thrown at us one after the other we simply can't take them all in, and even when they all may be exceptional, when put together in a massive collection we start losing our capacity to appreciate them.

There was a Dutch artist—let's call her Amelia Spoor—who experienced a somewhat paradoxical turn in her career because of what I describe.

At some point in Amsterdam there was a rumor about this artist who had spent twenty years making a single painting. The painting in question was shrouded in mystery and few people could claim to have seen it. When it was finally unveiled, after years of rumors, people were in awe. The artist wouldn't talk about it, but it was also a work that arguably documented a series of tragic events in her life, which included having survived an abusive childhood and a terminal illness from which she had miraculously recovered. The painting was hailed as a symbol of courage and determination.

Soon after, though, when she had reached great notoriety, other paintings of hers started emerging in the market, very similar to the one that she had been arguably working on for 20 years. They were first two, then four, then ten and then nearly fifty. At first the market took them enthusiastically, but later when it became clear that there were so many works similar to each other, the original piece started declining in value along with the interest around it. Finally one day, Spoor declared in an interview that she had never had an abusive childhood or a chronic illness—these were unsubstantiated rumors that had been developed, who knows how, and she had allowed them to continue to "make my story more interesting." She also claimed in that interview that while she had been working on that painting indeed for 20 years, she also did the same with hundreds of other paintings, some of which she would paint in matter of a few hours and leave around, only to make a few minor changes a few years later, here and there.

This is how one work that at some point, at face value, was considered a masterpiece, soon after was considered just one more painting by one more artist in search of acceptance.

Yours,

Pablo

71

September 16, 2014

Allan McCollum
New York, NY

Dear Allan,

Yesterday I was talking to an art student who was quizzing me on the meaning of what I do and how I can transmit that meaning to others. It is a recurring subject amongst young artists, who often overthink the premises behind art works and have a hard time getting over what I would describe as the cause-effect nature of art: I believe all of us, when we start studying art, somehow retain the idea that everything an artist does has a particular intention and purpose, and that a successful art work is the one that accomplishes that original intention or purpose. Of course over the years one learns that it is impossible to work in such a programmatic way as an artist, let alone control what a myriad of viewers may think of your work. Ultimately I believe we all, as artists, operate at varying degrees of intuition and experience, making works that we expect will generate a particular range of responses but never quite knowing how it all will unfold in the end. It may forever remain an unattainable goal, that whole idea that art is essentially a form of communication that replicates the exact feelings of the artist within a viewer.

There was once an artist who devoted his career to doing just that. Back in the late teens, Bernard Laliberté was a psychiatrist in Zurich who became directly involved with Dada artists. The passion that this awoke in Bernard caused him, in later years, to devote himself to the study of art making and perception. He believed that the response to an artwork was almost entirely the result of social conditioning, similarly to how religious beliefs are transmitted in a society. If one were to grow up in front of one kind of art, one single painting even, and be told it was the greatest and only kind of art possible, this would become this individual's frame of reference to judge any kind of art in the future. This idea is nothing extraordinary if you think about how time and place affect our aesthetic taste: Rubens' fleshy models and their beauty and desirability in their time is a case in point.

Laliberté was a good administrator and at some point in his career managed to land the directorship of an orphanage in a remote village in the Alps. As he was in charge of determining the entire regimen for this orphanage, and since there was no real supervision by a professional eye other than his, he could do as he wished with the program. This is how sometime in the summer of 1921 Laliberté decided to do an experimental curriculum where all children were taught to appreciate and make art based on a single painting he had made. Laliberté was not a remarkable artist, but it didn't matter to him; any painting would do. The painting he chose was some kind of mechanistic fantasia; a bad Giacomo Balla imitation perhaps.

No other painting nor any other art forms were ever discussed or displayed in the orphanage, and because it was such an isolated area, there were practically no other ways to learn about the existence of any other kind of art.

The orphans grew up breathing and digesting Laliberté's painting and ideas. Laliberté took special pains to make every kind of opportunity to copy that painting, and to convince them that creativity amounted to copying one painting.

Laliberté was so enthralled by the fact that he had impacted the aesthetic sensibility of his orphans so deeply that he couldn't bring himself to stop.

One day, Laliberté collapsed outside of the small orchard outside of the orphanage, breaking his neck. He died four days later at a nearby hospital.

It was a tragic event, and soon the village tried to get someone to take over the orphanage.

A few days later, another doctor who had known Laliberté in

the past came to visit to assess the situation. He encountered the most curious scene: all the youth in the orphanage dressed and spoke like Laliberté; they had his same gestures, his movements. Laliberté's painting, or original copies thereof, were hanging all over the building; hundreds, thousands of versions of the same rather forgettable composition. Everyday all the orphans main evening activity was to paint, over and over again, that same painting.

The doctor was overwhelmed with sadness, witnessing how the forsaken children of this orphanage had become the victims of Laliberté's theories of emotional conditioning of art.

He considered it critical to undo Laliberté's delusional experiment. He brought together all the youth—some of them were already in their late teens—to the common room of the orphanage. He gave them a long lecture explaining that they had never been shown the depth and richness of art. He pulled out art history books with plates showing Michelangelo sculptures, paintings by Rafael, Rembrandt and Velázquez.

The kids looked at the books with indifference. "That is not art", they concluded. Most of them walked away.

Yours,

Pablo

72

September 18, 2014

Estela Helguera-Tegeder
Brooklyn, NY

Querida hija,

This week many people are going on vacation. I envy them, as we can't go on vacation right now. Some people have religious holidays this week as well—another thing I can't be part of because I am not religious. So I am doing what I can to pretend that I also am on vacation, that I also can create, in an imaginary way, perhaps, that existential parenthesis where the everyday rules don't apply.

In the letters that I have been writing this actually has become a recurring subject—the notion that we can create spaces for ourselves where we can feel free, unconstrained. I have been reflecting on the capacity of art to create those spaces of freedom, where you are given the opportunity to not be who you usually are, where you can experience things in ways in which you don't usually experience them, and where you can reimagine relationships or discover new ones in unsuspecting places.

So if art gives us freedom by the mere ability of allowing us to think of ourselves in a different environment from where we usually are, could I use art to take myself on vacation mentally? Could I convince myself enough, through an art work, that I don't have to live my life as it is required this week? And if I were to succeed, wouldn't that experience of the imagined vacation be even better than a real one?

The answer may lie in our capacity to self-induce beliefs in ourselves, but also in the real implications of this type of escapism.

We once met a man who excelled at these tasks. You won't remember him, which is why I wanted to tell you about him in writing. Let's call him Gregory Zatar.

Zatar was a balloon salesman. I often wondered how you can survive by selling balloons—but then again, any activity must be more financially viable than the career of an average artist like me.

We met Zatar at a family restaurant, amidst a children's party to which you had been invited. Zatar was the balloon guy, making all sorts of balloon animals for the children. He was a small man of undefined age, which made him somewhat appropriate for a children's party context. He did have an uncanny ability to make complicated shapes out of those elongated balloons: dragons, piranhas, unicorns. We somehow struck up a conversation, and I was taken aback by the depth of his knowledge. As we spoke about animal shapes, he made a reference to Henri Bergson that seemed more appropriate of a philosophy professor.

Zatar had been, in fact, a philosophy professor from an Ivy League university. His classes were memorable and deeply influenced his students. He was an expert questioner, and prodded his class often into unsolvable dilemmas, almost pushing his students into desperation.

Turned out that this desperation was something he personally felt. Over the years, Zatar became disillusioned with philosophy. He increasingly found it pointless to lead a life consisting in reflecting about life instead of living it. He told me: "I came to the conclusion that there is no point in reflecting if you are not capable to act upon the things that you are reflecting on."

Furthermore, Zatar had also concluded that the activities that he engaged in should bear no relationship whatsoever to how he constructed his own mental reality. "All, that is, with the exception of living off teaching or writing philosophy". Why, I asked him. "It is very simple"—he replied. "When you try to make a living out of the activity that you are most interested in, and when it becomes your mission in life to teach it to others, that runs interference with your ultimate goal in life, which would arguably be to dedicate your mind to that activity." In Zatar's view, the reason why the best teachers of a particular discipline were not the best themselves in that discipline was because they didn't really love their discipline, but only the process of teaching it, which precluded them from loving it. His somewhat surprising conclusion is that we can be most dedicated to an activity, and even excel at it, when we are detached from it. "We humans, we are strange human beings"—said Zatar, as he was quickly twisting a purple balloon with his hands, turning it into a purple dinosaur for an excited five year old. "Our entire psychology revolves around prohibition and reward. That which we cannot have access to, becomes desirable; that which we have always access to, we despise. I have taken upon myself to create restrictions to those things that I deem most important. Twisting balloons for children's parties is not one of them, so here I am."

As I was still trying to grasp the full meaning of Zatar's words, it was time for him to pack up. With a wave of his hand he placed his balloon materials in a bag and walked out from the restaurant, mixing with the crowd from the street.

I promise we will go on vacation soon.

Yours,

Pablo

73

September 20, 2014

Laura Raicovich
New York, NY

Dear Laura,

I have always been suspicious of the artist that appears to be too self-assured and articulate about his or her work. I am very much aware that when I think I know what my work is about and believe I am able to articulate it very well to others, I have stopped making art. This is a sense I get from certain artists who have constructed air-tight discourses about their works, readings that may well have been written by a critic or art historian. You could call this "the third person syndrome". The problem, however, is not the implicit narcissism in this strategy, but the almost inevitable fact that when an artist focuses so much in constructing the reading of the work, this usually comes at the detriment of the work itself. If art is a language, why is it so important to translate it into another language?

I often think of the case of Emmett Sinopoli, with the fear of becoming him one day.

Sinopoli's work was hailed at some point as the greatest of his generation, with one particular critical and cunning work that was written about by many critics and theorists. He was always an articulate artist, but one could say that those early years when he made the work that made him renowned he spent more time making the work than discussing it. He nonetheless became a familiar figure on the lecture circuit—everyone loves to hear an articulate artist—and shortly after was offered a tenured position at a university. He continued working, but increasingly became more involved in lecturing and teaching on the ideas that made him originally famous. At some point the urge to continue to make art faded away.

Today he serves on several art organization boards and one can see him in most art conferences, discussing the work he made thirty years ago.

Yours,

Pablo

74

October 5, 2014

Luis Croquer
Seattle, WA

Dear Luis,

I've been confined in a uncomfortable economy class airline seat for the last 8 hours, unable to even rest my elbow on the arm rest. Flying has become the most efficient method to diminish our dignity as humans and make us feel kinship with caged animals.

I often ask myself why I subject myself to these experiences. I know it is important to travel, but my life is now dominated by demeaning experiences like this so that I accomplish something that is not very clear to me. I understand the sacrifices of art making—the struggles that one goes through inside the studio—but those struggles do have a bright point, namely that it is possible to welcome and even enjoy that struggle in the larger sense in which one is engaging with art.

But the experience of being a caged animal to do an exhibition in Europe?

What are the sacrifices that we are willing to do for art and what lengths are we willing to go to?

Seymor Tilsdale is a case in point.

Of all the things that people could say about Tilsdale, no one could say that he was not devoted to his work. Nor could anyone ever say that he would not be willing to sacrifice anything on behalf of his work. By most accounts, he lived in a miserable room in a dangerous neighborhood so that he could afford a studio; he took the most gruesome jobs to make enough money to make his art.

He accumulated enormous credit card debt by producing expensive and cumbersome sculptures and installations that no one would help him fund. In the end, these works would have to be discarded as they were cumbersome and Tilsdale was not an artist with a collector base. In fact to say that is an understatement: Tilsdale had never sold a single art work in his career. But he was still a determined mind.

It is this determination that had often made me wonder about how one should go about pursuing art making as an act of faith. Tilsdale believed too much in his own work, doing exactly what one is told in art school—believe in yourself—be true to yourself. But pursuing his true self and being willing to sacrifice it all in that pursuit did not serve Tilsdale well. In fact it only contributed to his undoing.

In contrast, his contemporary, Timothy Filler, did not have a sentimental relationship with his work. For all one may gather, he did not seem to care about what he did—he was, shall I say, rather indifferent about the process of making, entirely calculating in what he should say about it, and very attentive to whoever looked at or valued the work. He market-tested his projects. Tilsdale, in contrast, could have never done that—the very idea of satisfying anyone else would have repulsed him.

And I know what you are thinking: Tilsdale is the kind of artist that you and I would like. The true-to self, sincere, dedicated maker whose passion and obsession translates and becomes tangible to an informed viewer. But no. Despite our romanticism about the story of someone like Tilsdale, his work, I am very sorry to say, is not interesting at all—it presents all sorts of undesirable commonplaces, derivations, and unimaginative approaches to all too familiar topics. While Filler's work is easy to like, prompts lots of conversations, and makes curators and critics feel wonderful when they write about it. Filler, not Tilsdale, is the artist of our time.

Yours,

Pablo

75

October 10, 2014

Alissa Firth-Eagland
Guelph, ON

Dear Alissa,

You may have noticed that the world is in chaos. Unjust wars, killings of innocent people in the Middle East, children dying or being abandoned by governments and their societies. And the polarizing discussions that emerge on social media quickly devolve into a barrage of insults bordering on racism and outright dehumanization of the other. The violence and irrationality with which I feel we are confronted often makes me wonder about what the true measure is of normalcy in the world. For I consider myself an individual with a standard set of liberal values, but in the social context of where I find myself in this country and this period of time, I would be described by most as radical and even an extremist.

Which is an interesting thing to think about, because these days it is so easy to be considered a rogue thinker or an extremist in political terms, but to be so in art is no longer possible—if anything, perhaps, because the discipline itself of art has exploited the idea of radicality so much that in order to go beyond it needs to stop being art. So I often wonder, should we as artists stop pretending to be radical, or at least recognize that the two notions are not compatible anymore?

I know that I will be told that this is a conservative position; that I am simply not recognizing the radicality of the art of my time. But the changes that we see today in art seem to me to relate closer and closer to the way changes operate in the fashion system.

Because there is nothing of substance to dismantle, we only recycle previous ideas in imaginative ways.

You know that I will give you an example. And indeed I am thinking of the situation that recently arose with the work of Sebastopol Lind-Seltzer.

You wouldn't know Lind-Seltzer's work; in fact practically no one got to know him in the art world. After studying art in Amsterdam in the 1970s, Lind-Seltzer was a pioneer conceptual photographer that started making very radical gestures that influenced his peers. However, he was always unsatisfied with the insufficient "cultural lexicon", as he liked to call it, that the language of art offered. He, like many others of that generation, wanted his work to have a direct impact in the world—in his case of a political or social nature.

He thus left soon to Cuba where he vanished and lost contact with most of his acquaintances. Many thought he had died. But years later, toward the late 80s, Ingrid Sonquist, an ex-girlfriend from his years in Amsterdam by chance saw a picture of him as part of the Sendero Luminoso insurgent organization in Peru. The revelation was a shock to her: she had become a video artist of certain recognition for her political work, but the steps that Sebastopol had taken in his life seemed so much more radical than anything she could have imagined to do with her life.

While she abhorred the politics and violent approach of this organization, she nonetheless continued to be fascinated by her discovery and thought of Sebastopol often. Finally, through intermediaries she managed to establish contact with him and they initiated a correspondence. Sonquist wrote: "I know that you may think I would condemn you for having taken such a violent direction in your life. But when I saw you in that photograph, I instinctively knew that everything I had done with my art for twenty years was nothing in comparison with what you have done to engage with the ideals of social change that we had in our youth. I may disagree with your politics, but I envy the wholeness and integrity of your principles."

A long time passed by after Sonquist sent her letter. She had become convinced that it had never arrived. But one day she saw a letter on her mailbox, coming directly form Peru. It was a rather succinct response of only one line:

"I have killed men. I have burned down villages. I sleep every night with a rifle at my side. I live in fear; I survive from instigating fear into others. Please tell me—I need to believe—that what I am doing is art."

Yours,

Pablo

SOME RESPONSES

I.

Christian Viveros-Faune
Dear Christian,

Thank you so much for your email regarding my letter. You are right—I will not respond to it online, as I am trying, for once, to resist the immediacy of that medium to hold a conversation. It may appear a romantic impulse, but I also find that it allows me to be more careful in my thinking when I write.

I can see how it may seem inevitable to find real-life or specific parallels in what I write about: I apologize if my writing may appear to intentionally hurt others. Nothing could be farther from my intention. When I write, as I am sure you must do when you do your own writing, my aim is to go beyond specifics, to try to get to a certain understanding of what governs the art world we operate in. For some reason, as far as I can remember, I was always interested in what one might describe as the "outside context" of things: what I observe or hear about and how those observations and information may interconnect or form patterns that can help us better understand why we act the way we do in the world.

Ultimately I believe it is the result of a great frustration that I have, as well as an ongoing fascination, that regardless of how much you try to understand and explain art, it remains ever more inscrutable. This is perhaps something that you may have experienced when writing art criticism: the feeling that the more you write about something, the farther away it seems to be. It is a disquieting feeling for me, because the word is so familiar to thought and to the notion of truth that to use it improperly can dissuade people in ways that may prevent them from seeing whatever it is you write about on their own.

This reminds me of the case of Eleazar Rolson.

Eleazar Rolson was one of the most influential critics of his generation. He mainly was a diplomat and a writer: a poet. He came from a country and a time where art criticism was not a fully developed discipline, so it mostly corresponded to poets to act as art critics. There is obviously an illustrious tradition of this, coming from Baudelaire and others as I am sure you are aware; and for a while the marriage between poets and painters seemed ideal (for some painters and poets, it still is). A poet would contemplate a painting and write an inspired text about it; those texts would be either poetic prose or an interpretive flight of fancy that was less concerned with trying to find an objective common ground to describe a work or situate it in a particular historical or theoretical context and more an affirmation of the idea that the best way to interpret an art work is by creating another art work although in a different genre.

This was the kind of criticism that Eleazar Rolson used to practice. And because he was such a huge name in the world of letters as well as such a powerful intellect, most artists sought his approval, most writers imitated his style, and most members of the public regarded him as the final word on art. He even appeared on television at some point when he tried to do a series on the history of art, often lecturing as he walked down the galleries of a museum, or as he was sitting in the middle of a historic building.

But there was a moment when the apparent marriage of this kind of criticism and the new kind of art that started emerging had to clash. Artists started to rebel against the idea that the interpretation of an artwork was external to the artwork itself, and thus started to make the interpretation the art work itself. It was the moment of the explosion of conceptualism, as you may gather. There were no lyrical brushstrokes to interpret as feelings, there was no emotional investment in the piece that could be construed poetically as a biographical message, there were no sharp edges or strong colors that invited ambiguous readings. To these new works, Eleazar mainly reacted with indifference. He was certainly aware of Marcel Duchamp, but, unable to bring himself to discredit the French master, he claimed that this work was simply impossible to repeat, and that all conceptual art that followed was, in fact, an imitation.

But this judgment didn't do much to prevent the transformative wave of creativity that was taking place all over the world. Artists simply ignored the Rolson camp and the Rolsonians kept writing about those artists who had remained loyal to the previous aesthetic regime, making wonderful paintings that would invite poets to decode.

Eleazar Rolson, as brilliant as he was, was by no means perfect, and one of his greatest defects, aside from not recognizing the value of the art that "wanted to think for itself, instead of having others to think on its behalf" as one of those artists put it, was his unwillingness to admit his own biases. Digging in his heels, he started writing more and more extensive essays arguing against what he saw as artists' misplaced efforts of creating art as ideas. In his view, if the ideas were not contained inherently in the art works, these were worthless. He went on to write a large tome entitled "What Art is Not", essentially arguing for a unified theory of aesthetics.

Rolson's book became a key publication for the art world of his country, but for unexpected reasons. Instead of convincing others with his argument, he instead incensed the local conceptual artist community, who took it upon themselves to make works that contradicted every single statement that he made in his book about what art should be.

In this way, one can say perversely that this was the most inspiring book for art in memory.

The artist's reaction only made Rolson more determined. It was the moment of his true breakup with art. He now declared an open battle of aesthetics against this generation of artists. He organized symposiums with writer-critics that thought like him; he published more books, made another TV program, and initiated a foundation to fund the work of poet-friendly artists. This, as you may imagine, was a boon for the conceptualists, who saw themselves inadvertently being put by Rolson at the same level of the discussion. At the same time, more and more writers who actually had an art historical background and had specialized in these subjects, started to question Rolson's viewpoints. They started practicing a kind of criticism that primarily aspired to aid the viewer and protect the autonomy of the artwork—a sharp contrast to the authorial weight of the Rolson camp.

Rolson passed away and the new generation of true art critics took over. The writers who still wrote in Rolson's style gradually wrote less and less, mainly focusing on traditional painters who still held the old aesthetic models.

But this generation of art critics, when they finally became dominant, started to write in a way that, while it appeared objective and impersonal, was increasingly biased by their ideology and indirect imposition of their theories on the works they were describing. They would shroud their supposedly objective descriptions with heavy-duty theory that had little to no relation to the works upon which they were commenting.

So artists, perceiving that this way of writing was less and less connected to the work they were making, started to rebel again. A new generation of makers started rejecting the current criticism, inviting poets to write about their works.

One can imagine how the story continues unfolding.

All yours

Pablo

II.

Elaine Angelopoulos

Dear Elaine,

Thank you so much for your extensive, sincere response to my letter, and for the information about your current projects. I feel I should start by apologizing for two counts. One is for replying via regular mail, which takes longer and feels out of place; however as I did say in my first letter, this is the rule of the project.

The second apology is related to the nature of my story. After reading your response, I started realizing how what I am writing about sounds very negative and critical, depicting a kind of art world that at first glance is all about careerism and insincerity. You are absolutely right that there are plenty of authentic and sincere individuals in our midst, of which I consider you one—otherwise I would not have written to you in the first place. I thank you for reminding me of this. I also share your concern for remaining authentic, as I often wonder whether I have also become a person dominated by insincerity. Yet I often think about my father, who was a transparent, generous and sincerely effusive individual, but who also kept his deepest emotions to himself, because he felt that these didn't need to be shared. Which brings me to the perhaps self-evident thought that there is a point at which we can only take that much sincerity.

This reminds me of an anecdote from art school. I had an Italian architecture teacher—I will call her Antonia Rigotti. She was an outspoken Roman, always impeccable in her looks as every Italian woman. Overall she was a good instructor, if slightly hyperbolic, but always passionate. At some art critique at the end of the year she was looking at all our projects. She could be ruthless if she didn't like something. She would tear it apart bit by bit like a forensic doctor calmly teaching an anatomy lesson on a corpse. And this is exactly what she did to one of my classmates, a young and attractive woman. She certainly did not fit the mold of an art student as I recall—she had designer clothes and one would have a hard time imagining her struggling at the studio at night, versus partying. The professor in any case tore apart her concept, questioned her commitment, critiqued the realization of the piece, and ultimately didn't leave a single component without ruthless criticism. The poor woman was devastated, crying, but this did not deter professor Rigotti. Toward the end, when she lay inconsolable against the wall, Rigotti held her and told her: "but look at yourself: you are beautiful!"

She went on to say, if I recall correctly, that if she paid as much attention to her art as she did to her appearance she would be a better artist. Yet the comment, in her heavy Italian accent, rather sounded like a cynical line from a Fellini movie. It also suggested an implicit perception about her, as if she were saying, "just become a model and forget about art."

I often think about that incident when I phrase my comments in front of art students. I wonder what would have happened to this woman. Maybe the experience did her good. Maybe she is now a successful artist. Or a powerful fashion editor.

All yours

Pablo

III.

Laura Raicovich

Dear Laura,

Thank you so much for your response to my letter. As you know already, I will only respond via regular mail, so I apologize for the delay and the inconvenience.

The desire to be relevant in the world while at the same time feeling out of sync with it is a common issue that I believe we all are dealing with on an everyday basis, as well as the question of knowing that we are connecting with the right thinkers.

What I have often wondered is whether we are thinking things backwards. That is, we always assume that there is an audience that we are missing. "If only the right people saw this work", we hear someone say. "If only I was in the 'in' crowd." If only.

It reminds me of the story of Stuart Carradon.

Carradon grew up in Shetland, Scotland, and very early on his family knew that he would be a performance artist. He was constantly in search of an audience for his performances. Because he was the youngest of a large family, he sort of had an audience growing up. But his family was eccentric, and outside of the norm in comparison with everyone else. So when he left his family and looked for another audience, he had a hard time finding it.

He moved to London to study. There he also had a difficult time making progress with his career. He later traveled throughout Europe and tried different audiences: Italians, Spanish, Portuguese, Russians. None of them seemed to connect with his work. He was tortured, not knowing what he was doing wrong. He was convinced that his work was exceptional.

Finally, he decided that the problem wasn't with his work but with audiences, who were not prepared to understand or appreciate his work. He decided that his career, from that moment forward, would consist not in creating a body of work in search of an audience, but in actually creating an audience.

He opened an audience school back in Shetland. It was at first difficult for people to understand the kind of school that Carradon was proposing; but in the end people liked the notion of learning to be a better audience member. They learned to laugh and to cry on command, they learned subtle references that at different moments of a performance they would be able to recognize. They learned to stand still for hours during endurance pieces, and to participate in an interactive piece in case it was required.

Needless to say, Carradon developed the curriculum so that his works would be the model to follow.

He managed to graduate 169 students. The graduation exam was a day-long performance, where all the students, sitting in a large auditorium, witnessed Carradon doing a comprehensive anthology of his performances, all of which his students had been trained to experience. They laughed, they cried, they participated; they clapped in a huge, delirious standing ovation that lasted twenty minutes by the end of the performance. Carradon was in tears, grateful and ecstatic; profoundly proud of how far his students had come along.

It was a picture to behold. It was, perhaps, the most unforgettable moment of communion between an artist and his audience in the history of the performing arts.

Yours,

Pablo

IV.

Paul Ramirez-Jonas

Dear Paul,

Thank you for your text message concerning my last letter. It is a powerful statement to hear that something you made, made someone cry. I imagine it was more of a figure of speech in your case, but maybe I am wrong. In any case I really appreciate it.

Your response makes me think about art that stirs strong emotions. I do like art like that, but as I get older I am afraid that I may have lost the youthful disposition to let myself be carried away by emotions.

I remember an uncle of mine who never laughed, yet he always read the Sunday comic strips. He always remarked that he never found them funny and yet every Sunday he read them, always searching for that ever elusive laugh.

Often I feel I am becoming my uncle in terms of serious art: I want something to stir me up, but it's harder to do so every time. Yet, I feel the general public always feels the opposite: they want happy endings.

Let's imagine a composer at the height of the Great Depression who composed a song that represented those hard times. The song was so achingly beautiful and devastatingly sad that he was accused of causing suicides left and right. Let's suppose he had reasons for making such a song: he had a miserable life back where he was from, which, let's say, was Hungary. He anticipated the horror of war—being Jewish, he was taken to the Nazi labor camps in Ukraine during World War II. He managed to survive that experience, and later worked in the circus. By this time, his song had become hugely successful and performed by some of the most famous singers in the world. He had accumulated huge royalties in the United States, but he was an avowed communist, and would have never considered traveling there to collect the money.

He would have preferred to stay put in his usual spot, playing the piano at a rickety restaurant in his home town.

No one knows what he thought of the sadness he triggered with his song, but let's imagine that it weighed heavily on him, and that at the end of his life it was too much to bear. His mother hadn't survived the labor camps as he had, and his own guilt of survival must have haunted him.

One can even perfectly imagine him one day, probably a Sunday—Sundays are gloomy—deciding this was enough, and throwing himself out the window of his house. Cruelly as one may imagine, he did not die, but was taken to the hospital, where he choked himself with a wire—this time, successful in his attempt.

Now, many years later, when the '30s feel like a distant and innocent time, this whole story about the song may sound quaint.

Almost funny.

But, I almost forgot to mention: the imaginary composer I described wasn't imaginary: his name was Rezső Seress. His composition was titled "Gloomy Sunday."

Yours,

Pablo

V.

David Greg Harth

Dear Harth,

Thank you so much for replying to my letter. You were the first person to mail me a physical response, and I am not the least surprised, knowing your commitment to mail art and your past work. I wanted to write to you in the first place because I respect the seriousness with which you take every communication.

I understand what you mean when, as I talk about the various ills the world in general and the art world in particular, you say that all you can do is produce your work. It is true that worrying about the problems of the world and society can easily paralyze one, and paralysis can be the worst thing that can happen to an artist. This paralysis can take many forms, such as the one that can be best described as the illusion of movement.

This is why I often think of the case of Song Yun Seok. I met Song Yun when we were art students. She was probably the hardest working student of the entire school. She had grown up in California, and had a steel discipline in practically ever activity she undertook. She was merciless with herself when she needed to complete a task; rail thin and petite, she seemed nonetheless to have inexhaustible energy to work on assignments. She would spend days and days in school, staying overnight for several days, sleeping only a handful of hours on the cafeteria couch. Her level of manufacture was great, and she always over-delivered by a huge amount, always doing five times more work than what was assigned.

Her Achilles heel was that her approach was largely programmatic: there was not a great deal of individuality or character in what she did. She had a hard time articulating her personal view on a subject or explaining what, if anything, generated passion in her other than the satisfaction of getting a job done.

Song Yun's great crisis came when she graduated—as it happens to several artists. Suddenly she had no structure. She almost immediately went on to do her masters, and then she did another masters. Ultimately, she followed the career of the eternal student, existing always in that parenthesis of college life where you live in a parenthesis and don't have to create a personal infrastructure.

I recently saw her again, 25 years after our student years. She was now in pursuit of her 10th degree. She talked to me about how she had tried to do other things like working at an artist studio, but she did not like doing another's person's work. I then asked her something to the effect of "isnt' art school a place where you do as you are told?" She smiled and said: "I do like when people tell me what kind of work I should do as my own work."

To this day, Song Yun is still at school, about to complete an artist PhD, perfecting her work.

Yours,

Pablo

VI.

Alissa Firth-Eagland

Dear Alissa,

Thank you so much for your kind and warm handwritten notes. Actually I didn't mention this before, but yours were the first handwritten notes that I received in the course of this correspondence project, which does involve quite a number of people—but I am not surprised that the first one of this sort came from you, knowing your sensitivity and your interest in mail art. I was particularly taken by one of your postscripts, which read: "there's not too much art, just a deficiency in the methodologies of sharing it all with those who need it the most."

This idea is definitely worth thinking about. Indeed I have encountered many situations where I encounter certain kinds of art that I know would be valued an even become priceless if seen and displayed by the right people. I also remember my mother's old saying, "siempre hay un roto para un descosido." ("There is always a broken one for an untied one", which translated to art it would mean that even art that is not exceptional under certain standards could be exceptional for others.) The problem of course lies in how this connection between the "right" art work and viewer can happen, if it can ever happen.

This reminds me of an experiment conducted by an artist who I will call Giovanni Rocca.

Rocca was an active artist in the 1960s, when he became fairly recognized as a painter in his native Milano. He soon became disillusioned by the art market and the art world. He particularly disliked the fact that his paintings would be primarily acquired by rich individuals who had no personal connection to him, and, he felt, no real appreciation or knowledge about art. He wanted to make art for the regular person. In his diaries one can see how this desire translated into a test for himself: "I can't consider myself a real artist until I learn to make works that will appeal to an average person. I want to understand viewers to the point that I can make individual works for each one of them and affect each all in their own individual ways."

No one really knows how it was exactly that Rocca somehow zeroed in on the janitor of his building as the ultimate test for his artistry. His janitor, a Polish immigrant named Zbignew Lato, had no knowledge, and little interest in art. But supposedly one day when Rocca was in his studio, Lato came in to fix a plumbing fixture and showed no interest whatsoever in Rocca's paintings. Rocca, as it is believed, was incensed at first that his paintings, which would normally awe collectors, would have no effect on the janitor. He inquired with him about this and ultimately made it into a lifetime project to make a perfect painting for Lato. The janitor agreed to be quizzed and interviewed about what aesthetic qualities he would look for in an art work, but he proved to be particularly picky and complicated about what he would like. Rocca presented him with all sorts of art work—realistic, abstract, expressionistic—but none seemed to satisfy Lato. Rocca would furiously destroy the canvasses after they would be rejected by Lato. After all the attention and the adulation from rich collectors, curators and dealers, suddenly Rocca had made his entire career dedicated to satisfying someone with no interest or knowledge in art.

This back and forth went on for years. Rocca was descending into some kind of madness, drinking heavily, showing erratic behavior. One day, after a drinking binge, he fell down the stairs and suffered a concoction from which he never recovered. He passed away a day later.

When interviewed about Rocca's works, Lato said he was saddened about the tragic end of Rocca. When asked about why he hadn't liked all the paintings that he had tried to make for him, he replied: "I know nothing about art, but when Mr. Rocca wanted to make something for me, I thought my job was to be as tough as possible. I grew up with a father who was stern and never satisfied with me. I thought I needed to play the role of the unsatisfied customer with Mr. Rocca, so he would become a better artist. I never thought this could cause his demise."

Yours,

Pablo

Ps. The enclosed art work is for your eyes only. I am sorry to say that it is only meant to be seen by you. You may display it at your house but it cannot be seen by anyone else—it would need to be hidden from any visitor, and if seen, it must be destroyed at once.

VII.

David Greg Harth

Dear Harth,

Thanks so much for your response to my letter from February 22nd, 2014. You are correct in suggesting that we as artists seem to face a stark choice: either we find monetary backing to propel our practice or we become propelled, and maybe, fall prey of, our own madness. Shia LaBeouf appears to be a third case: one where fame and money made him prey to madness. And many artists can be mad, but to be mad is not to be an artist.

There is a wonderful quip from Camus in *The Myth of Sisyphus*:

> "I once heard about [. . .] a postwar artist who, after finishing his first book, committed suicide in order to draw attention to his work. It drew, in effect, attention, but the book was considered poor."

This is to say that fame indeed draws attention, but there is little benefit when you don't have much to show when what you are doing is critically scrutinized.

And yet I know what you may say: it's better to receive the attention and have no talent, than having talent and no attention. For what is the use of talent if there is no one to appreciate it? To which my answer would be: it is always better to have talent rather than money, unless if you know what to do with your money even if you don't have talent.

Which reminds me of a story that I would like to share with you.

Ebenezer Poole was perhaps the most famous ice skater of his generation. His dream, however, was to be a psychoanalyst. He used his entire fame and fortune to open a psychoanalytic institute. The psychoanalytic community regarded him with respect—he in the end had a foundation that supported a lot of their work—but deep down everyone knew that Poole was not capable of discussing theoretical and scientific issues connected to the discipline. It was an uncomfortable situation for everyone, and Poole suspected it.

Finally one day Poole wrote a book about psychoanalysis using ice skating metaphors. This inspired many ice skaters who wanted to follow Poole's path. Since an ice skater can't do the sport forever, many of them started following Poole's example and started becoming therapists themselves. Without realizing, Poole had invented a new specialty in the world.

Yours,

Pablo

VIII.

Sheetal Prajapati

Dear Sheetal,

Thank you for your very touching and sincere letter. Your experience as a child traveling to India is so vivid that I felt I was there with you, next to your swing. While I never experienced as a child the kind of trans-continental dislocation that you lived, I can relate to the need of a place of safety.

When I was my daughter's age, I did not want to go to school. I was afraid of other children. Come to think of it, because my siblings were much older I did not have much daily exposure to kids my age. I wanted to stay home with my mother. For me, the house was a very safe and happy place. I remember proposing to her that I could stay home every day and sweep the leaves off the patio we had. I loved that patio. It always represented freedom to me.

Years later, we moved to another house with a garden. By this time I was already resigned to school. One day—I believe it was my birthday—my parents organized a "Kermesse", which was essentially a party with various activity stations. My father was a bathroom supplies salesman, so we used toilet crates as tables. The strongest recollection from that day is that on that morning I accompanied my father to the hardware store to buy some color light bulbs and some electric cable to illuminate the garden a bit. He hung the lights around the garden walls, which were covered with ivy. Those lights were left there after the party, and in fact they stayed there for as long as we owned the house, which is when I was 17.

At night, after dinner, I would usually go out to the garden and turn on those lights. It was a miracle that they still worked after all those years, despite the rain and the outdoor weather.

I would sit there and look at those lights—the colors, the way they projected shadows against the leaves. I deposited memories in them, secrets, fears, anxieties, experiences of unrequited love from adolescence. When I was about 16, after going to the movies with my closest four friends, I invited them to the garden. We sat there and spoke about very deep and important issues for us—usually dealing with loneliness, and with that ever elusive love that none of us seemed to ever conquer. The experience of being in that garden and having those conversations profoundly marked us, and to these day, more than a quarter century later, it is still a bond that we share.

My family moved to Chicago when I was 18. We sold that house. It was difficult for me to part from that garden. I clearly remember how we left the lights hanging there; my parents had forgotten about them and I couldn't bring myself to take them down. All those memories were contained in them. I wanted to part from that garden with the fantasy that perhaps they would stay there forever, guarding those memories.

There is a poem, I believe from Fernando Pessoa, that both I and my brother loved. I have lost track of it, but it went something like this:

> I know that
> When we were children
> We all had a garden,
> Of or own or the neighbor's,
> Where the only rule was to play,
> And that sadness only belongs
> To the present.

Yours,

Pablo

IX.

Alissa Firth-Eagland

Dear Alissa,

Thanks so much for your last note. You are becoming my most loyal interlocutor. Which is not surprising to me, knowing your sensibility and your capacity to listen to others. I feel lucky having known you for all these years.

Thank you also for your comments about my letter on Justiniano. I like your observation that we need perhaps to be more selfish, but also that in the case of Justiniano, he was indeed becoming art.

I want to think about that idea for a bit. Merging life with art has been a longtime obsession for artists, especially over the last fifty years. Yet there is always a bit of a contradiction in that plan: if art and life are completely merged, doesn't art disappear altogether? Isn't the very success of that merging the very negation of art? It seems the problem to me of the notion of "stealth art", invented by your fellow Canadian Stephen Wright, who basically argues that art has to erase itself to save itself. The paradox is, if that erasure is successful, it is also a defeat, because art disappearing amounts to having no art. And if art still is there, in any form, then the disappearance has been a failure as well.

Aldinar Gruber was an artist who, some years ago, attempted to solve this problem. A professor at the kunstakademie in Dusseldorf, he spent his life trying to make art that was and wasn't there at the same time. He somewhat zeroed in on the use of the international affective system—a system of images used by psychologists for perception tests. These include images of violence and disgust but also of sex and pornography, as well as benevolent images of flowers, puppies, etc., all with the intention of inserting subliminal messages in the minds of the viewer. Gruber believed that this process of inserting subliminal images in the mind, if handled properly, could well influence aesthetic judgment and the emotional reaction that a person would have toward a work.

Gruber created his own images and devised a subliminal system to feed these to influential individuals in the art world. He chose to start with an influential curator in Dusseldorf. Over the course of a year (Gruber was very patient) he followed this curator, studied his routines and his habits, and made sure to insert in his daily life images of his work—putting one inside a magazine that he read at the dentist, putting a poster of the image outside of his house, sending him emails that appear to have been sent by a news or information service. He played songs outside of his house with words that fed him descriptions of the images that he had seen in those other contexts. None of these images contained Gruber's name. When Gruber finally had an exhibition, this curator appeared and seemed at home, repeating the words that he had heard in that song played outside of his house. He became a staunch supporter of Gruber's work.

Gruber then realized that he had devised a powerful system to brainwash those who could become supportive of his work. He then proceeded to employ the treatment onto others, choosing approximately fifteen important figures in the art world who could help advance his career.

The problem with Gruber's plan was that this became such an arduous task that, almost without realizing, he ended up investing much more energy in inserting the subliminal messages about his work amongst his subjects than in thinking about the kind of images and messages that he was inserting—probably not the most interesting.

After five years of this exercise, these fifteen people, all expenses paid, were invited to a grand solo exhibition he presented at a local gallery in Dusseldorf. Most of the guests did come to the opening and observed the works with great attention. This was, for Gruber, probably the most important moment in his life.

The consensus, however, was fairly negative. They all agreed with each other that the work was not truly innovative, that they all had seen that kind of work before.

Yours,
Pablo

THE PARABLE CONFERENCE

SCRIPT

The following performance was presented at the Brooklyn Academy of Music on October 18 2014 with the following cast:

Host 1—Brian Linden
Host 2—Rossella Matamoros
Host 3—Greig Sargeant
Host 4—Equiano Mosieri
Host 5—Laura Lona
Host 6—Corey Tasmania
Host 7—Candace Thompson

The production was directed by Pablo Helguera with the assistant direction of Sarah Hughes.

[*Guests arrive in the space. The space is arranged like a benefit or a wedding, with flower arrangements, birdhouses and images of birds hanging from the ceiling. Music from the 1930s plays in the background.* PABLO, *will be singing with a pianist in accompaniment.*

A group of ushers, with white bow ties and gloves, delivers place cards to each guest, and they are directed to different tables.

At the tables, there is wine and food. A group of 20 waiters, also described here as "Hosts", walk around the space, facilitating introductions amongst those at the table and making sure everyone has what they need. Each Host will have detailed information of the guests at each table, including the letters each guest received, things that one guest should know about the other ("Mr. Finkelpearl is the Arts Commissioner", for example).

When all guests are sitting at tables and have spoken for a while, the HOSTS, *who have been acting like waiters so far in the evening, start speaking from different sections of the space.*]

HOST 1
Dear Gabriela,

HOST 2
Dear Sheetal,

HOST 3
Dear Michael,

HOST 4
Dear Dannielle,

HOST 5
Dear Andras,
HOST 6
Dear Thierry,

HOST 7
Dear Juan,

PABLO
I am writing to invite you to be an audience member at an event that will take place on October 18th, 2014 in New York City. This will not be a typical event, due in part to the fact that as soon as you sign up to attend you will start receiving individually-written letters from me. You are under no obligation to respond to any piece of mail you may receive leading up to the performance. We only request that you do commit to actually attending the event itself, as there will be significant effort invested in communicating with you leading up to it.

I fully understand that this invitation may initially appear too vague and perhaps unclear in its intention. You may want to know more about what will happen, or not happen, on October 18th, 2014, before agreeing to attend. This lack of clarity, for better or worse, is an inherent aspect of this project. I can say that I have given a great deal of thought to this invitation and promise you that, should you decide to attend, I won't betray your trust.

Please also note that communication for this event will always and exclusively be conducted via regular mail.

I sincerely hope that you may be available and in New York City on October 18th to join me. I anxiously await your response.

Truly yours,

Pablo Helguera.

HOST 3

You may wonder why am I choosing to write letters when there are so many other more expedient ways to communicate with people.

HOST 4

Today, as on many other days, I think about my father, about his hopes and expectations for me and whether I am fulfilling them in the same way he hoped to fulfill his own father's expectations.

HOST 2

This Saturday morning I thought about the excessive importance that is placed on the art market, and the spurious art that suddenly arises, when the truly substantial art is largely ignored—mainly because it requires people's brains and attention.

HOST 6

I am often bothered by a particular question that, were I to ask it out loud, would probably not garner much me much of a serious response. This is why I like to write letters: they allow us to ask questions that can be difficult to elaborate on in everyday conversation.

The question in this case is: is there too much art in the world?

HOST 7

If there is something that defines the lives of most people around us it is the experience of being permanently overscheduled. This is certainly true for me—I feel that every hour of my life has to be accounted for. Which makes me wonder: how in such a state of mind can one give enough time to art?

HOST 4

I know I shouldn't be living my life according to my interpretation of someone else's ideas of what it should be, and especially when that person is not here anymore to bear witness (my father passed away a decade ago). But I still feel compelled to live up to that expectation, as some kind of mission I have been assigned.

HOST 5

I have been learning quite a lot about myself through the simple act of writing letters. It surprised me to realize that it is very difficult to write in this format without becoming very personal, and, at times, confessional—a word that I have always feared when it comes to art. So I have been thinking these days about what I would term as the "art as confessional" problem.

HOST 1

Ed Koch, the recently deceased former mayor of New York City, was a colorful character. My favorite comeback line of his is "I can explain it to you; but I can't comprehend it for you."

HOST 3

The answer has to do with what it means to receive a physical letter these days, since what we get in the mail is no longer real correspondence, but mostly bills.

Furthermore, when one writes a letter, one has to be more thoughtful of what is necessary to include versus what is irrelevant.

HOST 7

I think about that question when I observe certain visitors at the museum, most of whom seem focused on looking at all of the art as if it were a job, or a checklist to complete; often taking pictures of every artwork and contemplating their own phone screen for most of their visit.

I understand them. I am also not the contemplative type. It makes me think about whether the fact that we continue exhibiting artworks in a lineup format, in this chronological, Cartesian fashion, somehow translates to the sensation that we are in a production line of experience, and we become factory workers of perception.

HOST 5

First: why would being overly generous about displaying our most intimate hopes and fears to the public be problematic? The answer is, I think, that it is not the personal revelation that becomes problematic, but the rather narcissistic expectation, first, that these hopes and fears are relevant to others, and moreover, that they deserve to be elevated to the realm of art. And we all know that when it comes to evaluating the importance of our personal issues, objectivity is impossible.

HOST 1

I often think of this in terms of art. As you may know, a good portion of my professional life as an art educator has to do with precisely the sort of thing Koch is joking about: helping people experience art in a meaningful way. I confess that I often verge on desperation when I encounter people who are so closed and nearly incapable of letting themselves venture into engaging with an art work.

HOST 3

In any case, thank you for your text message concerning my last letter. Saying that letter made you cry is quite a powerful statement. I imagine it was more of a figure of speech, or that you were maybe joking. But in any case I really appreciate it.

This makes me think about art that stirs strong emotions. I do like art like that but as I get older I am afraid that I may have lost the youthful disposition to let myself be carried away by emotions.

HOST 1

Still, I often wonder what it would be like to devise a way in which we could, as Koch suggests, "comprehend" things for people.

HOST 3

I remember an uncle of mine who never laughed, yet he always read the Sunday comic strips. He always remarked that he never found them funny and yet every Sunday he read them, always searching for that ever elusive laugh.

HOST 1

And this leads me to the story of Justiniano Quiles.

HOST 3

Often I feel I am becoming my uncle in terms of serious art: I want something to stir me up but it's harder every time. Yet I feel the general public always feels the opposite: they want happy endings.

HOST 4

A similar question arises regarding fulfilling someone else's expectations when we make art. According to some, modernism is an ongoing, frustrating attempt to maintain dialogue with someone who isn't there anymore, followed by an attempt to replace them with a—perhaps also frustrating, in another way—surrogate, collective, faceless and anonymous interlocutor.

There is at least one artist I know of who attempted to break apart this communication scheme. Let's call her Ivana Korshnoi.

HOST 2

One has to wonder why this is the case. Is it a problem with art itself, or is it a problem with those making art today?

I can offer a small story that may help us reflect on this topic.

HOST 7

Once I heard a story from a museum researcher whose name I have forgotten; I will call her Francesca Walton. Francesca, for many years, studied museum visitors in galleries. As you may suspect, visitor behavior in museums is fairly predictable: we generally know how long they will linger, what they will spend more time looking at, what they may miss altogether. But there was one visitor in particular that this researcher encountered who was particularly unique. Let's call him Takeshi Hikari.

HOST 5

Most of us who have been to art school are familiar with the scenario of sitting and standing around while a student goes on and on talking about himself or herself in a situation that feels more like group therapy than a real critique session. The confessional impulse, it seems to me now that I think of it, may be a defense mechanism against the normal scrutiny and critique that comes with making art. If the work is based on a deeply intimate and fragile emotional experience, it becomes very hard to critique tactfully.

Let me tell you a story that may help illustrate some of these issues.

HOST 6

Let's think about this for a second. For that we need to imagine a story—a story of someone who I will call Sister Alison Parr.

Sister Alison was a Shaker, and lived pretty much her entire life in New Lebanon, New York, where her family converted to the Shaker faith when she was seven. Born around 1816, her life paralleled the rise of the Shaker faith. It was sometime in the 1830s when the Shakers experienced something called the Era of Manifestations, a wave of spiritual revival that appeared in the form of strong visions amongst a few Shakers. It mainly affected young women in the community, and Sister Alison was amongst them. One morning, after her daily milking duties (she worked on the Shaker dairy farm), she collapsed on the ground. While she was being assisted by other Shakers, her body started to convulse violently. She was in bed for three weeks, during which period she had high fevers; at night she experienced powerful visions, some of which lasted hours.

HOST 1

I will never forget Justiniano, whom I had met in art school in Chicago back in the early 90s. He was a cheerful painter from Lima, Peru, with a thick shock of black hair. He was a painter, as well as an art educator in a local children's art program. He was older than me, having finished a clinical psychology degree before coming to art. I also recall that he was a fervent reader of John Dewey (long before Dewey became fashionable in the art world) and was very interested in figuring out what he, somewhat cryptically, described as the "holy grail of communication."

HOST 6

After this period, Sister Alison produced several drawings that described those elaborate visions—ornamented representations of angels, trees and birds. These drawings, along with many others that were made by other Shakers with similar experiences, are called gift drawings.

Now, the Shakers did not accept the notion of art in its conventional sense. Art in the Shaker faith, for example, could not be without a purpose; as every action, being as it is a tribute to God, needs to be purposeful, and for that matter, useful. Pure aesthetic pleasure, it seems, could not count. Art could also not be purchased or displayed. In 1845, the Shaker Laws ruled that "no maps, charts, and no pictures or paintings, shall ever be hung up in your dwelling-rooms, shops or office. And no pictures or paintings set in frames, with glass before them, shall ever be among you."

HOST 2

A long time ago, in the ancient world, word came that there was a city, Elzaia, whose citizens had developed the ability to communicate with birds. It started with a wise man who had studied birds all his life and had an immense love for them. This love triggered his desire to communicate with the feathered creatures. Over the years, he taught this difficult art to others, who in turn also had disciples. At some point, communication with these animals became a central aspect of the culture of Elzaia. Every citizen of this city was a bird communicator. Soon many other cities became curious to know how this rare art was done.

HOST 5

Fray Bartolomeu Balcells had joined the Benedictine Monastery of Montserrat, in the vicinity of Barcelona. In his youth he had studied art but his religious calling pulled him towards joining the order. He always thought of art nonetheless, writing personal notes to himself about its potential as a means for communication.

HOST 4

Ivana Korshnoi was a painter obsessed with art history. She made a living as a night guard in an encyclopedic museum—imagine something like the Hermitage. The graveyard shift suited her well, since she was not a people person, and it allowed her to study a painting for months at a time. As primarily a painter of landscapes, she had a particular affinity for the work of Jean-Baptiste Camille Corot, which she obsessively studied and about which she knew practically every detail. She memorized his every painting, down to the brush stroke. She read every piece of writing and every bit of biographical information about him. She often felt she shared a supernatural connection with Corot.

HOST 7

Mr. Hikari was a successful retired doctor with a great passion of art. He was not a collector per se—he collected pictures that he himself took of art in museums. His goal in life was to see every art museum in the world and to take pictures—with or without permission—of whatever the museum had on display. He was remarkably skilled at this—so much so that even the most suspicious and alert museum guard would be fooled by his tactics. He went to great lengths, even having secret cameras installed on a lapel pin and on a cane he walked around with. His impeccably discreet demeanor, and the fact that he was quite a distinguished-looking gentleman, made him practically undetectable. It could take him a few minutes to go through an entire small museum. When he could, he would also videotape the galleries.

HOST 2

Some Elzaians started to travel to make demonstrations of their abilities. Because the public was eager to see these demonstrations, the Elzaians started to charge sums of money. Tourism poured into Elzaia, and theaters were built to accommodate more and more spectacular demonstrations. A neighboring city, Islaya, built its own theater and promoted its spectacles in competition with Elzaia.

HOST 1

One day over coffee on Belmont Avenue, Justiniano explained his theory of art interpretation to me. Art interpretation, he argued, is a flawed concept. It is not useful to share your interpretation of an artwork with others; as what you are transmitting is not at all related to the actual artwork but only to your own ideas. Truly experiencing art could only happen for the seasoned art professional that is deeply engaged with art, and who could form an interpretation that is unique and specific to the self. "So, what to do with the masses of people who are not art experts? Are they destined to never truly experience art in its fullest sense?" I said.

"I have a solution for that", Justiniano said. "Over the years I have developed a technique for experiencing art."

HOST 4

At some point, Ivana became interested in the ideas of theosophy and spiritualism in the writings of Helena Blavatsky. She believed that each painting had a spiritual force contained in it.

HOST 6

It is known that the Shaker leadership, while excited about all the powerful visions that came during the Era of Manifestations, was also perplexed, and possibly jealous, of the fact that these visions were coming only to young women in the community, and not to them. This may have been a reason for them to prohibit the artworks' display. It is known, however, that these "gift drawings" were nonetheless often given amongst Shakers and then kept privately.

HOST 5

Fray Bartolomeu was also a superb listener, which made him an excellent confessor. Everyone, it seemed, wanted to confess to him. He was famous for being a wise advisor. He started writing and thinking a lot about the practice of confessing, lamenting to himself that monks didn't really know how to confess their sins. Eventually, arguing that a monastery is "a school in the service of the lord", he proposed the creation of a confessional program inside the monastery. The prior was intrigued by Fray Bartolomeu's proposal and after reflecting on it, gave his blessing to him to pursue the endeavor.

HOST 7

Francesca approached Dr. Hikari and convinced him to be interviewed for her study. Dr. Hikari invited Francesca to his apartment on the Upper West Side. What she saw was hard for her to believe.

Dr. Hikari's apartment was packed with disks, video tapes, and various other forms of documentation of art works in museums, as well as every kind of museum souvenir imaginable: snow globes, posters, catalogues. By his own calculation, he had visited 7,300 museums in his lifetime, and photographed all artworks on view in every single one of them. To him, the holy grail was the collection that was never on view; this caused him a great deal of grief, like the mountaineer who has dreamt all his life of climbing that inaccessible peak.

HOST 3

Let's imagine a composer at the height of the Great Depression who composed a song that represented those hard times. The song was so achingly beautiful and devastatingly sad that he was accused of causing suicides left and right. Let's suppose he had reasons for making such a song: he had a miserable life growing up, say, in Hungary. He anticipated the horror of war: being Jewish, he was taken to the Nazi labor camps in Ukraine during World War II. He managed to survive that experience, and later worked in the circus. By this time, his song had become hugely successful and performed by some of the most famous singers in the world. He had accumulated huge royalties in the United States, but he was an avowed communist, and would have never considered traveling there to collect the money. He would have preferred to stay put in his usual spot, playing the piano at a rickety restaurant in his home town.

[ADDRESSEES INTERLUDE]

DEBORAH FISHER
Dear Pablo,

HARTH
Dear Pablo,

ALISSA
Dear Pablo,

DEBORAH
When you write that you are perhaps writing these letters out of a sense that you want to become more grounded in your communication with others, are you serious? Because there is nothing grounding about receiving these letters. I look forward to them, they are a gift! But they are in no way grounded, concrete or tangible on this end.

HARTH
I don't know where your mind comes up with stories or facts. I don't know how you balance certain obstacles or happenstances in your life.

ALISSA
If being open to an artists' message requires a capacity for feeling within a viewer, does being a "good receiver" of art require empathy, specifically?

DEBORAH

They are personal and intimate. I have almost started to feel that you are clearly talking to me, and only to me. But I also know that this is not really the case because they also allude to a public that is also receiving these letters—the conference. I know and am describing some of this public by talking about these letters with the friends we have in common.

ALISSA

On the part of both the maker and the viewer this requires letting go of control. Say, releasing assumptions to the wind and shedding expectations. That's what frees the human heart. Children seem far less burdened by assumptions and expectations than adults. Perhaps it is because they hold no illusions that they are in control?

HARTH

But what I say to you is actually quite irrelevant. To you. To your next letter. The power of irrelevance comes forth within the concentration on how is held at a higher value than the concentration of the future.

DEBORAH

When I engage in this, we talk a lot about how you are doing the work. We share parables. I can't speak for the others, but when I talk about these letters, I am careful. I talk a lot about process. I imagine how you must be writing them. But I avoid talking about the intimacy of receiving them. I avoid talking about how perfect the fit sometimes is between what I am struggling with and the parable you share. I avoid saying that I hear your voice reading them to me.

ALISSA

Humanity has figured out how to cut stone, mold metals, and forge new materials. Yet changing our minds is nearly impossible, especially on a collective level. The challenge is simultaneously to think of ourselves as individuals and as part of something larger.

HARTH

This reminds me, I recently had a discussion about how roses are a poor choice of a flower to give to a love. I prefer tulips. While Holland is often known as the large tulip producer, most seeds come from Turkey. That's according to someone I have a crush on.

DEBORAH

It's interesting, the form you are making, not because it is grounding but because it is sleight of hand. You are establishing an intimate relationship with me that I buy completely, but I know it is not an intimate relationship at all—it's public. Based on a few signifiers—warm-toned paper, a blue ink signature, the fact that I know that nobody I know has gotten my parables yet, their flanking relevance to what I think about things . . . I conjure an intimacy that I know, rationally, is false.

ALISSA

As much younger people, we could not make a move without some kind of approval. In many cases, this is family. How we respond to art is how we assert our individuality to ourselves.

With much warmth,
Alissa

HARTH

It's been a while since I had a solid crush on someone. She doesn't know this. So if you ever make these letters public, and then she finds out, then she'll know.

DEBORAH

I've been reading about the history of magic, the craft of which is essentially about guiding the public to believe what it wants to believe.

There is no way to do this but to actually put yourself out there.

And yours,
Deborah

HARTH

With deep regret that I have gained weight again,
Harth.

HOST 4

One day Ivana Korshnoi attended a lecture by a Hungarian spiritist, Georg Sulyok, which deeply affected her. Sulyok argued that artworks were uniquely positioned to be passages to the spirit world. She approached Sulyok and asked him to teach her his techniques so she could try them out. Sulyok agreed to work with her and they decided that they would try to summon Corot's spirit at the galleries of the museum.

HOST 1

Despite my puzzlement, Justiniano explained his theory of "art experiencing". Instead of wasting time trying to teach someone how to experience art, he would experience it for them. First he would interview the individual, getting a sense of his or her interests and passions, gathering a complete psychological profile of them. Afterward he would go to experience art on their behalf, literally becoming a surrogate viewer. He had done some initial experiments and he was very excited about its potential. He wanted me to join him.

I was curious about his proposal but I never took him up on his offer. The project seemed too elaborate and I had too much going on in any case.

HOST 5

Fray Bartolomeu based his confessional program around art classes, starting with painting and then expanding to photography, video and performance art, which Fray Bartolomeu found particularly conducive to confessing deep and troubled experiences.

The beginning of Fray Bartolomeu's confessional school was very successful. Many monks from other monasteries joined and became very involved in creating their confessions. Here I should point out that Fray Bartolomeu was adamant that this was a religious school, a place of faith and reflection, not an art school, but it attracted art-inclined monks all the same, especially after the school's reputation started to spread throughout the region.

But every enterprise runs the risk of falling victim to its own success.

HOST 7

And what did he do with all that material, Francesca asked him? Did he look at it? Dr. Hikari wouldn't ever give a straight answer. But it was apparent that, like a regular pack rat, the thrill was in owning the thing, not in looking at it or experiencing it later.

Francesca and Dr. Hikari stayed in touch. I don't discard the notion that given that Dr. Hikari was a lonely older man and Francesca an attractive young woman, he might have fantasized about having a romantic relationship with her, a fantasy I highly doubt she would ever have shared. The fact of the matter is that when he passed away, he left in his will his entire collection of images to Francesca.

HOST 2

Other cities followed in imitating Elzaia's bird communication techniques. Elzaians took an aggressive approach by creating a school for bird communicators that everyone around the ancient world joined in order to learn the bird language. The art began to be used in battle, as it was recognized that one could send coded messages using birds. After a few decades, the art of bird communication had fully developed for war and for spectacle. Communicating with birds had stopped being a labor of love; it now was a profession and a business career. So those who joined this practice now were those who had in mind either money and success, in the case of the business-oriented; or the destruction of the enemy, in the case of the military students.

HOST 6

Sister Alison Parr passed away in the late 1800s. It turns out she had kept many of her gift drawings to herself, not knowing who to give them to, or rather, believing that she had not yet met the person to whom they belonged.

Sometime in the 1920s, as the numbers of the Shaker community in New Lebanon started to decline, one of the Shaker buildings was sold and its contents vacated. Boxes of books and hymnals were sent to a local library. It was there where the daughter of the librarian, while assisting her father in opening boxes that contained several of the Shaker books, encountered one of Sister Alison's drawings. It is said that she was immediately fascinated by the drawing and secretly took it home, staring at it for several hours that same night. It is also said that the following day she woke up with a high fever and convulsions in her body, and was found speaking in tongues while embracing the drawing. Her father tried to take the drawing away from his daughter, which generated loud protests, cries, and desperate pleas from her. She was eventually allowed to keep the drawing.

HOST 1

Years later, I saw Justiniano again. He not only had continued pursuing his "art experiencing" project, but he had turned into a business. Modeled after art consultancies, Justiniano's "art experiencing" business was primarily geared at rich individuals who wanted to be part of the glamour of the art world but didn't have the time, or quite honestly, the interest to spend their lives looking at exhibitions, reading books, or even watching films. He was thinking of copyrighting this method of art experiencing. I believe he wanted to call it "VAE—Visual Art Experiencing."

HOST 2

But it so happened that the more this practice became spread out and the more different methods it spawned, the more limited the communication with the birds appeared to become. Birds seemed more and more reluctant to communicate now with the citizens of Elzaia and the surrounding cities. It was almost as if the birds began to find the humans boring.

HOST 4

As a portal to the connection with the artist they picked a painting titled *Bridge at Mantes*, a painting that Ivana had copied numerous times. They decided to conduct the séance on a Christmas Eve, when the very few guards in the museum were celebrating, distracted and drinking in another wing of the museum. Ivana and Sulyok entered the building with her painting tools. Sulyok believed that as Ivana commenced painting the landscape, he would sense vibrations from the portal and they would thusly be able to ask the spirit of Corot to direct Ivana's hand onto the canvas.

HOST 5

As much as Fray Bartolomeu opposed the idea of the monks exhibiting their art publicly, many of them stated doing so anyway, usually under pseudonyms, exhibiting and performing in local galleries. The leadership of the monastery started looking at Fray Bartolomeu's experiment with trepidation, but Fray Bartolomeu convinced them that the project's results were only positive.

However, things soon got more complicated when a fellow monk who had joined the sessions had the poor judgment to show a 2-channel video installation with strong sexual overtones and involving young children at a local alternative space. The piece triggered an investigation that proved that this monk had been abusing minors over a period of several years, with the full knowledge of the prior. The monk went to prison and the prior was removed and sent to Algeciras.

HOST 6

Upon hearing the news of the librarian's daughter, a few of the dwindling number of elder Shakers knew that sister Alison's gift drawing had found its true owner. It was believed that the drawing would not evoke the same reaction in anyone else; as the piece was specifically created to address one individual. And in truth, as far as we know, no one since that time who has seen that drawing experienced the same reaction.

HOST 7

It was an overwhelming behest; it took five large crates to empty the entire apartment. Francesca tried to find a place to donate this incredible wealth of material—some kind of library or foundation. But once it was examined, it was clear that it would be useless for any purpose. The surreptitiously taken photographs were of poor quality and none of them were labeled, which made it a practically impossible task to identify them, many of them were in formats that were difficult to transfer, and others were already corrupted or unreadable.

HOST 2

The city of Elzaia began a slow decline.

HOST 1

The next time I saw Justiniano, at some non-profit arts organization benefit, I hardly recognized him.

HOST 2

The elders complained that the love for the birds was now gone; the birds were now treated like instruments.

HOST 1

He seemed to be twenty years older, almost frail. He told me that he had continued with his art experiencing business, and it was still going strong.

HOST 2

The few of those who shared the love of birds that their grandparents had had didn't like the options of a military or a business path, so most of them left for other cities to pursue other endeavors.

HOST 1

"The only problem", he told me, "is that it is very taxing, physically and emotionally."

HOST 2

But as it happens with elders, no one ever pays attention to what they are saying, dismissing them as senile or intolerant.

HOST 1

Justiniano was like a Dorian Gray in reverse: he was absorbing all the anxieties, fears and hopes of his clients, and using art to sublimate those experiences. His sessions with his clients could be very emotional, and as he recounted his experiences to them many times he would collapse in tears.

HOST 4

It is believed that they began the experiment around 11pm on Christmas Eve, when Sulyok started reciting a variety of spiritist phrases that were meant to open communication with the deceased artist's spirit. Several hours later, nothing yet had happened, but closer to 2am Ivana felt a twitch in her arm.

HOST 5

As you may imagine, this was the end of Fray Bartolomeu's school. It did produce a couple of artists of certain local renown. One of them became a monologuist in the style of Spalding Gray. Another monk, who left the order shortly thereafter, became known for exploring nudity and sex in public spaces as part of his work.

HOST 6

It is unclear what became of the librarian's daughter, but some say that she never recovered from the experience. There are rumors that in later years she joined a religious order.

[PABLO comes to center stage]

PABLO

There was a man who liked to write parables; in fact it appeared that anytime he wanted to say something he would use a parable to explain his idea. This man—who by the way, is not me, because this one story I am telling you is not a parable—anyway, this man was a great thinker. And like any other great thinker, he was conflicted, feeling that he somehow didn't fit in his own time and in the world in which he had grown up. His father, a businessman, had great expectations for him, and was a great influence on him, to the point that even after his father died our parable writer struggled for the rest of his life with rebelling against that paternal influence. He rejected the religion of his time, but at the same time the only practical job he could ever have was being a pastor of that religion; he was deeply in love, and in fact the woman he loved also loved him and they were engaged to be married, but in his contorted reasoning he believed their love was a mistake, and thus canceled the wedding two days before it was to take place.

He took various pseudonyms to write his parables, but it was all transparent. Like Sister Alison Parr, he went through great suffering; like the residents of the city of Elzaia, he was speaking a language that was not understood by others. Like Ivana Korshnoi, he spent most of his life speaking to spirits. Like Bartolomeu Balcells, he used the Catholic art of confession in his own twisted way to understand his own subjective reality and concluded that this, was, in fact, the only truth one could ever attain. Like Doctor Hikari, his life was a ceaseless, but ultimately futile, attempt, to capture the present. And like Justiniano Quilez, his grandiose image of himself made him think he could be a kind of savior to others through his thoughts, only to encounter a contradiction in his own philosophy: that the subjective truth that one finds for oneself, if it is indeed truthful, sometimes isn't useful for the world—it doesn't save it, it doesn't help it in any way. So it is with art, where we struggle to become ourselves, but that struggle is for the most part uninteresting to others. We try to reconcile what is ultimately an organic need to communicate, like the song of a bird, with the idea that it may be something else, that it may have a transcendental dimension.

Thus our parable writer, philosopher, ultimately fell out of favor with the world that he constantly quarreled against; he declared war on the church of his time and became persona non grata, eliminating any chances of fitting in the world. Sick and penniless, he lost the will to live, dying at 42. His writings and his hundreds of parables were forgotten for half a century.

But they were revived one day by a German philosopher by the name of Edmund Husserl, who was trying to create a philosophy that incorporated the contributions of the subconscious, a subjective philosophy, and who found in the parables of this writer a foundation for what became the major XXth century philosophy built on the subjective, known as existentialism.

That parable author, that conflicted man, was named Søren Kierkegaard.

The world, long ago, I think, said goodbye to that philosophy—leaving it to the realm of adolescence. Yet in art we have not yet resolved how we tie the subjective to the world. This is perhaps what I was trying to do with these letters with these parables. But what I found, and perhaps you found it with me, and perhaps Kierkegaard would agree, is that a parable never really answers a question; it only opens many more. And when its truth is in the eye of the beholder, what is to be done with that truth?

Maybe it's a good thing that we have stopped writing physical letters.

HOST 1

The last time I saw Justiniano he was remarkably slim and fit. Yet he looked a bit strange: his hair was somewhat ridiculously styled, as if he were a teenage idol. He told me that he had left the art world, as well as abandoned his art education theories. He had a new relationship with a man down in Miami, a successful wine exporter. He didn't have to work any more. I asked him at some point why he decided to leave his work with "art experiencing". What he told me stuck with me ever since:

"I have discovered the joys of selfishness."

HOST 2

Finally came the day when bird communication was so ineffective that it could no longer support any kind of reliable show-business or military activity. As a result, schools started closing, armies developed more effective weapons and communication strategies, and cities redirected their efforts to attract tourism revenue.

A generation later, Elzaia was reduced to a few scattered huts, and a generation later, it no longer existed as a city.

To this day, nobody knows how to communicate with the birds.

HOST 4

What happened later is a matter of conjecture. The guards, who were still in the midst of their celebration, heard a noise in the

Corot gallery and ran to see what was going on. They bumped into Sulyok, who was running down a hallway with a terrified look on his face. He ran away, never to be seen again. As they arrived at the Corot gallery they found Ivana on the floor, lifeless, still holding the brush, eyes open, with an enigmatic smile on her face. At the center of the gallery, in front of Corot's painting, was Ivana's easel with the paint set up, and a perfectly made painting, a remarkably authentic Corot night scene that served as a perfect complement to the original *Bridge at Mantes.*

Lab tests later determined that this painting had been made sometime in the 1850s, right around the time of *Bridge at Mantes.* Yet no one could explain the provenance of this work, nor how it could have made its mysterious appearance in the museum's gallery.

HOST 5

Fray Bartolomeu himself left as well and never returned to Spain. I heard that he now lives in San Francisco, where he runs a local arts healing program.

HOST 6

It is said that the rest of Sister Alison Parr's drawings are kept in a restricted archive only for scholars to study. There is a particular warning that young women should look at these drawings only at their own risk.

HOST 7

In the end, Francesca had no choice but to dispose of it all, through a Staten Island waste management company that took it to a landfill. And in matter of a few hours, Francesca saw that entire collection be taken away—a lifetime of chasing artworks all over the world, millions of images documenting one viewer's journey through all imaginable museums, all pointless, all of them never opened nor seen by a human eye.

HOST 3

Now, regarding this hypothetical composer of the saddest song in the world: No one knows what he thought of the sadness he triggered with his song, but let's imagine that it may have weighed heavily on him, and that at the end of his life it was too much. His mother hadn't survived the labor camps, and it must have been haunting for him to live with the guilt that he had survived while she didn't.

One can even perfectly imagine him one day, actually, a Sunday, deciding this was enough, and throwing himself out the window of his house. Cruelly as one may imagine, he did not die, but was taken to the hospital, where he choked himself with a wire—this time successfully.

Now, many years later, when the 30s feel like a distant and innocent time, this whole imaginary story about the song may sound quaint.

Almost funny.

But I almost forgot to mention: the imaginary composer I described wasn't imaginary: his name was Rezső Seress. I think you know what song I am talking about.

Yours,
Pablo

[*final musical interlude, with "Gloomy Sunday"*]

[*image of Corot's "Bridge at Mantes"*]

[*house lights*]

About the Author

In a methodical way and recurring to strategies connected to the baroque fugue and ars combinatoria (combinatory art), Pablo Helguera (Mexico City, 1971) often draws improbable relationships between human histories, biographies, anecdotes and historical events, always bringing them all together in a cohesive whole and making all serve as a reflection on our current relationship with art as a society. Helguera often focuses on history, pedagogy, sociolinguistics and anthropology in formats such as lectures, museum displays, performance and written fiction. His project *The School of Panamerican Unrest* (2003-2011), an early example of pedagogically-focused socially engaged art, consisted in a nomadic think-tank, physically crossed the continent by car from Anchorage to Tierra del Fuego. He has exhibited widely internationally (MoMA, Havana Biennial, Performa, Reina Sofia, amongst many others) and has been recipient of the Guggenheim, Franklin Furnace and Blade of Grass Fellowships and the Creative Capital and Art Matters grants. He was the first recipient of the International Award of Participatory Art of the Emilia Romagna Region in Italy. His book *Education for Socially Engaged Art*, (2011), a primer for social practice has quickly become adopted as a main textbook for art schools and university programs internationally. He is also author of several other books including *The Pablo Helguera Manual of Contemporary Art Style*, *Theatrum Anatomicum (and other performance lectures)*, *What in the World*, and *Art Scenes: The Social Scripts of the Art World*, a book on the sociology of contemporary art. In 2013 he launched the project *Librería Donceles*, consisting in creating the only Spanish used bookstore in New York, a non-profit project intended to draw attention to the perceptions of Latin American culture in the U.S. The bookstore has traveled to Phoenix and San Francisco. He was named the first artist in residence for The Site Santa Fe biennial, New Mexico, where he is developing a 4-year project titled *Nuevo Romancero Nuevomejicano*. He is married to artist Dannielle Tegeder and they live in Brooklyn with their daughter Estela.

Other Books by Pablo Helguera

Endingness: Prolegomena for a New Art of Memory
The Pablo Helguera Manual of Contemporary Art Style
The Boy Inside the Letter
The Witches of Tepoztlán (and Other Unpublished Operas)
Artoons (*I*, *II*, and *III*)
The Juvenal Players
Suite Panamericana
Hacia una Estética de la Burocracia
Estela y las Hojas
Theatrum Anatomicum (and Other Performance Lectures)
What in the World (a Subjective Museum Biography)
The School of Panamerican Unrest (an Anthology of Documents)
—with Sara Demeuse
Urÿonstelaii
Education for Socially Engaged Art
Pedagogia No Campo Expandido
—with Monica Hoff
Art Scenes: The Social Scripts of the Art World
Onda Corta
He Was Elan
Artunes

www.ingramcontent.com/pod-product-compliance
Lightning Source LLC
LaVergne TN
LVHW091108080826
845145LV00008B/1846

* 9 7 8 1 9 3 4 9 7 8 8 2 5 *